T0351414

STUDIES IN WELSH HISTORY

Editors

RALPH A. GRIFFITHS   CHRIS WILLIAMS
ERYN M. WHITE

20

SOCCER AND SOCIETY:

SOUTH WALES, 1900–1939

SOCCER AND SOCIETY

SOUTH WALES, 1900–1939

by

MARTIN JOHNES

*Published on behalf of the
History and Law Committee
of the Board of Celtic Studies*

CARDIFF
UNIVERSITY OF WALES PRESS
2002

British Library Cataloguing-in-Publication Data
A catalogue record for this book is available from the British Library.

ISBN 0-7083-1741-3

Every effort has been made to trace the copyright holders of the illustrative material in this volume, but in case of query please contact the publishers.

Jacket design by Jane Parry
Typeset at the University of Wales Press
Printed in Great Britain by Dinefwr Press, Llandybïe, Carmarthenshire

EDITORS' FOREWORD

Since the Second World War, Welsh history has attracted considerable scholarly attention and enjoyed a vigorous popularity. Not only have the approaches, both traditional and new, to the study of history in general been successfully applied to Wales's past, but the number of scholars engaged in this enterprise has multiplied during these years. These advances have been especially marked in the University of Wales.

In order to make more widely available the conclusions of recent research, much of it of limited accessibility in postgraduate dissertations and theses, in 1977 the History and Law Committee of the Board of Celtic Studies inaugurated a new series of monographs, *Studies in Welsh History*. It was anticipated that many of the volumes would originate in research conducted in the University of Wales or under the auspices of the Board of Celtic Studies. But the series does not exclude significant contributions made by researchers in other universities and elsewhere. Its primary aim is to serve historical scholarship and to encourage the study of Welsh history. Each volume so far published has fulfilled that aim in ample measure, and it is a pleasure to welcome the most recent addition to the list.

CONTENTS

CONTENTS

PREFACE

Cardiff [City] showed how true football should be played and what a fascinating, attractive sport it is.

Western Mail, 4 October 1910

Rugby union may have dominated popular views of south Wales but, as for this reporter, soccer is the 'true football' for many people in the region. This book explores the history of association football in the context of the society that played, watched, talked and read about it. It is based on my doctoral thesis, which was undertaken at the University of Wales, Cardiff.

I am indebted to many people for their help during the writing and researching of both the book and the thesis. Chris Williams was a model of a doctoral supervisor and, despite his preference for the oval ball, he has been a continuing source of advice and support. That this book ever saw the light of day owes much to him. Ian Garland provided numerous leads, sources and encouragement and, especially in the early days, convinced me that there was a point to the project. Similarly, Derrick Jenkins was always ready to answer obscure queries, chat about footballing giants past and present, and lend me the fruits of his own research into football in Cardiff.

Colleagues and students at University of Wales, Cardiff; University of Glamorgan; University of Wales Institute, Cardiff; Nuffield College, Oxford and, most recently, St Martin's College, Lancaster, have listened and contributed to my thoughts on sport, history and Wales. Special thanks are due to Andy Croll, Mike Huggins, Bill Jones, Iain McLean, Keith Strange and Amanda West. Friends and colleagues from the British Society of Sports History and the wider field of history have commented on my work and ideas, and have been a source of inspiration. Most notably, Tony Mason and Gareth Williams were the thesis's astute examiners and the source of many suggestions. Specific thanks are also due to Huw Bowen, Alun Evans, Richard Holt, Geraint H. Jenkins, Gavin Mellor, Dave Russell, Matt Taylor and Wray Vamplew. The following have all provided important advice, leads and encouragement: Tony Ambrosen, Gareth M. Davies, David Farmer, Ceri Stennett and Dave Twydell.

The staff of libraries and record offices across south Wales and beyond have all found and fetched for me innumerable books, newspapers and documents. I would particularly like to thank the staff of the Local Studies Department at Cardiff Central Library for never tiring of my repeated requests for copies of the *Football Echo*. Carolyn Jacob at Merthyr Central Library, and Brian Lile and John Jenkins at the National Library of Wales, Aberystwyth, also provided invaluable help, while the FAW and South Wales FA kindly allowed me access to their archives. I am most grateful to Western Mail & Echo Ltd for their permission to reproduce the four cartoons.

Friends and family have provided varying forms of support, made countless cups of coffee and patiently listened to my musings. Special thanks are due to Grant Abt, Nigel Blackamore, Janice Coyle, Neil Goodman, Meedru Khan, Will Mepham, Petar Petrovic and Stef Williams. Swansea City FC, my brother Richard, Claire, Arthur and the rest of the North Bank first taught me that what went on off the field was just as (or even more) interesting as what happened on it. They continue to remind me of my roots and that football is not just about the past. I hope they can forgive me for calling the game soccer throughout and, worse still, giving Cardiff City more mentions than the Swans. Heather Moyes joined this journey when it was still a thesis and is still aboard at the publication that marks its end. Somewhere along the way we got married and, without her love, the trip would have probably run aground.

When I was somewhat younger, my parents overcame the cold and their apathy towards the sport and first took me to the Vetch. More recently, they never once questioned the value of a Ph.D. in the social history of football in south Wales or a career in sports history. In gratitude for this, and much more, I would like to dedicate this book to them.

Martin Johnes

LIST OF TABLES

LIST OF ILLUSTRATIONS

Between pages 80 and 81

ABBREVIATIONS

AFC	Association Football Club
AL	*Aberdare Leader*
BWSF	British Workers' Sports Federation
CCC	County Cricket Club
FA	Football Association
FAW	Football Association of Wales
FC	Football Club
FE	*South Wales Football Echo*
FIFA	Fédération Internationale de Football Association
GWR	Great Western Railway
ME	*Merthyr Express*
NLW	National Library of Wales, Aberystwyth
NU	Northern Union
PRO	Public Record Office
RFC	Rugby Football Club
RG	*Rhondda Gazette*
SWA	*South Wales Argus*
SWDN	*South Wales Daily News*
SWDP	*South Wales Daily Post*
SWE	*South Wales Echo*
SWEP	*South Wales Evening Post*
SWMF	South Wales Miners' Federation
SWMFA	South Wales & Monmouthshire Football Association
WFU	Welsh Football Union (title officially used by the WRU until 1935)
WM	*Western Mail*
WRU	Welsh Rugby Union
WSFA	Welsh Schools Football Association

INTRODUCTION

WALES TRIUMPHANT IN THE WEMBLEY CUP FINAL

. . . Then, 30 minutes after the restart came the deciding goal. FERGUSON, from close in, drove hard, and [Dan] Lewis was brought to his knees. Len Davies rushed up, and in turning over to avoid the Welsh forward, Lewis lost his grip on the ball, which rolled slowly into the net.

South Wales News, 25 April 1927

'NINETEEN-TWENTY-SEVEN – the year Cardiff City first won the Cup'. That is how Welsh football history and, perhaps, some other history too, will come to be dated in the future.

Western Mail, 25 April 1927

And so, with a shot from a Scottish centre forward that slipped through the hands of an Arsenal goalkeeper from the Rhondda, Cardiff City won the FA Cup. The irony of the professional football labour market was not lost on contemporaries, some of whom even insinuated that Lewis's apparent error was rooted in some kind of national sympathy with the Cardiff team. Yet the goal was enough to win the cup, and Wales united in jubilation. Two days later a crowd, estimated at 100,000, turned out to welcome the victorious team home to Cardiff. For those on the streets that day, and for the rest of Wales, it was a rare triumph during a period of economic depression. Four months earlier, the miners of south Wales had returned to work defeated after a long and bitter strike. Others were less fortunate and unemployment was at an unprecedented level as south Wales was engulfed by an economic blizzard. For the people enduring that storm, Cardiff City's victory was a brief moment of sunshine.

SPORT IN WALES

In the late nineteenth century, south Wales experienced its own industrial revolution. The rapidly expanding coal industry imposed economic, environmental and social transformations on the region, creating an evolving and vibrant world. The new society needed new entertainments, and rugby gave them just that. Thousands of in-migrants from England's West Country brought with them a love of the oval ball, helping rugby, rather than soccer, to establish itself as the sport of south Wales. In 1905, the national Welsh rugby team defeated the otherwise all-conquering New Zealand All Blacks at Cardiff Arms Park. Contemporary Welsh writers saw it as a moment of glory for a triumphant nation and race; contemporary Welsh sports-lovers were probably more down-to-earth about the game but equally joyful.[1] That match laid down the basis of the relationship between rugby union and Welsh national identity. Not surprisingly, it has been at the centre of Welsh sports history. Using the match as a symbolic focal point, the work of Gareth Williams and Dai Smith has begun to unravel the complex meaning and status of rugby in south Wales.[2] They have shown how a middle-class game from England developed into an integral part of working-class culture and a popular expression of nationhood across the region. The leaders of the new south Wales liked to see the popularity of rugby as a symbol of the unity of a society and its people. To them, the Welsh successes at the game were further evidence of the achievements and virtues of the nation: a metaphor for the wealth and confidence that industrialization had brought. Rugby thus became part of the distinct and confident national identity that was created in late Victorian and Edwardian Wales on the back of a period of economic buoyancy. At a popular level, this new Welsh nationalism rarely took on a political slant. Instead, it was more concerned with achieving recognition within a British context, and sport offered a perfect vehicle for this: an opportunity to get one over the English neighbour without any of the uncertainties or extremes of a political movement.

---

[1] In particular, see the editorial of the *South Wales Daily News* (hereafter *SWDN*), 18 December 1905.

[2] See Gareth Williams, *1905 and All That: Essays on Rugby Football, Sport and Welsh Society* (Llandysul, 1991); David Smith and Gareth Williams, *Fields of Praise: The Official History of the Welsh Rugby Union, 1881–1981* (Cardiff, 1980), and David Smith, 'People's theatre: a century of Welsh rugby', *History Today*, 31 (1981), 31–6. Also see David L. Andrews and Jeremy W. Howell, 'Transforming into a tradition: rugby and the making of imperial Wales, 1890–1914', in A. G. Lingham and J. W. Loy (eds.), *Sport in Social Development* (Leeds, 1993), pp. 77–96.

Rugby in south Wales stood apart from the game in England because of its cross-class involvement. The Welsh middle classes promoted the sport with a sense of pride as an emblem of the cohesion and values of their society. Many of the other symbols of Welsh nationhood were limited in their appeal but rugby was more embracing and further reaching than Nonconformity, the Welsh language, the Liberal Party, or any of the new national institutions that it created. Rugby gave a south Wales that was becoming increasingly diverse through the effects of industrialization and migration, an accessible and successful banner under which to unite.[3] Thus rugby was turned into a central pillar of industrial Wales, and an afternoon in 1905 cemented that. It became part of the invented traditions used by the Edwardian middle classes to legitimize Welsh nationhood in both a historical and a contemporary sense. More recent events have entrenched this notion of rugby as the Welsh national sport. The often spectacular grand slams and triple crowns of the 1960s and 1970s ensured that the game remained an outlet and symbol of Welsh national pride in the eyes of both its own people and those looking in.[4]

So where does this leave association football? Kenneth O. Morgan dismissed it as 'not really a Welsh institution' and saw the irony of the winning goal in the 1927 cup final as rather appropriate.[5] In his efforts to emphasize the otherness of Wales, he saw soccer as never becoming popularly associated with notions of Welshness in the way that rugby had. By 1900 soccer in England and Scotland had developed into a central element of working-class culture, 'the people's game'. In south Wales, association football may not have been able to claim such a pivotal role in working-class culture, but the game did nonetheless have a history in the region. Brian Lile and David Farmer have shown how, from

---

[3] Although, as David Andrews points out, the new Welsh national identity was very much a male construct which ignored females and reinforced the patriarchal nature of society. The importance of rugby was particularly illustrative of this. David Andrews, 'Sport and the masculine hegemony of the modern nation: Welsh rugby, culture and society, 1890–1914', in John Nauright and Timothy J. L. Chandler (eds.), *Making Men: Rugby and Masculine Identity* (London, 1996), pp. 50–69.

[4] For a wider view of sport and national identity in Wales, see Martin Johnes, 'Eighty minute patriots? National identity and sport in modern Wales', *International Journal of the History of Sport*, 17, 4 (2000), 93–110.

[5] Kenneth O. Morgan, *Rebirth of a Nation: Wales, 1880–1980* (Oxford, 1982 edn), p. 237.

1890 to 1906, soccer was developing a following across the region.[6] From this footing, the game's popularity grew throughout the rest of the Edwardian era. The first fully professional clubs were established and thriving junior leagues developed, but, having not yet enjoyed any success on a British platform, the Welsh game remained overshadowed by its more established sister code of rugby union. Soccer's popularity may have been increasing but it had yet to offer the kind of significant success against outside teams that would reflect well on Wales and enable the game to become a symbol of national pride. It was in the short-lived economic boom of the early 1920s that professional soccer belatedly matured in south Wales. By 1921 the region could boast senior professional clubs at Aberdare, Cardiff, Merthyr, Newport and Swansea which raised the popularity and profile of the game in the region immensely. Success followed quickly, most notably at Cardiff City which established itself as a leading first-division side and narrowly missed out on the championship in 1924. The following year it was beaten at Wembley in the FA Cup final before returning more successfully in 1927. Swansea Town too enjoyed some successful cup-runs and in 1925 won the third division (south) championship. Yet these achievements were not sustained. Cardiff City had plummeted into the third division by 1931, while Aberdare Athletic and Merthyr Town both lost their Football League status before slipping out of existence altogether in 1928 and 1934 respectively.

At international level, Wales first won the British home championship in 1907 and repeated the feat three times during the 1920s. In the 1930s, the Welsh team was the outright winner on three further occasions and joint winners once. Yet the national side never fully became a symbol of Welsh nationhood. Victories were celebrated but, with most of the players earning their living in England, never with the same intensity as Cardiff City's FA Cup triumph. After 1945 European and world competitions superseded the home championship in importance. The English base of so many Welsh players began to matter less since the most important games were being played against non-British opposition. However, qualification for the 1958 World Cup and

[6] Brian Lile and David Farmer, 'The early development of association football in south Wales, 1890–1906', *Transactions of the Honourable Society of Cymmrodorion* (1984), 193–215.

a quarter-final place in the 1976 European championship stand out as Wales's only major feats in international soccer since 1945. While the national rugby team has offered as much glory as despair, the national soccer team's moments of triumph have been fleeting episodes in a general story of failure. Wales has produced some world-class players like John Charles and Ryan Giggs, but they have been forced to play alongside a succession of journeymen, thus denying them the opportunity they deserved to perform on the international stage. Such individuals may have become extremely popular in Wales but, with their personal achievements being largely with English teams, they alone were not enough to transform the image of Welsh soccer. Nor have the clubs of south Wales fared much better since the Second World War. Both Cardiff City and Swansea City have produced some great players and enjoyed brief stints in the first division, but neither has been able to establish itself as a leading British club. In today's world of premier leagues and multimillion pound players, both languish at the lower end of the Football League. Newport County meanwhile has closed down, a victim of the increasing divisions of wealth within the game. This modern situation has shaped our perception of the past. Welsh soccer is overshadowed by rugby in historical accounts and 1927 has been reduced to a sentence in textbooks and a logo on flags at lower-division games at Ninian Park.

Yet to call rugby the principality's national sport is to ignore north Wales, where soccer is the more popular game. There, the feats of the national rugby side have never been followed as closely as in the south, and even Wrexham FC, the region's senior club, has enjoyed a measure of success in recent years through some brave cup-runs. The idea of rugby as the Welsh national game demonstrates how the south has dominated both contemporary and historiographical ideas of Wales. Arguably, since 1945 the south has provided the bulk of the nation's people, money and historians, and thus its image has often been transposed into a picture of Wales as a whole. This brings us to the crucial point of how national identities are invented or constructed rather than being a true reflection of the lives of the people who live there.[7] Soccer's large following in Wales is not

---

[7] The classic work on this subject is Eric Hobsbawm and Terence Ranger (eds.), *The Invention of Tradition* (Cambridge, 1983).

enough to create a perception of it as a Welsh sport. After all, the game enjoys widespread support the world over. Had Wales ever enjoyed sustained success at the sport then this would not have mattered: a small nation living in the economic, political and cultural shadow of a larger neighbour latches on to any claim to glory with which it can associate itself. But Welsh soccer has not provided that success whereas, in rugby, Wales has a game at which it is (or at least was) good and whose cross-class involvement makes the sport clearly different from elsewhere in the world.[8] Thus it was the unique, all-embracing sport of rugby that came to be seen as the national sport rather than a game played by most of the developed and developing world, in which context a small country like Wales could not hope to make a significant impact.

SPORT AND HISTORY

As Richard Holt has pointed out, it is the winners who write history, and thus soccer has been central in European sports history.[9] In the corner of Europe that is Wales, rugby's claim to be the national sport means that it has dominated academic sports history. The work of Dai Smith and Gareth Williams has shown the importance of rugby in Welsh society, but, as they fully acknowledge, it was not the only component in a Welsh sporting identity. In particular, boxing, athletics, cricket and even rugby league have played their part in a rich Welsh cultural life, as of course has soccer, and each deserves attention from historians.[10] Academic work on the history of soccer has steadily

---

[8]   Although professionalism means that Welsh rugby union is now being incorporated into a wider commercial sphere, perhaps losing some of its popular and democratic characteristics in the process.

[9]   Richard Holt, 'Sport and history: the state of the subject in Britain', *Twentieth Century British History*, 7, 2 (1996), 234.

[10]   For Welsh boxers, see Dai Smith, 'Focal heroes: a Welsh fighting class', in Richard Holt (ed.), *Sport and the Working Class in Modern Britain* (Manchester, 1990), pp. 198–217. Andrew Hignell, *A Favourit' Game: Cricket in South Wales before 1914* (Cardiff, 1992), is a valuable beginning to the study of Welsh cricket. Martin Johnes, ' "Poor man's cricket": baseball, class and community in south Wales, c.1880–1950', *International Journal of the History of Sport*, 17, 4 (2000), 149–62, is an exploration of a minority sport in Wales. Andy Croll, *Civilizing the Urban: Popular Culture and Public Space in Merthyr, c.1870–1914* (Cardiff, 2000), is a wider study of popular culture that is historically relevant far beyond the town it examines; ch. 4 looks specifically at sport.

grown and developed since Tony Mason's pioneering book,
Association Football and English Society, 1863–1915, was published in
1980.[11] We are now beginning to understand something of the
economic, social and political significance of soccer in Britain. As
Russell concludes in his overview,

> a local football club absorbed some of the energies of a remarkably large
> number of the local male community and, as such, served as a 'natural'
> community focus . . . [The game] has undoubtedly been the source of
> immense social, aesthetic and emotional pleasure (and not a little pain) to
> its numerous devotees. Very few modern cultural forms have stirred the
> passions of quite so many individuals as football.[12]

In its importance to individuals alone, soccer is historically
significant.

This book is a study of soccer in south Wales in the years from
1900 to 1939.[13] It examines the game from its grassroots through
its semi-professional levels to its pinnacle in FA Cup finals and
international matches. The different sporting relationships that
exist within a region provide a recurrent theme throughout the
work. Be they between different sports, clubs, spectators or
directors, such associations shed light on how the game operated
and what it meant to people. As a result, the ideas and themes
about a club and the community raised in Korr's work on West
Ham United are built upon.[14] Similarly, the general interpretations made about the game, particularly by Fishwick on the
inter-war years, will be examined and expanded.[15] Smith's and
Williams's work on Welsh rugby has focused on the question of
national identity and it is an important theme in this work too.
Identities are complex and heterogeneous, with different meanings for different individuals. What the Liberal middle classes
regarded as Welsh was not necessarily the same as what was

---

[11] Tony Mason, *Association Football and English Society, 1863–1915* (Brighton, 1980). For
a recent review of the state of academic soccer history, see Holt, 'Sport and history'.
[12] Dave Russell, *Football and the English: A Social History of Association Football in England,
1863–1995* (Preston, 1997), p. 240.
[13] Football was a contemporary generic term that collectively described soccer and
rugby and is used as such in this book. Thus soccer, a contemporary rather than an
American term, is used to refer to the book's subject. South Wales is defined here as the
geographical area that incorporates the pre-1974 counties of Glamorgan and
Monmouthshire and the industrial zone in eastern Carmarthenshire around Llanelli.
[14] Charles Korr, *West Ham United: The Making of a Football Club* (London, 1986).
[15] Nicholas Fishwick, *English Football and Society, 1910–50* (Manchester, 1989).

thought by the rest of the population of south Wales. Sport plays an important role for many individuals in shaping and reflecting how they see themselves, and this book contributes to our understanding of the myriad of faces that Welsh national and other identities embraced.

The discussion of national matches, competitions and associations facilitates conclusions that are applied to north and south Wales. Nonetheless, the focus on south Wales allows the avoidance of many of the generalizations that the plurality of Welsh society enforces on studies of the nation as a whole. Indeed, the inspirations and aspirations of football in south Wales lay not with compatriots in the north, but across the border in England. Thus, this work is a regional study of soccer at all levels which aims to illuminate our wider knowledge of the game. However, south Wales is not like any English region. Its regional pride was often articulated in the language of nation and thus the question of Welshness makes it unique. This does not detract from its worth as the basis for a regional critique of soccer. South Wales has as much in common with England as it does in contrast, and there are obvious parallels with other regions dominated by heavy industry. Indeed, the question of national identity adds to the richness of what can be unearthed by giving an insight into the contradictions and complexities of a class-based yet patriotic society.

The history of Welsh soccer has begun to be mapped by a number of worthy publications. A broad framework has been established for the national team, the national cup and the leading clubs, and it is from this platform that this study begins.[16] It draws upon extensive research using the region's press, complemented by a variety of manuscript, oral and other sources. The most popular south Wales newspapers were produced in

---

[16] Peter Corrigan, *100 Years of Welsh Soccer* (Cardiff, 1976), provides a general outline of the history of the game in Wales. Gareth M. Davies and Ian Garland, *Who's Who of Welsh International Players* (Wrexham, 1991), examines those who have donned the Welsh shirt. Peter Stead and Huw Richards (eds.), *For Club and Country: Welsh Football Greats* (Cardiff, 2000), explores some of the nation's most famous players. Other useful contributions to the literature of the game in Wales are Derrick Jenkins and Ceri Stennet, *1927* (Cardiff, 1985), and Ian Garland, *A History of the Welsh Cup, 1877–1993* (Wrexham, 1993). There are also some useful club histories: in particular see Tony Ambrosen, *Amber in the Blood: A History of Newport County* (Harefield, 1993); John Crooks, *Cardiff City Football Club: The Official History of the Bluebirds* (Harefield, 1992); Grahame Lloyd, *C'mon City: A Hundred Years of the Bluebirds* (Bridgend, 1999); and David Farmer, *The Official 'Biography' of the Swans, Town and City* (Swansea, 2000).

Cardiff and, thus, often focused on the city's affairs. This means that, throughout the book, there is a tendency to use Cardiff as the main example where it is typical of the region. However, the other urban areas of south Wales are examined and clear distinctions made where their experiences differed. South Wales was not (and is not) a unified body. The Rhondda Valleys and the seaport of Cardiff may not be miles apart geographically, but in terms of community and tradition they are distinct. During the riots of 1910, Tonypandy High Street was a long way from the suburbs of Cardiff and, by the outbreak of war in 1939, they had not come much closer. This book tries to acknowledge both the variations within and beyond individual communities, as well as the ties that bind them to the broader concepts of region and nation. With sport being one of the most obvious agents in shaping the meaning of place, soccer provides an ideal vehicle to shed light on the nature of these communal, regional and civic identities.

This book is a history of soccer's place in society rather than a history of the game itself. It is not an account of matches and players but rather of what they meant to people and the society in which they lived. It attempts to place the game firmly within the wider historical context that shaped it. Yet soccer was not simply a mirror of the world around it. As Russell points out, 'we should acknowledge a little more circularity in the relationship between social and economic base and sporting superstructure, and football's capacity to engender social change. Football, like all cultural forms, must always be allowed a certain autonomy.'[17] The book begins by looking at the Edwardian development of the game and the agents that promoted and hindered the growth of professional soccer. Chapter 2 takes the narrative of the professional game through the First World War and inter-war years. It explores the often devastating effect that the economic depression had on clubs, players and spectators alike. The third chapter considers the multi-layered amateur (usually referred to by contemporaries as 'junior') game from street kickabouts to the network of local leagues from which professional clubs drew players and spectators. Chapter 4 examines soccer's supporters. It explores what the game and its clubs meant to them and pays

[17] Russell, *Football and the English*, p. 237.

particular attention to the question of class in soccer. Chapter 5 is an exploration of the professional clubs and civic identity in soccer. Through the motives of directors, the wider reception of clubs' successes and the involvement of external figures such as local politicians, soccer casts important light on what towns meant to the people who lived there. The final chapter addresses the question of national identity in soccer in south Wales. What was actually an expression of regional pride was often equated with, and articulated in, the language of national identity. This was seen neither as a matter of tension nor contradiction. People in the south celebrated the achievements of the region as national triumphs without feeling any close empathy with the remote, and often rural, world of north Wales.

NEWSPAPERS AND HISTORY

Sports history has been criticized for an over-reliance on news-paper sources.[18] Whilst not denying the importance of a broad base of sources, newspapers offer more than a convenient and rich vein of information. As Hill argues, the press is also 'a medium through which images of the past are refracted to the historian'.[19] Through paying semiotic attention to how newspapers told their stories, we can glean something of how people read and received the world beyond their immediate horizons. The media may not tell people what to think, but they are integral in informing what they think about.[20] Yet the press offers historians more than a window through which to gaze at (rather than reconstruct) the past. It was also an integral actor in the whole local culture of soccer.[21] Newspapers not only stimulated interest in the sport through match reports, but also acted as a forum and leader for information, debate and financial appeals. The *South Wales Echo*'s

---

[18] Peter Beck, *Scoring for Britain: International Football and International Politics, 1900–1939* (London, 1999), p. vii.

[19] Jeff Hill, 'What the papers say: sports history, the newspaper press and narrative theory', paper given at the British Society of Sports History conference, Lancaster, 2001.

[20] Gary Whannel, *Fields in Vision: Television Sport and Cultural Transformation* (London, 1992).

[21] Fishwick, *English Football*, ch. 5; Mason, *Association Football*, pp. 187–95; Tony Mason, 'All the winners and the half times . . .', *Sports Historian*, 13 (May 1993), 3–13. In south Wales coverage did concentrate on local clubs although some attention was given to the national game and particularly to the FA Cup.

extensive use of soccer as a theme or metaphor in political cartoons meant that even those who would not normally read an article about the game were aware of it and its happenings.[22] Thus, the public's perception of the game was as much shaped by reading newspapers as it was by their own experience. Club directors were acutely aware of this and liaised closely with reporters, passing on inside knowledge and using the local paper as their club's public voice. In return, newspapers were generally supportive of clubs in the years preceding and following the First World War. The papers won readers through their access to exclusive information, while the clubs ensured that they were not criticized too frequently. In 1920 the *South Wales Echo* felt it could not devote space to publishing the large number of letters complaining about Cardiff City's decision to raise prices for a forthcoming cup-tie. Instead, the directors' reasoning was printed and supported. A year later it could be found refusing to publish a letter criticizing the City captain. In 1922 the paper responded to Cardiff City's lack of close-season signings with an article on the advantages of an established team whose members knew each other. The article claimed that no one could question the judgement of the directorate and manager.[23] The press would print letters critical of a club, and constructive criticism by reporters was not unknown. But papers preferred to talk of the mutual responsibility of directors and supporters in an effort to appear neutral and not alienate its readers or the club.

From the late 1920s onwards, the relationship between clubs and the *South Wales Echo* began gradually to change. While soccer coverage in papers like the *Western Mail*, with a more middle-class audience, continued to concentrate on match and news reports, the *Echo* introduced opinion and gossip columns. The leading correspondents of mass newspapers, although retaining their *noms de plume*, became personalities in their own right. They liked to think of themselves as experts on the game and thus advised players in their columns. 'Citizen' of the *Echo* even talked personally to Cardiff City players in 1931, giving them advice on where they were going wrong. The tactical advice offered was not always very sophisticated ('Better to shoot and to miss than

---

[22] For example, see the cartoon about the Abyssinian crisis and the football season in *South Wales Echo* (hereafter *SWE*), 17 August 1935.

[23] *SWE*, 9 January 1920, 29 August 1921, 8 August 1922.

never to shoot at all') but was probably no worse than that given by the directors.[24]

As Cardiff City slid down the league ladder, a less cosy relationship developed between the club and the press. 'Citizen' argued that it was unfair to blame players and that the onus should be placed on the board. Such criticism generated public pressures and expectations that could not be ignored by directors. The press's influence was such that, in 1931, a Cardiff City director admitted that 'Citizen's' criticisms had forced the club to abandon its policy of not signing any new players. Through stirring up public criticism, 'Citizen' forced the directors to reveal the extent of the club's financial problems during the following season. The severity of the club's monetary crisis led to a truce in the attacks. By the mid-1930s, with the club in a healthier financial situation, 'Citizen' was again publicly criticizing the board and urging it to buy players. Later, the club actually signed one junior player whom the reporter himself had brought to its attention. In 1936 'Citizen' was attacked by the directors and others over his criticisms of Cardiff City. Accused of wanting to dictate to the club, he was called the 'Mussolini of Welsh football' and the 'Hitler of Cardiff City'. He placed the blame on the club for telling the national press that its troubles were over, while trying to give the local papers another, more sober, message. Correspondents were essentially caught between two stools. As 'Citizen' pointed out, 'If I criticise players fearlessly I am told I am undermining their confidence, if I praise them I am told by the public I am an agent of the club.' 'Citizen' received letters blaming him personally for everything at Cardiff City from team selection to the captain's decision to play against the wind![25] Other supporters saw him as their spokesman. He was urged to convene public meetings, set up a supporters' club and even organize a boycott of matches.[26] Yet, despite what was perceived as his regular interferences, he declined to get too involved in the internal affairs of the club.

These changes at the *Echo* were part of broader developments in the press. By the 1930s, national newspapers, particularly the

---

[24] *SWE*, 11 April 1931; *South Wales Football Echo* (hereafter *FE*), 5 January 1935.

[25] *FE*, 21 November, 19 December, 21 February 1931; 3, 17 October 1936; *SWE*, 14 December 1935, 19 October, 3 February 1938. 'Citizen' claimed that he got more letters than a glamorous film star. *FE*, 14 September 1935.

[26] See, for example, *SWE*, 23 February 1937; *FE*, 12 February, 23 April 1938.

Sunday press, were treating soccer in a more sensational manner.[27] The local press had to compete with this but without endangering its special links with clubs. After all, it was this access to inside information that gave local papers an edge over their national rivals in the competition for readers.[28] Welsh rugby coverage, in contrast, with no popular competition from the national press, remained more conservative, with little gossip or speculation about internal club affairs. Meanwhile, the professional soccer clubs still needed the help of the press to portray a positive public image. Thus, despite periodic disputes and animosity, the two sides continued to co-operate, even if sometimes in an atmosphere of mutual mistrust. Clubs used the press as their official voice for everything from the announcements of signings to denials of rumours and the thanking of supporters.[29] Sometimes, this would be through a letter to the paper but, more commonly, by asking a reporter to write a story. In times of financial crisis, the local newspaper took the lead in promoting fund-raising and stressing the gravity of the situation and the supporters' duty to help.[30] Newport County directors once even used the press as a forum to fight out their internal disputes in public. Such contacts ensured that local reporters had a strong knowledge of the inside workings of clubs. 'Citizen's' claims that he knew more about Cardiff City than anyone outside the club were probably true. On occasion he almost seemed to take delight in telling readers how he knew the identity of a potential signing or a player's wages but that it was not diplomatic to reveal the information. Yet, on other occasions, he could still feel that the board was not being open enough with him.[31]

This interaction between clubs and newspapers means that the press is an invaluable source for soccer history. The *South Wales Echo* and its Saturday evening sister paper, the *South Wales Football Echo*, have been the main sources for this book. Their soccer coverage was typical of the biggest-selling local daily newspaper

[27] Fishwick, *English Football*, pp. 100–7.
[28] In 1925 both the *Western Mail* (hereafter *WM*) and *Evening Express* sold record numbers on the day of Cardiff City's FA Cup final. *WM*, 27 April 1925.
[29] See, for example, *SWE*, 8 January 1937, 22 November 1935.
[30] See, for example, *South Wales Evening Post*'s (hereafter *SWEP*) help for Swansea Town, 15 June 1935.
[31] See, for example, *SWE*, 9 April 1935 and 19 October 1938.

in a large town. Other reporters may not always have been so
critical, especially at smaller clubs where expectations were not
so high, but they remained key actors in the local soccer scene.
The *Western Mail*'s Newport County correspondent was even a
leading member of the Newport County supporters' club.[32]
Clubs outside the Football League perhaps suffered from not
having a daily newspaper on their doorstep with which they
could develop a close relationship. Thus, any press coverage by
the main regional papers was welcome. An Ebbw Vale AFC
director actually wrote to the *Echo* to thank them for covering
one of the club's matches and writing a fair report about it.[33] He
was evidently not used to such treatment.

SOUTH WALES, 1900–1939

The export-driven, coal-based economic boom of the late
nineteenth century reached an apogee in the Edwardian era,
bringing a peak in the in-migration to the south Wales valleys
and coastal towns. A mass proletariat was created as workers
from rural Wales, England, Scotland, Ireland and even beyond
arrived in search of work. In the burgeoning communities,
housing and health problems were rife, but a vibrant culture was
forged through Nonconformity, music, sport, pubs and institutes,
Liberal politics and, increasingly, trade unionism. This popular,
religious and political culture crossed class boundaries and
helped to keep a 'frontier society' together. At the head of this life
was a small but influential middle class which helped to bind the
culture together by appealing to and promoting the calls of community and nation. The widespread loyalty to the Liberal Party,
which reached its apogee in the 1906 general election, symbolized this unity. Although eager to promote its Welshness, south
Wales also had pride in being part of the motherland of a huge
empire. Wales was as much a part of Britain as it was its own
nation.
   However, cracks and contradictions were beginning to
appear in the Welsh 'Edwardian High Noon'.[34] An increasingly

---

[32] Ambrosen, *Amber in the Blood*, p. 30.
[33] *FE*, 14 November 1931.
[34] Morgan, *Rebirth of a Nation*, ch. 5.

commercialized popular culture and English in-migration were threatening the popularity and influence of Nonconformity and its institutions. Despite the wider evidence of economic and cultural prosperity, the drive for profit in the south Wales coalfield had its victims. The industrial disputes and riots that swept south Wales in 1910–12 were a rude reminder that no combination of beer, tries and hymns was going to make the working class accept the status quo if they felt that their interests were being neglected. Support for the Labour Party and the unions swelled, threatening the Liberal hegemony. However, when war was declared in 1914, south Wales joined the rest of Britain in standing as a people united against a foreign aggressor. When the guns fell silent in 1918, the region moved quickly through a short economic boom into the depths of the depression. New trading patterns, overseas producers and technologies were developing, robbing the south Wales coal industry of many of its markets. The long-term shortcomings in its production methods were exposed and its prosperity collapsed. Being so reliant on one industry, the result for south Wales was mass unemployment. Faced with falling wages and lengthening dole queues, the mining union fought back but, after the disaster of the General Strike and the subsequent lockout, its power was crippled. After a number of brief revivals, the terminal nature of the change was confirmed by the shock waves that followed the Wall Street crash. The coal industry was brought to its knees, and the early 1930s saw unemployment reach cataclysmic levels. Although pockets of relative stability existed, particularly in the western anthracite coalfields and the more economically diverse coastal towns, the mass in-migration of the Edwardian years went into reverse as thousands of Welshmen and women left for the greener economic pastures of the Midlands and the south of England. The vibrant culture of the Edwardian period was battered but did not collapse. Musical, religious and sporting pursuits continued, albeit on a smaller scale, offering some relief to the suffering communities. Meanwhile, a new communal protest against company unionism, the ravages of the dole queue and the means test emerged, providing a glimmer of hope and self-esteem.

Soccer and people's experiences of it were naturally shaped by this wider context. Yet, at the same time, it offered people a distraction from the problems of daily life. J. B. Priestley's classic description of the 'conflict and art' offered by Bruddersford United may be laden with clichés but in it is the essence of soccer's appeal: the sense of fun, escape and belonging that it engendered.[35] When Fred Keenor lifted the FA Cup in 1927, the torment south Wales was experiencing made the impact of the achievement so much greater. Temporarily at least, it gave a region back its pride. It is the aim of this book to show that soccer could and did play such a role in society in south Wales. It attempts to reclaim the sport as an integral part of the history of the region's popular culture. In doing this, it contributes to the recognition that, while there is much in south Wales that sets it apart from the rest of Britain, there is also much which unites them.

---

[35] J. B. Priestley, *The Good Companions* (London, [1929] 1976 edn), pp. 13–14.

I

'IT'S COMING, AND IT'S COMING FAST':[1] THE DEVELOPMENT OF PROFESSIONAL SOCCER IN EDWARDIAN SOUTH WALES

> There can be no reasonable doubt that 'Association' Football is *the* game of the present and of the future. It is rapidly gaining favour by leaps and bounds – even in localities which in the past have been regarded as Rugby strongholds.
>
> Tredegar AFC, Prospectus, 1910[2]

In 1901 soccer had been a professional sport in England for sixteen years and was regularly attracting crowds of over 20,000 for its most glamorous league games. That year Tottenham Hotspur won the FA Cup before a crowd of 110,820. It was the first time a southern club had won the competition, and the match signalled the place that soccer had assumed in an English national popular culture. In south Wales, however, the sport was on the periphery and overshadowed by rugby union. A South Wales League had been formed in 1890, while St Helen's in Swansea hosted the region's first soccer international in 1894 before a crowd of 6,000. Such was the local ignorance of soccer that the *Western Mail* published a plan of the pitch before the match. Attendances in the league rarely rose above 1,000 but the competition was fierce enough for clubs to turn increasingly to underhand payments so as to attract better players.[3]

In 1899 the South Wales and Monmouthshire Football Association (founded in 1893; henceforth SWMFA) voted against legalizing professionalism despite accusations that it already existed in 'covert form'. A year later, a special meeting of the association was told by its chairman that he

> remembered a time when they could not obtain an Association ball in Cardiff . . . The popularity of the game had since then advanced by leaps

---

[1] *South Wales Daily News* (hereafter *SWDN*) quoted in Lile and Farmer, 'Early development', p. 199.

[2] PRO, BT31/13277/110013.

[3] See Lile and Farmer, 'Early development', for further information on the 1890s.

and bounds, and he did not see why they should not now go a step further, and let themselves loose by legalising professionalism. At present in South Wales several clubs suffered owing to other clubs, who covertly adopted professionalism, offering inducements to these players and taking them away. 'Professionalism', contended Mr Sandiford, with warmth, 'is not only rife in South Wales but rampant.'[4]

Not everyone shared his warmth and the meeting voted to legalize professionalism by a single vote. The SWMFA's secretary tried to claim that the meeting was invalid and invoked the support of the association's founding president, one Captain Morgan Lindsay, grandson of the first Lord Tredegar and a member of the Royal Engineers' FA Cup final team of 1878. Lindsay was serving in the Boer War and thus had been unable to attend. Yet, in reality, with the Football Association of Wales (henceforth FAW), the Wrexham-based senior association founded in 1876, already sanctioning professionalism, the SWMFA had no power over the matter beyond its own cup competitions.[5]

Professionalism brought improved playing standards and the press claimed that the 'style of the game' had 'undergone a great change for the better'.[6] In 1901, Bill 'Barber' Jones of Aberdare became the first player from the South Wales League to play for Wales. A year later he was playing for West Ham United in the Southern League. Further evidence of improving standards came in 1902, when Manchester City paid Aberaman £50 for 'burly full back' Hugh Jones. Better standards naturally boosted interest in the game, but there was also already an appetite for a higher class of soccer. The GWR claimed that it was not unusual for a thousand people to travel from Cardiff to watch Bristol City play in the Football League.[7]

In 1906 Wales entertained England at Cardiff Arms Park before 20,000 spectators. A 1–0 defeat meant that Wales had not beaten England since 1882, but the enthusiasm which the audience showed for the match was a sign that association football had a future in south Wales. The Welsh team that day contained

[4] *SWDN*, 22 October 1900.
[5] See *SWDN*, 22 October, 27 November 1900.
[6] Quoted in Lile and Farmer, 'Early development', p. 207.
[7] *WM*, 24 August 1910.

no players born or employed in south Wales and was picked (to the annoyance of the south) by the FAW, a supposedly national association dominated by northern officials. Nonetheless, that year the SWMFA had seventy-four affiliated members. Although only eleven of them were classed as senior clubs, it was evidence that soccer in the region was beginning to develop an infrastructure that would ensure that the success of future matches like the international at Cardiff would not be down to novelty appeal alone.[8] It was from this position that soccer in south Wales would grow impressively through the late Edwardian era. By 1914 there were 375 clubs, thirteen leagues and nearly 10,000 registered players affiliated to the SWMFA.[9] The development of the game was far from smooth and required patience and much hard work on the part of its pioneers. But ultimately their efforts were successful and led to a significant shift in the popular culture of the region. Soccer's rise had its origins in the evolving social and economic conditions of Edwardian south Wales. This chapter looks at how and why the game developed in south Wales.

MAKING 'IT GO': AGENTS BEHIND THE DEVELOPMENT OF SOCCER, 1900–1910

Edwardian south Wales was a region undergoing massive demographic change. Over 127,000 people moved into the region between 1901 and 1911. The majority were young men, the primary, sports-playing sector of society.[10] While many came from west Wales and the rugby-playing south-west of England, there was also a considerable influx from regions where soccer was well established. In-migrants from the Midlands, south-east England and the north of Wales provided large numbers of spectators and players for the soccer clubs of south Wales. As the *Western Mail* pointed out, there was a 'large colony of North Country people' who 'undoubtedly are clamouring for a game to which they are accustomed'. Copies of the football edition of the *Wolverhampton Express and Star* were sent to Newport every Sunday

[8] *SWDN*, 23 July 1906.
[9] SWMFA *Annual Report*, 1913–14.
[10] Figures calculated from census information in John Williams, *Digest of Welsh Historical Statistics* (Griffithstown, 1985).

for the many migrants from the West Midlands living in the town. This influenced Newport FC to choose amber, the colour of Wolverhampton Wanderers, for its strip in 1906.[11] Players from the Bristol area dominated the South Wales League in its early years, while Ton Pentre's team of *c*.1910 was largely composed of players who had moved south from the soccer-dominated Wrexham area to work in the coal industry.[12] When men found no club to fulfil their desire for soccer they could always form one. J. W. Thorpe, a leading light in the foundation of Swansea Town, served his legal articles in the Ruabon practice of Llewelyn Kenrick, the founder of the FAW, before moving to south Wales. Bartley Wilson, who oversaw the transition of a small Cardiff club known as Riverside FC into Cardiff City, originated from Bristol where he had followed soccer. George Thorneycroft, a founding director of Newport County, had moved to the town from West Bromwich to work as an iron mill manager. An early chairman of the SWMFA, Jack Sandiford, was from the north of England, as were other early promoters of the game in Cardiff.[13] The impact of in-migration was not always so positive for soccer. In 1906 Pontypridd United, already in financial trouble, closed after dissension in the team caused by the introduction of players who had only recently moved to the district.[14] Nonetheless many of the thousands of migrants to south Wales brought with them a love of soccer, which they were keen to maintain, be it as spectators, players or officials.

At the heart of the efforts to promote soccer was the SWMFA and its South Wales Senior Cup. The excitement of a knock-out competition and frequent derby matches between growing towns and communities, together with resultant press coverage, rapidly stimulated interest in the game. The size of the crowds took many by surprise:

> To recall such intense interest, keen excitement, and such a large crowd in the Rhondda as was present at Treherbert on Saturday to witness the

[11] *WM*, 24 August 1910; Richard Shepherd, *Newport County Football Club, 1912–1960* (Chalford, 1997), p. 10; *SWDN*, 3 September 1906. The fact that the local rugby club played in amber also contributed to the decision. Newport County also chose the colour when it was founded in 1912.

[12] Garland, *Welsh Cup*, p. 81.

[13] George Lerry, *Association Football in Wales, 1870–1924* (Oswestry, 1924), p. 15; Garland, *Welsh Cup*, p. 92; Derrick Jenkins, 'Football in Cardiff, 1888–1939' (unpublished MS, 1984), p. 54; Shepherd, *Newport County FC, 1912–60*, p. 22; *WM*, 24 August 1910.

[1908] semi-final for the South Wales Cup, one must go back many years . . . Saturday's crowd made the Rugger enthusiasts envious and was beyond the most sanguine expectations of the Soccerites, for who would have dared to prophesy a couple of seasons back that two local clubs would draw a gate of £100 in the Valleys. The attendance was a revelation, and those who witnessed the encounter had every cause to feel satisfied with the exhibition, though cup matches are not always conducive to scientific football.[15]

Alongside the unscientific football of cup competitions were the South Wales and the Rhymney Valley Leagues. Formed in 1890 and 1903 respectively, the two senior leagues gave clubs regular competitive matches against nearby rivals, further popularizing the game. Success in either cup or league was warmly celebrated with both spontaneous and organized receptions:

Naturally there was a great jubilation at Treharris on the success of the team, and as soon as the news of the victory [in the 1907 South Wales Cup final] was flashed over the wires crowds began to assemble near the railway station in order to give a hearty welcome home to the team. By the time the train arrived the crowd had assumed such huge proportions that all the traffic in the vicinity was suspended, and as Hughie Williams, the popular captain, emerged from the station gates with the coveted trophy in his possession a mighty cheer rent the air. He was immediately hoisted on the shoulders of some stalwart supporters, a procession was formed, and headed by the St. Cynon's brass band, paraded through Perrott Street to the square and thence to the headquarters of the club at the Commercial Hotel.[16]

The highly visible, audible and ritualized nature of such celebrations further raised the profile of soccer and ensured that its achievements took on a wider significance as something of a civic event. Public processions were already part of religious and other sporting celebrations and their extension to soccer was a natural part of the game's incorporation into the local popular culture.[17] Soccer's advances were becoming increasingly hard to ignore.

[14] *SWDN*, 22 January 1906.
[15] *SWDN*, 9 March 1908: Ton Pentre v. Cwmpark, at Treherbert rugby ground.
[16] *SWDN*, 8 April 1907: Treharris v. Merthyr Vale, at Aberdare.
[17] Other processions in popular culture are examined in Croll, *Civilizing the Urban*, pp. 200–13.

The SWMFA was well aware of how important matches stimulated interest and excitement, and it did its best to stage such games in towns where soccer was weak. At a meeting held by the SWMFA after the 1908 South Wales Cup semi-final in Merthyr, the local athletic club, impressed by the size of the attendance, decided to form a professional soccer club.[18] The following year, the final was held at the Northern Union ground in Tonypandy, attracting over 6,000. After the match, the chairman of Mid Rhondda Northern Union club announced that the sport had not been a financial success and that he wanted the club to take up soccer, which was the 'coming game'.[19] The SWMFA also worked hard to persuade the FAW to stage international matches in the south, for which it had negotiated the use of Cardiff Arms Park. The 1906 international against England, which set a new gate-receipts record for a soccer match in Wales, was testimony to the association's success in promoting such matches.

Relations between the SWMFA and FAW were not always cordial owing to the latter's hesitancy in assisting the development of the game in the south. This was partly because of its own financial instability, but also because it felt that its status as the national association was threatened by the growing SWMFA. Disputes between the two associations arose over representation on the FAW council, the selection of the national side and the venue of Welsh Cup and international matches. After persuasion and pressure from the SWMFA, the FAW sanctioned the holding of eight international matches in south Wales, compared with fourteen in the north, between 1900 and 1914. Although this led to new arguments between the two associations over money, the matches did much to boost soccer's southern profile. The FAW's Welsh Cup was also crucial in assisting the game's development in the south. Wrexham FC dominated the competition, but Aberaman reached the final in 1903 and Aberdare in 1904 and 1905. Just six south Wales clubs entered the 1905–6 competition, but by 1909–10 thirteen of the forty entrants were from the south. The performances of the early south Wales teams reminded the FAW of the progress of the game in the south and boosted the more successful clubs' finances and popularity.

---

[18]   *SWDN*, 27 March 1908, 3 April 1909.
[19]   *SWDN*, 5 April 1909. Northern Union was the name given to rugby league before 1922.

Soccer's development was also helped by the stagnation into which rugby was slowly falling. Since its symbolic zenith in 1905, Welsh rugby had drifted into complacency, and accusations that the game had become too defensive with little emphasis on exciting and open back-play were commonplace.[20] A Swansea RFC official claimed in 1907 that, with the exception of matches against Cardiff and Newport, there were no difficult or challenging games for his club, which was causing gates to fall as people lost interest. Like many, he feared that soccer would fill this void.[21] Senior rugby had no cup or league competitions to add any excitement or meaning beyond pride to its matches, and increasing numbers of spectators seemed to be transferring their allegiances to the more competitive arena of soccer. While rugby faced problems on the field, off the field it met with crisis. In 1907 allegations of professionalism and match fixing were rife. Accusations that players were paid were nothing new, but the extent of the exposures emanating from Aberdare did much to harm Welsh rugby's reputation and self-esteem.[22] Soccer could only profit from the recriminations and negative publicity that rugby was attracting, and its growing sense of confidence represented a notable contrast to the crisis in its sister code. It also benefited from being a simpler game, with fewer rules, making it easier to play and follow than rugby.[23] By 1910 there were warnings that soccer was threatening the very existence of rugby in the Rhondda and other localities.[24] Such predictions may have been somewhat premature, but they indicated the momentum that the dribbling code was gaining.

Although improving, the general standard of soccer in south Wales was far from being on a par with that in the senior English competitions. To give people an opportunity to see a more attractive and higher standard of soccer, leading English clubs, such as Aston Villa, Manchester City and Wolverhampton Wanderers, accepted invitations to play exhibition matches across south Wales against local sides.[25] The promoters of

[20] See, for example, *SWDN*, 29 April 1907.
[21] *SWDN*, 7 June 1907.
[22] See Williams, *1905 and All That*, pp. 159–66.
[23] Russell, *Football and the English*, p. 20.
[24] *WM*, 3 October 1910.
[25] Such games had been played in the region since the 1890s but increased in frequency during the Edwardian years. Established south Wales clubs also played exhibition games in local towns where soccer had not yet taken off.

Cardiff City organized three matches against leading English teams to gauge and stimulate interest in soccer in the city, before launching the club as a fully-fledged professional outfit. While the visiting teams were often largely reserve sides, the matches helped to develop both media and public interest in soccer, and gave the game's promoters confidence that there was potential support for professional clubs.

For soccer to establish itself fully, a consistently high standard of attractive play was needed. Central to achieving this was the hiring of better-quality players from England and north Wales.[26] The experience and talent of such professionals, and the beneficial impact they had on the performances of local amateurs, made soccer far more appealing and were key to its establishment as a spectator sport. The actual spread of professionalism was gradual and uneven. The pioneering club was Aberdare, and neighbouring clubs, such as Aberaman and Treharris, followed it. Once some clubs had taken the step, others had to follow if they wanted to continue to compete on equal terms. Although full-time professionals were not unknown in south Wales, most clubs before 1910 simply employed a limited number of part-time professionals who were probably no better off than many of their 'amateur' peers in rugby union who received generous expenses and broken-time payments.

FINANCE, LAND, CHAPELS AND AMATEURS: PROBLEMS AND OPPOSITION

Employing players involved a considerable financial outlay which the early professional clubs struggled to meet. Despite reaching Welsh Cup finals and enjoying league success, both Aberdare and Aberaman found themselves struggling to cope with their wage bills. By the end of the 1906–7 season, financial difficulties had forced the two clubs, together with Ebbw Vale, Porth and Rogerstone, all leading teams in the early years of the

[26] Employing players from afar was not, however, straightforward. Many of the players first signed on by Merthyr Town claimed to have scored important goals and played for top teams. Later, the club's officials admitted that their lack of knowledge of the game may have allowed them to be misled. *Merthyr Express* (hereafter *ME*), 12 March 1921.

century, to fold.[27] An official of Merthyr Town said that had the club's promoters known the troubles and pitfalls ahead, he doubted whether they would have set up the enterprise.[28] The financial cost of professionalism was immediate, but the rewards were slower to come, and clubs were not yet well enough established to sustain the losses.

Finance was not the only hurdle holding back the development of soccer. Securing a suitable ground was the initial, and often the biggest, problem that new clubs faced. Professional outfits required enclosed grounds where admission charges could be enforced. Ideally, such a site would be located centrally in a town to ensure that spectators could easily reach it. The industrial and population expansion of the period meant that land was at a premium in urban areas. What vacant or under utilized space that did exist was expensive and usually owned by rich individuals or large companies. The region's aristocratic landowners were not opposed to sport, and some actively encouraged it in an effort to foster social and industrial harmony. However, with rugby having developed first, it had already secured much of the available land, either on lease or as a gift from paternal landowners.[29] A few landowners were not so willing to help either code of football because of the games' associations with drink and unruly behaviour by both players and spectators.[30] Soccer's position was exacerbated by its professional associations. Much of the aristocratic landowning class of south Wales had been educated in English public schools. In later life, some retained the ideals of sport for sport's sake that their education had instilled and were thus reluctant to foster professional sport. Some members of the local aristocracy, such as the SWMFA's first president, Captain Morgan Lindsay, did hold honorary positions at soccer authorities or clubs, but they were not actively involved in the game on a daily basis and nor did they help to ease the land shortage. The situation was not helped by the fact that most of the rich industrialists lived away from the towns and valleys that were occupationally dependent

[27] Lile and Farmer, 'Early development', p. 211; *SWDN*, 6 April 1907. Aberdare reopened the following season.

[28] *ME*, 12 March 1921.

[29] The marquess of Bute's benefaction of Cardiff Arms Park is a notable example.

[30] See Croll, *Civilizing the Urban*, pp. 144–6.

on their enterprises. Such men also had links with many communities across south Wales, a trend which developed with the Edwardian amalgamation of coal companies.[31] This meant that industrialists often lacked the kind of strong association with a specific town that could kindle an interest in promoting it through a professional soccer club. Thus, because control of the land was in the hands of a minority, soccer was unable to develop as quickly as its supporters wanted. The ruling classes were exerting some control, deliberately or not, over the leisure of the masses, using the same material dominance that gave them power over their employees' lives at work.

Similarly, the Cardiff Corporation was determined to use its control of land to ensure that the introduction of professional soccer did not bring unsavoury practices with it. A proposed lease for a soccer ground on the eventual Ninian Park site in 1907 forbade betting, rabbit coursing and the sale of alcohol on the land.[32] In Edwardian south Wales, the politically dominant middle classes and traditional aristocracy were keen to try to keep a rein on the burgeoning working-class culture, and regulating the use of public space for leisure was one method easily utilized. Companies that owned land were not held back by any moralistic concerns, but they did want a profitable return on leases. However, the financial instability of the early professional game made potential new clubs reluctant to commit themselves to expensive leases.

Instead, many small clubs reclaimed vacant and rough land on the edge of towns. In the Rhondda, some junior teams of both codes were forced to play on 'bleak mountain tops'.[33] Throughout the south Wales valleys, land was available on the adjacent hilltops, but a professional club could never hope to draw crowds large enough to cover its wage bill when spectators faced a trek up a hillside to watch a game. Even when grounds were secured, there was often no guarantee of continued tenure, and such problems were central to the disbandment of some early

---

[31] Many other charities and activities, often dependent on philanthropic support, faltered in Cardiff and other towns because of a lack of locally based industrialists. See Neil Evans, 'Urbanisation, elite attitudes and philanthropy: Cardiff, 1850–1914', *International Review of Social History*, 27 (1982), 290–323.

[32] Finance Committee minutes, 7 March 1907, in *City of Cardiff: Reports of Council and Committees* (hereafter Cardiff Corporation).

[33] *SWDN*, 29 April 1907.

professional clubs such as Porth and Aberaman.[34] In the rapidly expanding communities, landlords often found new and more lucrative uses than soccer for their land. Long-term leases were unaffordable for clubs and offered landlords a poor financial return.

One obvious answer to ground problems was to share an enclosure with a rugby club. Before 1906, Cardiff RFC had been happy to allow the occasional international or exhibition match to be held at the Arms Park. But as attendances in the Valleys rose and the exhibition and international matches in the large towns proved a success, it became clear that soccer represented a threat to the popularity of the handling code. This led to some bitterness creeping into the rugby fraternity's relationship with the soccer authorities and clubs. In Swansea the local rugby authority was even considering banning junior soccer players from participating in its matches.[35] Such tensions meant that the rugby fraternity was reluctant to enter into any ground-sharing arrangements. Agreement was also held back by potential logistical problems caused by fixture clashes. Cardiff RFC did allow one more exhibition match at the Arms Park in 1909, but that was the end of the association game there until the modern era. The extra income in rent that a soccer club would provide meant that some of the smaller rugby clubs, particularly when the ground was owned by a syndicate or welfare organization, agreed to ground-sharing schemes. But the rugby clubs of the larger towns, enjoying greater financial security, could afford to be more distant in their relations with the upcoming soccer clubs. Merthyr Town initially shared Penydarren Park with a local rugby team.[36] The arrangement showed the fears of the rugby fraternity to be justified when, after just one season of the two codes sharing, the rugby team was disbanded when the athletic club, which owned the ground, decided to concentrate its energy on soccer.

Other professional sports were more willing to come to ground-sharing arrangements. Through athletics, boxing, and, to a lesser degree, cycling, professional sport was widespread in

---

[34] *SWDN,* 29 April, 27 May 1907.
[35] *SWDN,* 24 September 1909.
[36] Trevor Delaney, *The Grounds of Rugby League* (Keighley, 1995), p. 199.

the south Wales valleys during the first decade of the twentieth century.[37] Being popular, openly profit-orientated and with fewer overheads (especially wages) and quicker returns than soccer, there had been limited investment by private companies in securing space, such as Taff Vale Park in Pontypridd and the Athletic ground in Mid Rhondda, for athletics and cycling. With the owners interested in maximizing profits, they were happy to allow professional soccer to share the grounds. This gave the code the initial boost it needed, and both grounds were eventually taken over by professional soccer clubs.

Out of the crisis over professionalism in rugby came the introduction of professional rugby to south Wales. In 1907–9, encouraged by promises of financial assistance from the game's governing body, six Northern Union clubs were set up in south Wales by individuals who either no longer wanted to be involved in the dishonest 'shamateurism' of Welsh rugby union or had been suspended by the WFU for having such transgressions uncovered.[38] Soccer and Northern Union were drawn together by a shared commitment to professionalism and the hostility and mistrust they suffered from rugby union. Aberdare AFC gave professional rugby an initial helping hand by letting the Northern Union club use its ground.[39] Although attendances were initially high, and interest was stimulated by the visits of touring sides from New Zealand and Australia in 1907 and 1908, Northern Union failed to establish itself in south Wales. Compared with soccer matches between rival south Wales clubs, Northern Union games against clubs from the north of England seemed increasingly unattractive, particularly as the Welsh teams lost more often than not.[40] Association football thus began to win

[37] Williams, *1905 and All That*, ch. 7. Cricket also had a tradition of professional players but was yet to develop fully its place in working-class culture.

[38] Williams, *1905 and All That*, p. 165; Geoffrey Moorhouse, *A People's Game: The Official History of Rugby League, 1895–1995* (London, 1995), p. 105. Tony Collins, *Rugby's Great Split: Class, Culture and the Origins of Rugby Football League* (London, 1998), is an excellent social history of early rugby league in England. For more on rugby league in Wales see Peter Lush and Dave Farrar (eds.), *Tries in the Valleys: A History of Rugby League in Wales* (London, 1998).

[39] Delaney, *Grounds of Rugby League*, p. 193; Williams, *1905 and All That*, pp. 160, 164; *SWDN*, 27 May 1907. Indeed, E. H. Rees, secretary of the Northern Union club, had previously been involved in the running of a local professional soccer club.

[40] Ebbw Vale and Merthyr were the most successful teams, winning a third of their games. Aberdare won just 5.9 per cent of its total matches, and Barry just 16.7 per cent. Wray Vamplew, *Pay Up and Play the Game: Professional Sport in Britain, 1875–1914* (Cambridge, 1988), p. 147.

over those whose sporting preferences lay outside amateur rugby. This, together with the financial burdens of having to play regularly in northern England, particularly after the governing body's subsidies were withdrawn, was too much for the fledgeling sport. The Northern Union clubs in Barry, Mid Rhondda and Aberdare failed to survive more than a year. In Treherbert, Northern Union lasted two seasons, the Merthyr club closed in 1911, while Ebbw Vale left the league in 1912.

Some of these sides had previously been amateur rugby clubs. This meant that their large grounds were now available to other professional sports. It was only through sharing a newly pro- fessionalized rugby ground that a senior soccer club could be set up in Ebbw Vale.[41] In Mid Rhondda, soccer gained access to the local professional athletics ground when the financially struggling Northern Union club that rented it decided to switch to the dribbling code. In Merthyr, Northern Union helped soccer by taking so much support away from the rugby union club that the latter's parent athletic club switched to the association code.[42] Soccer was not so lucky everywhere. In Treherbert, a rugby union syndicate secured the former Northern Union ground, leaving the soccer club with an unenclosed field.[43] After the demise of Northern Union, the grounds continued to be used by other professional sports such as cycling and athletics alongside soccer. This provided invaluable income for the association clubs. Thus, while rugby union may have been reluctant to help soccer's development, the game found other professional allies in the south Wales valleys and benefited from their failures and successes.

While professional soccer was developing in the Valleys, its progress was muted in the coastal towns before 1910. In 1906 Newport FC decided to take on a number of professional players and enter the Western and South Wales Leagues. The club closed a year later because of financial difficulties.[44] The biggest problem in setting up professional clubs in the coastal towns was

---

[41] *SWDN*, 7 October 1907; Williams, *1905 and All That*, p. 165. Ebbw Vale RFC took up Northern Union so that it no longer had to hide its payments to players. Also see *SWDN*, 13, 19 June 1913, 18 June 1914, for details of the relationship between soccer and Northern Union in Ebbw Vale.

[42] *ME*, 12 March 1921.

[43] *Rhondda Leader*, 29 July 1911.

[44] *Football Argus*, 1 September 1906; *SWDN*, 3 September 1906.

that of securing a suitable ground. With the rugby clubs unwilling to help and no privately owned athletic venues, any prospective ground would have to be purchased at considerable cost and was unlikely to be located centrally in the town. In 1906, after fourteen months of negotiations, the secretary of the South Wales League had to admit defeat in his attempt to rent a plot of land for a ground in Cardiff because the owner, Lord Tredegar, was unwilling to grant a long-term lease.[45] In 1907 there were attempts to secure land owned by the City Corporation on Sloper Road, the eventual site of Ninian Park, but agreement could not be reached on the financial terms and clauses of the prospective lease. The professional status of soccer, and its perceived potential profits, seemed to be leading to demands for an unreasonably high rent and other improvements to the land. The syndicate announced that without a ground, it could not proceed with the prospective club, and the scheme collapsed.[46] There was already enough evidence from the Valleys that professionalism alone was not enough to attract crowds big enough to support a club. Thus, until large suitable grounds could be found, south Wales's largest towns would remain without senior soccer clubs. In 1905, Cardiff was made a city and, within a week, a junior club called Riverside (Cardiff) FC applied to change its name to Cardiff City. The request was refused but, nearly a year later, the club applied again, claiming that it was the leading team in the city and deserved the title. Its assertion was challenged and permission denied by, first, the SWMFA and, then, by the FAW. The name was being reserved in case a senior team was set up in Cardiff which would better represent soccer and the city.[47] Despite joining the South Wales League for the 1906–7 season, Riverside remained an amateur club.

Soccer's development was also hindered to an extent by religious attitudes. In the late nineteenth century, many Nonconformist ministers preached against football in general, angry at its associations with drinking and gambling and at the distraction it

[45] *SWDN*, 8 January 1906.
[46] The syndicate felt that it was already being generous in offering £100 p.a. for what was in effect a 'rubbish heap'. *SWDN*, 2 May 1907; Cardiff Corporation, Property, Markets etc. Subcommittee minutes, 17 April, 1 May 1907.
[47] *SWDN*, 17, 21 September 1906; SWMFA minutes, 1, 15 September 1906; Lloyd, *C'mon City*, p. 24. The club had begun using the title Cardiff City without permission and was threatened with suspension unless it ceased doing so.

provided from religious activities. The competitive nature of sport was also seen as being at odds with the Christian ethos. Indeed, the rise of commercialized leisure *per se* was viewed as a threat by Nonconformity. The thriving music-halls, cinemas and football grounds offered a stark contrast to the chapels' half-empty pews.[48] Although the Welsh religious revival of 1904–5 had created some public hostility towards football, and even led to the disbandment of some clubs, its intensity was short-lived, and most Nonconformist ministers gradually grew to tolerate rugby's place in society.[49] Soccer, however, tainted by the sin of professionalism, was a different case. While some Nonconformist ministers had begun to accept and support the benefits of organized sport, playing for money was often seen as 'an unnatural and unwholesome life'.[50] Even elements of the Anglican church, which had been very supportive of soccer in its nineteenth-century amateur days in south Wales, began to have reservations about the game. A Cardiff vicar used the press to make public his fears that association football was injuring Christianity. He was angry that the city had been invaded by thousands on Good Friday for a match at Ninian Park, and complained that the noise of the crowds and a band had disturbed worshippers in his church.[51] How much of an impact such indictments had is unclear. Like the tirades against drinking, not all moralistic lectures emanating from the pulpits influenced the habits of even the listening congregations. Anglican support was limited in south Wales and, although chapel membership was still strong in the wake of the 1904–5 revival, Nonconformity's wider influence was in slow decline. It did maintain a strong following amongst the middle classes, and any hostility cannot have helped soccer, possibly discouraging potential wealthy and respectable backers. However, the momentum of the game's growth was greater than the influence of the chapels' antipathy.

The hostility was by no means universal amongst Nonconformist ministers, and some suggested a positive attitude towards

---

[48] See Croll, *Civilizing the Urban*, ch. 6.

[49] See letter in *SWDN*, 9 March 1910; Williams, *1905 and All That*, pp. 76–8. A minority of ministers did continue to preach against the sport. See Croll, *Civilizing the Urban*, ch. 6, and letter in *SWDN*, 11 March 1910.

[50] Revd E. Davies, quoted in Lile and Farmer, 'Early development', p. 204.

[51] *SWDN*, 25 March 1913.

sport to try to reclaim the 'thousands of our young men' lost to the churches.[52] As well as setting up their own soccer teams, various churches and chapels introduced an annual Footballers' Sunday when players of both codes took an active role in a service. A 1910 *South Wales Daily News* editorial, noting the involvement of the Welsh soccer international L. R. Roose in such a service in Ilford, advocated its introduction to south Wales:

> . . . the qualities that go to make fame on the playing field are those of the highest manhood. It is futile for the church to thunder against football; it is unfair to ignore the best in the game while attacking the worse. Why not, instead, bring the leading players into personal contact with the pulpit? It is misunderstanding far more than indifference that empties the pew. Preachers can do much to purify the atmosphere of popular amusements, and it is their duty to join forces, and not issues with the young men who uphold on the playing field the prowess of their nation. Football Sunday could be a national institution. The religious element should be brought into sport. Religion is 'the most manly possession' in the world, and the football hero in the pulpit makes for the higher welfare of the game and the cultivation of the nobler qualities of young manhood.[53]

It saw an association between sport and religion as the saviour of both. To what extent such ideas were adopted is unclear, although isolated examples were still being publicized in the early 1920s.[54] Whether the captain of Cardiff City talking about the qualities of football being useful in everyday life had any impact is questionable, but such events did help to overcome religion's opposition to professional sport.

Soccer's early years in England were dominated by conflicts between the advocates of amateurism and professionalism. By 1900 professionalism had established itself in English soccer and, while not welcomed by elements of the game's authorities, it was tolerated in order to ensure its regulation. Much of the conflict originated not from hostility towards professionalism, but instead from traditional middle-class adherents of the game who were unhappy at the way soccer was being turned into a mass,

---

[52] *SWDN*, 9 March 1910.
[53] *SWDN*, 8 March 1910.
[54] *SWE*, 16 April 1923.

commercial spectator sport.[55] Seeing their control of the game slip away, a group of amateur clubs, predominantly from southern England, broke from the FA and formed the Amateur Football Association in 1907. Although there was initial debate in the south Wales game over the rights and wrongs of being paid to play soccer, the issue did not cause the divisions that it did in England. In south Wales there was no significant group of former public school players keen to uphold the virtues of amateurism instilled by their education. Sport in Wales prided itself on its democratic nature. Its role in bringing together classes was revered, not reviled, by the middle classes. The amateurism of Welsh rugby owed more to a desire to continue playing for the Triple Crown than to any lofty ideals. Professionalism would have brought isolation from the other home nations and Welsh rugby was not willing to risk that. Instead, clubs were content to continue the underhand payments and liberal interpretation of expenses that made up their 'shamateurism'. Eric Hobsbawm has argued that amateur sport was often promoted by the middle classes in order to help emphasize their separate identity at a time when occupation and wealth changes were blurring social divisions.[56] In south Wales this process was not obvious, with rigid class divisions still very much evident within the wider framework of community and other identities.[57] Given both this and sport's function in highlighting these other identities, the middle classes of south Wales did not feel the need to assert their 'higher' status through amateurism. Society in south Wales was, in many ways, élitist. The working class and much of the middle class valued success, be it cultural, political or economic. In such an atmosphere, it was achievement that counted, not taking part.[58] The public school ethic of playing for the game's sake had no place in the evolving culture of south

---

[55] See Mason, *Association Football*, ch. 3.

[56] Eric Hobsbawm, 'Mass producing traditions: Europe, 1870–1914', in Hobsbawm and Ranger, *Invention of Tradition*, pp. 291, 299–300.

[57] There were severe restraints on social mobility in the region, with few outlets for individuals to advance. As a result, the Welsh middle classes made up only a small proportion of the local social structure and thus felt less need to exert their difference. See L. J. Williams, 'Capitalists and coalowners', in Prys Morgan (ed.), *Glamorgan County History*, vol. VI: *Glamorgan Society, 1780–1980* (Cardiff, 1988), p. 114.

[58] The strong competitiveness in the popular culture of south Wales can also be seen in the region's musical and choral festivals. See Gareth Williams, *Valleys of Song: Music and Society in Wales, 1840–1914* (Cardiff, 1998).

Wales. Thus, if the result was all-important, there would be no objection to being rewarded or paid for achieving it. Professionalism in sport was in line with the general ethos of life in south Wales.

Advocates of amateur soccer did exist in south Wales. The introduction of professionalism was controversial and the Welsh soccer authorities enforced the same strict distinctions between amateurs and professionals that their English counterparts insisted on. However, the Welsh amateurs did not seek isolation from the professional game and accepted it as a part of modern soccer. Thus the creation of the separatist Amateur Football Association had no repercussions in Wales. Cardiff Corinthians, founded in 1898 and the most famous of the south Wales amateur sides, wanted to play against the best opposition possible and took up competitive soccer in 1904. Its ambitions lay in joining the Southern and Welsh Leagues and not in stubborn isolation. Indeed, a number of its players made themselves available for Cardiff City should they be needed.[59] There were also strong adherents of amateurism in Welsh rugby, but they were unwilling to risk a repeat of the divisions that resulted from the 1907 'shamateur' allegations and were thus not too rigid in their definitions of what amateurism actually meant. It was concern over rugby's future that lay behind most of the game's attacks on soccer's professionalism. The real motive was not the morality of paying players but the threat that professional soccer posed to rugby's popularity.

Thus, by 1910, a culmination of factors put soccer in a position where it was beginning to rival rugby's pre-eminence in the popular culture of south Wales. There were now twelve league divisions, 262 clubs and over 7,000 players affiliated to the SWMFA.[60] The standard of play had improved sufficiently to develop a core of regular supporters, many of whom had been won over from the handling code. In some inland towns and the Rhondda Valleys, soccer was even beginning to oust rugby. Aberdare, Treharris and Merthyr Town were attracting healthy attendances of 3,000–4,000. Rugby was said to be virtually extinct in Merthyr and Aberdare and 'slowly but surely' falling

[59] *SWDN*, 8 October 1913. The club's English namesakes, the Corinthians, did not play competitive matches until 1922.
[60] SWMFA *Annual Report*, 1909–10; *WM*, 24 August 1910.

out of 'popular favour' in the Rhondda.[61] Schoolboy and junior soccer was also fast developing. In 1910 the new Cardiff City club said that the increasing demand for the game in the city was mainly down to the 'thousands' of soccer-playing boys who were being produced by the district's elementary schools. The press thought that many parents had started watching the dribbling code instead of rugby because of their sons. Indeed, in 1909, the *Western Mail* claimed that a growth in the love of soccer was inevitable because of the strength of the junior game.[62] From this base, talented youngsters began to emerge, allowing clubs to rely less on expensive imported professionals without a decline in standards. Testimony to the improving playing standards was that some of the region's best players left to join English clubs. Three of Aberdare's South Wales League winning side of 1904 went on to play in the Football League, including Billy 'Fatty' Wedlock, a future England captain. The junior game also ensured that soccer did not die out in towns where the financial burdens of professionalism had forced the closure of the senior club. Such financial problems indicated that progress had not been straightforward. Similarly, the 1908 Eight Hours Act, which led some companies to compensate for shorter shifts by not allowing miners to leave work early, meant fewer travelling supporters and smaller crowds at mid-week evening games.[63] Thus, in 1910, soccer still had a long way to go. Despite its stagnation, rugby remained immensely popular, while its national side continued to be successful, providing an outlet for Welsh patriotism and pride that soccer would find hard to rival.

ENGLISH LEAGUES

In 1906 Treharris and Newport FC joined the Western League, which consisted of teams from south-west England. Within two years they were joined by Aberdare Town and Barry District. This participation in English leagues was the beginning of a trend that

[61] *WM*, 24 August, 3 October 1910. In 1910, the visit of Cardiff RFC attracted less than 1,000 spectators to Treorchy. In the same month the visit of Cardiff City to nearby Ton Pentre drew five times that number.
[62] Cardiff City AFC Ltd, *Prospectus*; *WM*, 24 August 1910, 6 October 1909. See ch. 3 for more on Edwardian schoolboy soccer.
[63] See *SWDN*, 14 March 1910.

was to prove critical to the development of soccer in south Wales. The Western League matches provided a higher standard of play than local competitions and, crucially, had the added attraction of regular English opposition. As in rugby, matches against English teams had an element of international competition about them and were thus popular with spectators. This also appealed to the patrons of clubs who saw the leagues as a way of putting their towns on the British map. Heavy travelling expenses and some indifferent performances meant that the venture was not an immediate success, but by the 1909–10 season Merthyr Town and Ton Pentre had joined the competition's Welsh members.

In the summer of 1910 a dispute arose between the Welsh clubs playing in the Western League and its governing body over a proposed reorganization of the competition. Aberdare, Merthyr Town, Ton Pentre and Treharris (which that season had become the first Welsh club to win the league) all resigned from the competition, while applications to join from Mardy, Cwm Albion, Cwmpark and Tredegar Town were rejected.[64] This created a vacuum for a league competition that would enable Welsh clubs to play English teams regularly. A year earlier, the Football League had, for a second time, turned down the Southern League's request for a merger of the two competitions.[65] The stagnating Southern League was left with no alternative but to strengthen itself, and the most obvious area to expand into was south Wales. The growing popularity of the game in the south Wales valleys suggested that an enormous potential for professional soccer existed in the region's large coastal towns, a view reinforced by the healthy attendances at exhibition matches in Cardiff, Swansea and Newport. Ton Pentre, Merthyr Town and Aberdare were invited to join the Southern League when it was restructured for the 1909–10 season. The clubs were even promised that, provided they remained in the League for two consecutive seasons, they would automatically be promoted to the first division.[66]

---

[64]   *SWDN*, 20 June, 1 July 1910. At the heart of the dispute was the issue of finance, with English clubs complaining that the trips to south Wales were too expensive. Some Welsh clubs seem to have been promised financial guarantees about expenses that were not followed. *SWDN*, 5 July 1909.

[65]   Lionel Francis, *Seventy Five Years of Southern League Football* (London, 1969), p. 43.

[66]   The promise of automatic promotion was never fulfilled. Dave Twydell, *Rejected FC*, Vol. 1: *Histories of the Ex-Football League Clubs* (Harefield, 1992 edn), p. 15; *SWDN*, 16 September 1909.

Under the guidance of its secretary, Harry Bradshaw, the league's management committee visited influential men in junior soccer across south Wales to encourage the formation of new clubs. Riverside FC were asked to join the Southern League in 1910 and then, in the following year, approaches were made to individuals in Swansea and Newport. Like the Western League, the Southern League provided clubs with regular competitive matches against quality opposition from England, as well as against local rivals. Although, by 1910, the League could no longer claim the equality with the Football League it once had, it remained a prestigious competition with a strong first division that included famous clubs like Crystal Palace and Queen's Park Rangers. Spectators in south Wales were quickly attracted by the Southern League, whose fortunes, to the benefit of the game in the region, now seemed entwined with south Wales. When Aberdare AFC ran into financial difficulties in 1913, the Southern League promised to help the club, with Harry Bradshaw personally presiding over a supporters' meeting and trying to organize fund-raising matches.[67]

The overtures of the Southern League alone were not enough to develop professional soccer in the coastal towns of south Wales. There was still the problem of a lack of suitable grounds to overcome. It was in Cardiff that the first breakthrough was made with the elevation and transformation of Riverside FC. In 1908, at the third time of asking, the club had been given permission to change its name to Cardiff City, on the condition that it would relinquish the title if a first-class club was formed in the city. Yet the lack of a suitable ground was holding back the adoption of professionalism. The Southern League's 1910 invitation, however, gave the club new confidence. With entry to the League guaranteeing attractive and potentially lucrative fixtures, individuals were more willing to sign guarantees. A lease for land used as a rubbish tip was finally secured from the City Corporation, which had by now reduced its financial demands. Thus, with a suitable ground and a guarantee of entry to an attractive competition, the Cardiff City committee set about transforming the club from a small team in the South Wales League to the

---

[67] *SWDN*, 13 December 1913.

Table 1.1

South Wales clubs' entry to Southern League, pre-1914

1909–10	1910–11	1911–12
Aberdare	Cardiff City	Cwm Albion*
Merthyr Town	Treharris**	Mardy
Ton Pentre		Pontypridd

1912–13	1912–13	1914–15
Llanelly	Abertillery Town**	Ebbw Vale
Mid Rhondda	Caerphilly**	
Newport County	Barry	
Swansea Town		

*Did not complete 1911–12 season.
**Did not enter/complete 1914–15 season.

region's first full-time professional soccer club.[68] Established players from outside the region were brought in and the modern-day Cardiff City FC was born. Nine of the thirteen players in the club's first professional squad were from Scotland. None of the four others was a native of south Wales.[69] In Swansea and Newport, the men approached by the Southern League were not members of a single junior club, but individuals involved in the game in differing capacities. Thus, professional clubs had to be formed entirely from scratch. As at Cardiff, with the Southern League guaranteeing attractive fixtures, individuals were prepared to take a risk by personally securing a lease on available land. In Swansea, land in the centre of town was rented from the local gas company at a very expensive rate, while at Newport land was obtained on the edge of town. With grounds now secured, public meetings were called in both towns to raise the necessary money to make the new clubs a reality.[70]

The willingness of the Southern League to accept clubs from south Wales meant that, as well as new clubs being formed,

[68] Many of the Cardiff City players did actually find new part-time jobs outside football to supplement their income. Directors promised to find Jack Evans, the club's first professional, an extra job on signing.

[69] *SWDN*, 10, 12 August 1910.

[70] See *South Wales Daily Post* (hereafter *SWDP*), 17 May, 13, 15 June 1912.

existing teams also applied to join the competition. By the 1913–14 season there were fourteen south Wales sides playing in the League. The higher standard of play required better professionals who demanded higher wages, while the English fixtures meant more costly travelling expenses. The experiences of the first professional teams in south Wales had not been forgotten and many clubs took the precaution of becoming limited liability companies.

Thus soccer's expansion in south Wales after 1910 owed much to the efforts of the Southern League's management committee. It encouraged the formation of new clubs and made it known that applications from south Wales would be welcome.[71] Its vision ensured that soccer in south Wales would develop into the fully professional game that it was in England. Yet the league's confidence in soccer's potential in south Wales was remarkable. In the summer of 1912 the Southern League voted to accept applications from south Wales clubs that were non-existent in all but name. Newport County applied successfully to join, despite not yet having secured a ground, let alone any players. The club had been founded by a meeting of four people the night before the Southern League AGM.[72] At Mid Rhondda the formation of the club was particularly fraught, illustrating the risk which the Southern League had taken. The transformation of a local junior club (which itself had previously been a Northern Union team) into a professional outfit began at a public meeting in April 1912, organized with the idea of raising money and supported by the Cardiff City manager. Entry to the Southern League was secured, but raising capital proved to be a problem. At one point in mid-August the whole project was announced dead because of insufficient funds. Nonetheless, the promoters decided to carry on and, with just over a week until its first game, the club had a ground and a manager but very little money and no players. Yet it managed to secure a team of local amateurs with some

[71] English clubs in the Southern League's second division, which suddenly found themselves playing in a predominantly Welsh competition, expressed doubts about the wisdom of expansion into Wales. Luton Town and Leyton threatened to resign over the issue. Promises of travel subsidies alleviated some of their concerns but tensions continued, particularly after the subsidies were reduced in the following season. *SWDN*, 3 May 1912, 26 June 1913.

[72] Ambrosen, *Amber in the Blood*, p. 7.

imported professionals and, in its first game, entertained Ton Pentre before a thousand spectators.[73]

The Southern League's attempts to promote soccer in south Wales could not have succeeded without the efforts and ambitions of individuals in the new clubs. Cardiff City may have evolved out of a junior club, but all it had in common with Riverside FC was a handful of individuals: the players, ground and management were all different. Bartley Wilson, who had run the Riverside club and had been the force behind its ambitions, was secretary of the new Cardiff City club but not a director. Ambition was not enough; what professional clubs required was money. Thus Wilson and the rest of the Riverside committee could not progress alone and Cardiff City enjoyed few benefits from having evolved from something smaller. Similarly, in Swansea and Newport the clubs required individuals who were willing to take risks and invest money. Not having evolved from smaller clubs, the towns' soccer movements may have been slightly later in bringing together interested parties and securing grounds, but, once this was achieved, Swansea Town and Newport County were no more disadvantaged than Cardiff City. But all three clubs were dependent on the financial investment taken by the assortment of small business, professional and skilled men who became their first directors.[74]

The economic climate of south Wales during the Edwardian years was crucial to people's willingness to invest money in soccer. Despite some problems in industrial relations, it was a period of expansion and enterprise. The results of industrial success included a financially secure middle class and a wealthy élite. People were willing to take monetary risks in a climate where success and innovation were inherent. Soccer's vast popularity in England and the strong sporting culture of south Wales illustrated the potential for professional soccer in the region. Thus, there were people who were willing and able to invest the money needed by clubs. Soccer also began to attract

---

[73] *SWDN*, 27 April, 3 May, 27, 28, 31 August, 6 September 1912; *Rhondda Leader*, 11 May, 17 August, 24 August 1912.

[74] The occupations of the first directors were: accountant, ironworker, commercial traveller, building contractor, two licensed victuallers (Newport County); hotel keeper, coal exporter, solicitor, fish merchant, insurance inspector, two licensed victuallers (Swansea Town); dairyman, two clerks, stock keeper, electrical engineer, builder and printer (Cardiff City).

Table 1.2
Intended Welsh League Division One, 1914–15[1]

Bargoed	Llanelly	Pontypridd	Ton Pentre
Barry	Mardy	Port Talbot	Troedyrhiw
Cardiff City	Merthyr Town	Rhymney	
Ebbw Vale	Mid Rhondda	Swansea Town	

[1] The disruption caused by the First World War means that it is unclear if all these clubs actually competed during 1914–15. A club from Milford Haven had also briefly been a member of the Welsh League, showing that senior soccer was spreading deep into west Wales.

some famous patrons whose support, although limited to financial rather than active help, must have helped to win the backing of other potential investors. Lord Ninian Crichton Stuart, son of the famous third marquess of Bute and a future MP, was one of the guarantors of Cardiff City's lease on Ninian Park – hence the ground's name. The coal magnate D. A. Thomas was an investor in Mid Rhondda, Merthyr Town and Cardiff City. Such men helped soccer gain the respectability that their class's patronage had given rugby in its early days.

Merthyr Town set the standard for south Wales by winning promotion to the Southern League's first division in 1911–12. This did much to boost the profile of soccer in the region and had an impact on the expectations of the other large clubs. Cardiff City attracted healthy attendances from the outset and this, together with Merthyr's success, instilled impatient ambitions in the club's directorate. They claimed that the Southern League's second division did not offer a programme good enough to maintain a first-class team. Thus, at the end of its second season in the Southern League, the club applied for membership of the Football League, admitting that its application was based more on potential than on pedigree or history.[75] Not surprisingly, the application gained only one vote. Instead, the Cardiff City directors led the setting up of the new Southern Alliance competition which offered the opportunity to play Southern League first-division sides. The club also considered joining the Birmingham and District League and pushed for the

[75] *SWDN*, 13, 17 May 1912.

promotion of three clubs instead of two from the Southern League's second division.[76] In 1912–13 Cardiff City won promotion to the Southern League's first division, thus finally giving the club the standard of the play it felt it needed.

The developments in the Southern League were in danger of leaving the rest of local soccer behind. In an effort to ensure that the domestic game was not marginalized, the Glamorganshire League renamed itself the Welsh League in 1912. Its long-term objective was to rival the Football League, but there were problems from the start. Cardiff City and Newport County initially declined to join and other members saw the competition as secondary to their participation in the Southern League.[77] Many of the teams fielded by the top clubs in the league were, in essence, reserve sides. As long as Welsh clubs were achieving in English competitions, the Welsh League, which could only offer success on a local scale, would be perceived as inferior. Yet the rapid successes of Cardiff City and Merthyr Town had encouraged smaller towns to try to emulate their glories by forming semi-professional clubs, so furthering the development of the senior game in south Wales. By the outbreak of war, almost every large town in the region had a club in either the Southern League or the first division of the Welsh League (see table 1.2).

Beyond the league competitions, various cups continued to play an important role in the development of soccer in south Wales. Clubs from the region began regularly to enter the FA Cup, the oldest and most glamorous of all cups, which proved to be very popular with spectators. South Wales enjoyed its first success in the Welsh Cup when Cardiff City won the trophy in 1912. There were also appearances in the final for Llanelly (1914), Pontypridd (1912 and 1913) and Swansea Town, which, in its first season of existence (1912–13), became the second south Wales club to win the cup. Each success was greeted with public celebrations, publicity and increased support for the clubs and soccer in general. In Swansea, the editorial of a local newspaper noted:

---

[76] *South Wales Argus* (hereafter *SWA*), reproduced in Ambrosen, *Amber in the Blood*, p. 7; *SWDN*, 26 April 1911.
[77] *SWDN*, 30 May, 1 July 1912. The Glamorganshire League itself had been born out of a change of name by the Rhymney Valley and District League in 1909.

The winning of the Welsh Cup by the Swansea Association team has incidentally had the effect of disclosing the large proportions already reached by the local supporters of the dribbling code and the intensity of the enthusiasm. Thousands of people waited in the dribbling rain for the home-coming of the players, and a huge procession accompanied the latter from the Rhondda and Swansea Bay Railway to the Hotel, where the time-honoured custom of 'filling the cup' was observed.[78]

What the victory did more to disclose was how the public was attracted to success. Along with Merthyr Town, Swansea Town became the first Welsh club to reach the first round proper of the FA Cup in 1914. The club went one round better in 1915, knocking out the Football League champions, Blackburn Rovers, before 16,000 at the Vetch. Although it lost to Newcastle United in the second round, the club had achieved one of the game's biggest-ever upsets. The triumph may have been overshadowed by the war (and the takings reduced by the half-price admission of men in uniform), but the interest, publicity and gate receipts from its cup runs did much to establish Swansea Town, both in its own town and on the wider soccer scene. Success was a key to future stability.

Soccer's popularity developed quickly. Attendances grew rapidly and new records were set for south Wales and beyond. In March 1913 25,000 watched Cardiff City play Luton Town at Ninian Park, a record for the Southern League's second division.[79] Cardiff City was fast becoming one of the best-supported clubs outside the first division of the Football League. Its 1913–14 average league attendance of approximately 11,800 was higher than that of over half the clubs in the senior league's second division.[80] Meanwhile, in Swansea Town's first season, crowds were generally twice the size of those of Swansea RFC.[81]

With soccer's popularity increasing, there was bound to be a knock-on effect on rugby. One correspondent warned:

---

[78] *SWDP*, 25 April 1913.
[79] *SWDN*, 22 March 1913.
[80] Cardiff City average calculated from figures in John Crooks, *Cardiff City*, p. 176; Football League averages from Brian Tabner, *Through the Turnstiles* (Harefield, 1992), p. 73.
[81] David Farmer, *Swansea City, 1912–82* (London, 1982), p. 20.

> It has been my experience in other places that once you get a Rugby
> enthusiast to an Association match and interest him you can rely upon him
> bringing two more Rugby enthusiasts with him to the next match, and so
> on by the snowball method until you have the entire whilom [*sic*] Rugby
> crowd wondering what kept them in sporting darkness so long.[82]

An exaggeration maybe, but soccer, even with 'second-rate teams', was certainly having an impact on the popularity of its more established sister code as supporters switched allegiances. In 1910 even a Cardiff RFC player chose to watch a soccer match instead of turning out for his club's reserves. That year the SWMFA claimed that the earlier bitterness from the rugby clubs was almost dead as it was recognized that soccer was here to stay and organized by men with equal business ability and straightforwardness.[83] However, the optimism was somewhat misplaced, and the more soccer gained in popularity, the more the rugby fraternity felt threatened. In Swansea there were fears that rugby would die before Swansea Town had even kicked a ball.[84] Although editorials in both the Cardiff and Swansea press argued that there was room for both codes, the financial implications of the transfer in allegiances of hundreds, possibly thousands, of sports enthusiasts were obvious, and by 1912 the WFU was openly expressing concern.[85] The promoters of soccer declared repeatedly that their ambitions did not involve the ousting of the handling code and that they wanted the two games to exist harmoniously side by side.[86] However, the rugby fraternity of the coastal towns did not see it that way and tried to fight back with contemptuous remarks. There was particular ill feeling shown towards Newport County and its members by Newport [rugby] Athletic Club, much to the indignation of the soccer fraternity.[87] In Swansea the press was anticipating difficulty and prejudice from rugby circles over co-operation on fixture clashes

[82] *WM*, 29 August 1910.
[83] *WM*, 3, 4 October 1910; *SWDN*, 17 February 1910.
[84] David Farmer, *The Life and Times of Swansea RFC: The All Whites* (Swansea, 1995),
p. 109.
[85] *SWDN*, 29 April, 10 September 1912; *SWDP*, 6 May 1913.
[86] See, for example, the Swansea Town chairman's comments in *SWDN*, 14
September 1912.
[87] See *SWA*, 5 May 1913.

with Swansea Town.[88] Advocates of 'proper football' began to return many of the attacks with equally snide remarks about rugby. Swansea Town's chairman said that Swansea RFC was not supplying the public with the class of football it wanted and the new soccer club could give it much better entertainment.[89]

Rugby continued to be hampered by overly defensive and dirty play, and elements of the press even felt the established clubs' lack of enterprise was more dangerous to the game than was the rise of soccer. Faced with the growing threat, the WFU was accused of 'characteristic apathy and masterly inactivity'.[90] Belatedly it took steps to hinder soccer's growth by refusing to allow any player who had turned out for a professional soccer club to play amateur rugby and, during the 1911–12 season, by refusing grants to clubs which allowed the association code to be played on their grounds.[91] In Swansea it was hoped that the enthusiasm generated by Swansea Town's Welsh Cup victory in 1913 would stimulate a revival in rugby knock-out competitions. The following year, at the instigation of a Swansea RFC representative, a new cup was finally launched, but it was dogged by rough play and failed to inspire the intended revival.[92] Instead, at club level, rugby continued to flounder in the face of the rising tide of soccer. In 1910 Cardiff RFC faced the unprecedented situation of being unable to sell all its workmen's season tickets; the blame was placed on the new Cardiff City association club. The rugby club experienced its worst-ever season in financial terms in 1911–12. Despite the problems caused by the year's rail and coal strikes, people were quick to make the connection with the rising support for soccer.[93]

Outside the coastal towns, soccer's progress was not as smooth or spectacular, with finances a constant problem for the smaller Southern League clubs. Although most of their professional players were part-time, many earning little more than expenses, the payment of wages was a constant financial strain for such clubs. Treharris, Pontypridd, Ton Pentre, Caerphilly and

---

[88] In contrast, the Swansea Town directorate was keen to come to some arrangement. *SWDP*, 17 May 1912; *SWDN*, 18 June 1912.

[89] *SWDP*, 15 June 1912.

[90] *WM*, 3 October 1910.

[91] Farmer, *All Whites*, pp. 106, 115.

[92] Smith and Williams, *Fields of Praise*, pp. 181–4; *SWDN*, 29 April 1913.

[93] *WM*, 24 September 1910; *SWDN*, 29 August 1912.

Aberdare were temporarily suspended in 1914 by the FAW, for not paying wages owed in arrears.[94] Capital expenditure was also required on grounds to bring them up to the standard required by the Southern League. The reliance on gate receipts for their income meant that 1911–12 was a particularly trying season for many clubs, as a prolonged coal strike crippled the Valleys, compounded by a rail strike which prevented many spectators reaching matches. Cwm Albion saw its attendances tumble during the coal dispute when many of its regular supporters could not afford to attend matches. The club failed to complete its Southern League fixtures and was forced to drop out of the competition. It limped on for another season in the Welsh League before financial difficulties forced its closure. The old problem of security of tenancy reappeared at Aberdare. In 1912 Lord Merthyr, Aberdare AFC's landlord, gave the club six months' notice to leave the ground. He was unhappy that it was being used exclusively for one sport, but was willing to allow the club's tenancy to continue if a scheme were drawn up whereby the benefits of the ground were shared out. The club decided to branch out and run other games such as tennis, cricket and bowls in order to ensure its survival.[95] A year later, debts of £500 looked like forcing its closure. The club struggled on and re-formed in December 1913, this time belatedly taking the precaution of registering as a limited liability company. It proved fruitless, and the club folded at the end of the 1913–14 season, blaming a lack of support and poor management.[96]

With little financial security, facilities at the smaller Southern League clubs were very crude, much to the horror of some English observers. An Exeter newspaper accused Merthyr Town of being a disgrace in its old washed-out shirts.[97] A Portsmouth reporter was shocked at the ground of Cwm Albion:

> A guide was employed and led us to an unenclosed ground across two fields ankle deep in mud. The dressing room was a disused cowshed although the home team changed in the village, I was then shown a broken wooden box marked PRESS from which to write my report. The game was watched by a few hundred people most of them safely beyond the

94   *SWDN*, 26 May 1914.
95   *SWDN*, 31 October 1912.
96   *SWDN*, 20, 29 August, 9–11 December 1913; Twydell, *Rejected FC*, vol. 1, p. 15.
97   Undated (*c.* November 1911) *ME* cutting in Merthyr Tydfil Library.

reach of the collecting box, on the slopes of the hill surrounding the ground.[98]

Most of the smaller clubs continued to be based at hotels or public houses, which doubled as changing rooms and a meeting place. The Treharris ground had to be reached by steep steps with only a loose rope preventing a fifty-foot drop onto the street and roofs below. The club's pitch was 'a semi-bog in a hollow and lumpy with it' and its football 'utterly unorthodox and primitive'.[99] Despite their entry to the Southern League, the professional clubs from the south Wales valleys endured a constant financial struggle and remained a world apart from the Football League.

Despite their much higher attendances, the coastal town clubs did not automatically achieve financial stability either. In Newport County's first season, the weekly wage bill was £27 but the average fortnightly home gate only £20. The club only survived through the efforts of the directors and its supporters' club. By 1914, thanks to transfer fees, players' wages and heavy capital expenditure on the ground, the club was nearly £1,000 in debt and in serious danger of closing. Survival was only ensured after some substantial gifts from local dignitaries.[100] Even Cardiff City's large gates failed to stop it losing over £3,000 between 1911 and 1913.[101] Consequently, the directors felt insecure and were hostile to any development that might threaten their position. The club voted against the amateur Cardiff Corinthians' unsuccessful application to join the Southern League. In 1913 there were moves to set up a second professional club in the city. The syndicate responsible owned a new athletics ground known as Cardiff Stadium. The Cardiff City directors immediately set about vigorously trying to disrupt and discredit the plans, lobbying the Southern League management and pointing out publicly that members of the syndicate were bookmakers. The

[98] *Portsmouth Evening News*, quoted in Paul Harrison, *Southern League Football: The First Fifty Years* (Gravesend, 1989), p. 22.

[99] Ambrosen, *Amber in the Blood*, p. 9; *Portsmouth Evening News*, quoted in Harrison, *Southern League*, p. 22.

[100] *SWDN*, 13 January, 16 February 1914; Ambrosen, *Amber in the Blood*, pp. 8–11.

[101] *SWDN*, 24 July 1913.

Southern League rejected the application, and the syndicate abandoned its plans.[102]

CONCLUSION

By the outbreak of war in 1914, professional soccer in south Wales had come a long way. In 1900, there had been just 160 professional players registered with the FAW. By 1914, the figure was 431.[103] A strong club-scene had developed that was incorporated into English competitions. The standard of play had risen sufficiently for Swansea Town to beat the English champions and Cardiff City to become the best-supported club in England and Wales outside the Football League. Clubs were not completely reliant upon imported professionals as new young talent emerged that could hold its own with the best. Men from south Wales had become regulars in the English first division and the Welsh national side and attendances across south Wales were generally healthy and rising. Whereas, at the start of the century, soccer had been a minority pastime in south Wales, by 1914 it was an important part of the region's popular culture. The game's pioneers could look back with pride at their achievements.

Cardiff City's first professional was Jack Evans. A Welsh-speaker from Bala in north Wales, he moved to the Rhondda in search of work in the printing trade. Once in the south, he played for junior teams in Cwm and Treorchy before turning professional with Cardiff City for a 6s. signing-on fee. In 1912 he became the club's first player to be capped by Wales. As Peter Stead points out, his mobile career 'encapsulated much of the dynamic of Welsh society'.[104] In the first decade of the twentieth century, these demographic changes provided soccer with an audience already acquainted with the sport and willing to play, watch and run the game. With a vacuum in the English Southern League, Nonconformity's growing tolerance of sport, and rugby's crisis of confidence over the quality of its play and

---

[102] *SWDN*, 20 June 1912, 4, 21, 25, 28 April, 19–20 June 1913; *WM*, 19 June 1913.
[103] FAW *Annual Reports*.
[104] Stead, 'The Welsh football world', in Stead and Richards, *Club and Country*, pp. 4–5.

professionalism, the conditions were set for the development of professional soccer in south Wales and the publicity given by the press perpetuated its growth.[105] Once this happened, the game drew upon the same veins of popularity that had established rugby. Migration was about more than economic forces. It was a personal upheaval, and sport offered a shared experience that helped bond migrants into the new communities that were being forged. The press repeatedly stressed 'the innate love of the collier for manly sport'.[106] Soccer and rugby offered manual spectators and players physical entertainment and an opportunity for glory and unrestrained self-expression that was unattainable in work. Sport shared the camaraderie and values of the workplace but without the hardships and restraints. Like rugby, soccer's demands on time and space fitted with what was available to an industrial society, and the two games were perfect to help fulfil the needs of new competitive communities hungry for entertainment. Thus, while leisure was an escape from work, it was also shaped by the values and confines that work created. Contemporary ideals of social harmony, and the moral, economic and patriotic virtues of physical fitness, meant that the middle classes were willing to help sport and, thanks to the economic conditions, had the financial resources to do so. Yet support for soccer cannot be neatly explained in terms of class or community. Clerks, tradesmen, women and even ministers could all be found in the crowds. For all the importance of social and economic factors in professional soccer's development, it was the sheer excitement of what happened on the pitch that ensured the sport's success.

[105] The press was not particularly modest about its role in the popularization of the game. See, for example, *SWE*, 1 January 1920.
[106] *SWDN*, 29 April 1907.

II

THE PROFESSIONAL GAME, 1914–1939

It is unimaginable that people could look on at a game of football and forget themselves in the ecstasy of a winning goal at the moment when their comrades, maybe brothers, are making gallant and stupendous efforts at the front, even sacrificing their lives for the life of the nation.

Letter to *South Wales Daily News*, 3 September 1914

In August 1914 war broke out in Europe, driving Britain into a patriotic frenzy.[1] Within days, all rugby matches in England and Wales were suspended to help the nation to concentrate on the push for victory. There was no similar official suspension in junior soccer but, with so many players joining up, many competitions were abandoned anyway. By December 1914 1,217 players affiliated to the SWMFA had enlisted and nearly a hundred clubs had disbanded. At the end of the season, there were just seventy affiliated clubs still active, 325 fewer than the previous year.[2] The press looked to professional soccer's authorities to follow rugby's moral lead but, fearing financial losses and expecting it all to be over by Christmas, the FA and Football League decided to play on. The FAW followed this lead, with its president claiming that to interfere with football would be nothing short of 'panic legislation'. He argued that soccer fulfilled a large place in the organized life of the nation and that its discontinuation would only produce undesirable results.[3] Although many professional players had already enlisted, and some of the smaller professional teams disbanded, those clubs that did play on faced a battle of their own.[4]

The government and the War Office may have supported the continuation of professional soccer, but elements of the public

---

[1] For an account of Wales and the First World War, see Angela Gaffney, *Aftermath: Remembering the Great War in Wales* (Cardiff, 1998), ch. 1.

[2] *SWDN*, 4 December 1914; SWMFA *Annual Reports*, 1914–15.

[3] *SWDN*, 20 August 1914.

[4] For example, seven Cardiff City players enlisted immediately, and Risca District FC disbanded in 1914. 'Citizen', *A Short History of Cardiff City* (Cardiff, 1952 edn), p. 2; PRO, BT31/20119/116760.

and press saw things rather differently. The first two months of war saw letters and editorials in south Wales and national newspapers denouncing the playing of soccer during a time of crisis.[5] It was felt that since footballers were fit young men looked up to by much of the public, they should be setting an example by enlisting. Some critics believed that playing and watching the game were not necessarily wrong if the players and spectators were too young or too old to enlist. They accepted that sport had a role in relieving public tension and anxiety.[6] However, the more extreme antagonists felt that the whole concept of spectatorism was wrong in a time of war, and the sight of thousands of young and able men enjoying themselves at matches during wartime sickened them.

The south Wales press printed lists and pictures of famous, and not so famous, rugby players who had joined up, thus indirectly criticizing professional soccer. The decision of Swansea Town's directors to contest the military's decision to requisition the Vetch Field was subtly criticized after one member of the board suggested that the War Office could have the ground if it took over the club's liabilities. The implication that the club and the game were putting their own finances before the nation's needs was made clear by the press article then moving on to look at new recruits from the town's rugby fraternity.[7] In an effort to make a stand against the continuation of soccer, the *South Wales Argus* announced that it would not report any football news for the duration of the war.[8] The *South Wales Daily News* also chose not to print match reports in the first few weeks of the 1914–15 season but, as attendances showed that the public were still interested in professional soccer, the paper slowly increased the coverage it gave to the game.

Despite the allegations that professional soccer was unpatriotic, the game was helping the war effort. Grounds were made available to the military for drill or training at any time other than Saturday afternoons, most clubs gave their players rifle practice, and some even paid them in advance for the 1914–15 season to

[5] For example, *WM*, 23 November 1914.
[6] See, for example, the editorial in *SWDN*, 1 September 1914.
[7] *SWDN*, 8, 9 September 1914. The club was successful in its appeal against requisition after it was decided that financial compensation should have been offered.
[8] *SWA*, 4 September 1914.

allow them to enlist. On occasion, soldiers were let into matches half-price in an effort to show that the game was doing its bit, while spectators regularly found themselves the target of enlistment campaigns. The 7,000 spectators at a Welsh League match between Swansea Town and Llanelly in 1914, a third of whom were eligible for service according to a self-righteous reporter, were addressed by six different speakers, including the mayor and club chairman, on the virtues of enlistment.[9] The immediate impact of such appeals was limited in south Wales. *The Times* used the fact that only six recruits came forward after appeals at a Cardiff City match as an example of the selfishness of the game and its followers. However, as the club pointed out, hundreds of its supporters had enlisted, while the majority of the rest were involved in the coal and rail industries, integral parts of the war effort.[10] Nationally, soccer gave the state easy access to large numbers of potential recruits from working-class communities and thus became an important vehicle in the recruitment campaign.[11] The wartime hostility towards soccer in England was not widespread and actually represented the resentment of exponents of amateurism at the usurpation of the game by professionalism and the working classes.[12] In south Wales, antipathy towards soccer was even less common and given disproportionately large publicity by a patriotic press.

Restrictions on rail travel and a ban on mid-week games played havoc with fixture lists and soccer found it harder and harder, in both financial and practical terms, to continue. In November 1914, the FA estimated that, on average, attendances had fallen by approximately 50 per cent.[13] Cardiff City's average in the Southern League dropped from approximately 11,700 to around 9,300.[14] Other clubs, like Mardy AFC of the Southern League, already operating on tight budgets, suffered critical declines in their gates and closed before 1914 was out. The soccer authorities' increased restrictions on players' wages caused

---

[9] *SWDN*, 28 September 1914.

[10] *The Times*, 23, 28 November 1914.

[11] James Walvin, *The People's Game: A Social History of British Football* (London, 1975), pp. 88–90.

[12] See Colin Veitch, ' "Play up! play up! and win the war!" Football, the nation and the First World War 1914–15', *Journal of Contemporary History*, 20, 3 (1985), 363–78, and Fishwick, *English Football*, p. 145.

[13] *The Times*, 28 November 1914.

[14] Calculated from information in Crooks, *Cardiff City*, p. 78.

further tensions within clubs. Cardiff City players threatened to go on strike in 1915 over the issue of their benefits.[15] By the end of the 1914–15 season, it was clear that the war was going to be a long affair, and the FA decided to suspend league and cup programmes. Falling attendances and practical problems had achieved what the anti-soccer agitators could not.[16] A new makeshift league involving Cardiff City, Newport County and teams from south-west England lasted just a season because of low gates and rail restrictions. Cardiff City's average attendance during that season was a meagre 1,700.[17] The introduction of conscription in 1916 brought the call-up of most of the eligible professional players who had not enlisted voluntarily. Junior leagues did continue throughout the war, offering light relief from the hardships of the home and overseas fronts, but professional clubs spent the rest of the war playing the occasional friendly with teams of amateurs and guest professionals.[18] Without the regular income of popular matches, the expense of paying rent and ground maintenance proved difficult. Cardiff City, Merthyr Town and Swansea Town survived the war but few other clubs were so fortunate. Yet the real loss was the 35,000 Welshmen killed in the war, among them a host of amateur, professional and international players.

For those who returned, the war was a watershed in their personal lives. Fred Keenor of Cardiff City served alongside other professional players in the 17th Middlesex (Footballers') Battalion, and a leg wound threatened to end his footballing career before it had really started. In later years, he mostly refused to speak of his experiences on the Western Front. As his son put it, 'Dad blotted it out. He had lost too many friends. He often said that he was one of the lucky ones who came back.'[19] On being demobbed, the 'land fit for heroes' was no more immediately apparent to Keenor than it was to most other returning soldiers. He found work in a gasworks and on a milk round before rejoining Cardiff City when professional football resumed in 1919.

[15]   *FE*, 28 August 1937; *WM*, 16 October 1956.
[16]   Fishwick, *English Football*, p. 145.
[17]   Jenkins, 'Football in Cardiff', p. 83.
[18]   In 1917–18 there were still eight active junior leagues across south Wales. SWMFA minutebook, 1917–18.
[19]   Quoted in Lloyd, *C'mon City*, p. 57.

The post-war boom

For all the personal, social and economic turmoil of 1919, when soccer kicked off again there was a new confidence and optimism in the sport that reflected the post-war world's hopes for the future. Old clubs re-formed, new ones were set up and the south Wales game looked forward to building on its pre-war development. The early 1920s were to prove a golden period for soccer in south Wales. The number of senior clubs mushroomed, and a reorganization of the Southern League saw Merthyr Town, Newport County and Swansea Town join Cardiff City in an expanded first division, while the second division became an entirely Welsh body.

Table 2.1
Professional clubs in south Wales, 1922–1923

Aberaman Athletic	Llanelly
Aberdare Athletic	Mardy
Abertillery Town	Merthyr Town
Bargoed	Mid Rhondda
Barry	Newport County
Bridgend Town	Pembroke
Caerau	Pontypridd
Caerphilly	Porth
Cardiff City	Rhymney
Chepstow	Swansea Town
Ebbw Vale	Ton Pentre
Llanbradach	

At the end of the first post-war season, Cardiff City successfully applied for election to the Football League's second division. In supporting the application, the influential *Athletic News* asked 'why should South Wales, now a hot-bed of soccer, be outside the pale?' The club itself stressed the size of its support and its financial strength.[20] These were precisely the attributes to which the increasingly commercially aware Football League was attracted. That same summer, the Southern League's first

---

[20] *Athletic News*, 1 March 1920; *SWE*, 6 May 1920.

division, Welsh clubs and all, accepted an invitation to become the third division of the Football League. A year later, in 1921, Aberdare Athletic applied successfully to join the league. In just two years, five south Wales clubs had been admitted to the UK's leading competition and, with Cardiff City winning promotion in its first season, the region now had a representative in the country's premier division. The Welsh League also shared in the boom. By the 1922–3 season, it encompassed reserve sides from the Football League, teams from the Southern League clubs and a number of small professional sides. With the elevation of Pembroke Dock, the professional game spread beyond the industrial south and into the more rural west. That even small towns like Bargoed were setting up professional teams is an indication of the confidence within the south Wales game.

Wartime experiences fed the game's developing popularity. Many men who had served in the armed forces returned with a new or stronger passion for organized sport.[21] The game was actively encouraged by the army and played in every training camp, and even at the front, where it helped make the lives of soldiers more bearable. Many rugby enthusiasts from south Wales who had joined up may have found themselves playing the dribbling code for the first time. Once exposed to the game in this way, many may have developed a new appreciation of soccer.[22] As Gareth Williams observes of music, the war 'ended Wales's [relative] cultural isolation as her people came into contact with the wider world'.[23] The shared experience of war strengthened Britain's cultural unity and Welsh soccer was one of the beneficiaries. For some supporters the war offered an inspiration for the field of play:

[21] *The Times*, 25 September 1919; *Athletic News* cited in *SWDP*, 28 January 1915; Pierre Lanfranchi and Matthew Taylor, 'Professional football in World War Two Britain', in Pat Kirkham and David Thoms (eds.), *War Culture: Social Change and Changing Experience in World War Two Britain* (London, 1995), p. 189; Chief Medical Officer's Physical Training Report 1917, cited in E. J. Thomas, 'The history of physical education in Wales to 1970' (M.Ed., University of Manchester, 1979), p. 144; *SWE*, 1 September 1919.

[22] Similarly, it has been argued that the popularity of American football developed in the 1920s after the US armed forces played the sport during the war. See James Mennell, 'The service football program of World War One: its impact on the popularity of the game', *Journal of Sport History*, 16, 3 (1989), 248–60.

[23] Williams, *Valleys of Song*, p. 196.

> The 'old contemptibles' of 1914 were pushed back and suffered many casualties; their spirit could not be broken, with the result that victory was assured. Let critics and supporters of Cardiff City take heart, and if each will 'do his bit' the team will be able to demonstrate victories on Ninian Park.[24]

To many former soldiers the camaraderie of the army had been an enriching experience that made the horrors of war endurable.[25] Soccer and other sports offered an extension of that feeling of shared belonging and purpose. Even to those for whom the war had become a bitter memory, soccer promised excitement and escape in which one could temporarily forget the horrors of the trenches.

Despite its rapid growth, the resumption of professional soccer was not a smooth process. New or re-formed clubs needed finance for ground developments and players. Few clubs were as lucky as Aberdare Athletic, which enjoyed the support of a local mine owner willing to put money into the club and use his influence to find its professional players part-time jobs.[26] Instead, most clubs were reliant on public appeals and a few modestly affluent benefactors to raise the cash needed to match their ambitions. In 1920, in Port Talbot, a well-attended and enthusiastic public meeting was held to form a new professional club, but with no ground or wealthy backers the idea came to nothing. A professional club in Bridgend could only be formed because the new directors, 'well known business and professional men of the town', bought 6.5 acres for the considerable sum of £1,450. The new club, however, faced opposition from the local rugby fraternity, which was portrayed in the local press as a shopkeeper afraid of losing his customers (see Figure 1).[27]

Spectator sport was a business and there were only a limited number of potential clients. Once a club was actually established, the costs involved were still significant and required private backing. In Ebbw Vale the expense of setting up a professional team was borne predominantly by a welfare scheme established

---

[24] *SWE*, 10 September 1921.
[25] For example, see J. G. Fuller, *Troop Morale and Popular Culture in the British and Dominion Armies, 1914–1918* (Oxford, 1990).
[26] Aberdare Athletic minutebook, 1920–1.
[27] *SWE*, 16 April 1920, 21 June 1920, 29 March 1920.

by local iron and steel manufacturers to provide recreation for their employees and the district in general. Yet professional soccer represented a greater financial drain than the welfare scheme was willing or able to endure, and the club became a limited liability company after just one season, although it continued to use the welfare scheme's ground for free.[28] Such welfare schemes had given industrial south Wales a degree of democracy in its entertainment and culture through allowing workers to run their own recreation. But professional football required far greater resources and thus had to attract traditional middle-class patronage if it was to succeed.

When the Southern League's first division decamped to join the Football League, the clubs in the second division suddenly found themselves in a devalued competition. Some harboured ambitions of following Cardiff City and others into the Football League, and consequently spent heavily on ground improvements and players. Free from the restrictions of the maximum wage, some of the Rhondda clubs were said to have paid higher wages than Cardiff City and Swansea Town.[29] When a Football League club refused to release a player at the end of his contract, he could play in the Welsh or Southern League without his new club having to pay a transfer fee. Thus the high wages on offer made south Wales a tempting destination for a handful of leading players, until they could fix a return to the English league. In 1923, Llanelly AFC signed Jack Marshall, the Scottish captain, while Bridgend Town prised the talented Egyptian Tewfic Abdullah from Derby County. As Welsh and Southern League clubs employed more and more players, the number of professionals in south Wales rose rapidly from 371 in the 1919–20 season to 624 in 1921–2.[30] Yet too many of them were part-time journeymen who had failed to make the grade in England. As the *Merthyr Express* remarked in 1922, the Welsh League was becoming 'a dumping ground for superfluous

---

[28] *SWE*, 9 July 1921; Arthur Gray-Jones, *A History of Ebbw Vale* (Risca, 1970), p. 192; *ME*, 2 January 1926.
[29] *FE*, 25 January 1930. The maximum wage was enforced by the Football League to help to control clubs' workforces and help to protect their financial viability. It varied in the years up to 1922 before settling at £8 a week plus a £2 win and £1 draw bonus. See Fishwick, *English Football*, ch. 4, and Mason, *Association Football*, ch. 4, for a full examination of the status of professional footballers.
[30] FAW *Annual Reports*, 1921–3.

professionals'.[31] But others were just local boys who were never registered by their clubs and played for a few shillings under an assumed name.[32]

Abertillery Town, Pontypridd and Llanelly all unsuccessfully applied for election to the Football League in the early 1920s. None had either adequate financial backing or the potential support required to have any real chance of success. Instead, overambitious expansion left clubs in financial difficulties. At the end of the 1921–2 season, the FAW was worried that the 'fancy wages' being paid would lead to the bankruptcy of some clubs. The association had already suspended Mid Rhondda because of unpaid wages and debts to other teams.[33] Even clubs like Merthyr Town, already in the Football League, were struggling to achieve financial stability. The smaller senior clubs across Britain faced a constant struggle to cope with the economics of the professional game. The Football League may have brought increased receipts but it also meant higher wages and travelling costs. By 1921 the economy of south Wales was showing signs of impending collapse. South Wales's short-lived soccer boom was already overstretched, but the depression was to take it to breaking point.

ALL ROADS LEAD TO THE FOOTBALL GROUND

Soccer offered an attractive way to spend the increased disposable income that wartime inflation had brought, and it was in these heady days of the early 1920s that attendances at professional matches peaked in south Wales. Outside Cardiff and Swansea, crowds in these years ranged from less than one hundred to, very occasionally, as many as 20,000. In the region's two biggest towns, crowds compared favourably with more-established soccer regions and could be measured in tens of thousands (see appendix A). Crowds had exceeded those at club rugby since around 1910 and continued to do so. Attendances at Ninian Park could even outnumber those at rugby internationals. Across south Wales, with international results

---

[31] *ME*, 28 January 1922.
[32] Ivor Harris (Ton Pentre FC), interview with author.
[33] FAW *Annual Report*, 1921–2; *SWE*, 19, 24 November 1921.

fluctuating and the quality of Welsh club rugby still considered poor, more people turned to soccer for their pleasure. Rugby correspondents on the *Western Mail* even resorted to exaggerating attendance figures to conceal the fact that soccer was attracting more spectators.[34] The old appeals that there was room for both codes resurfaced (as did the recriminations), but rugby was undoubtedly feeling the effect of soccer's growth and successes. Hence decisions like that of Swansea RFC to change the time of one of its matches in 1926, so that it would not clash with a cup-tie at the Vetch, were sensible ones.[35] Many of the supporters at soccer matches in the coastal towns came from the surrounding area where football of this standard was not available. The Cardiff City management was later to claim that the club had received more support from the Valleys than it had from the city itself.[36] The rugby clubs of the coastal towns did not enjoy such large catchment areas since their rivals in the Valleys and smaller towns also played first-class rugby. Nor did Welsh club rugby have any prominent league or cup competitions that could provide glamorous games against English opposition. Thus, there was little to tempt rugby fans from the industrial Valleys or inland towns to watch Cardiff, Newport or Swansea RFCs. Different sports articulated different geographic identities.[37]

Yet the dribbling code too suffered because of the competition between the two sports. In 1923 Caerphilly Town, worried that a rugby club was to be formed in the town, warned that it would go bankrupt if its gates declined.[38] The competition between the codes was such that clubs across south Wales tried, with varying degrees of success, to come to arrangements with their rugby peers to ensure for the benefit of all that home matches did not clash. In 1922, a rugby international at the Arms Park between Wales and England was attended by less than 30,000. On the same day, 27,000 watched a first-division game at nearby Ninian Park. Both attendances represented a significant fall on the

[34] See, for example, *SWE*, 5 March 1921, 9 September 1921, 27 October 1922; Smith and Williams, *Fields of Praise*, p. 233.

[35] *SWE*, 3 March 1926.

[36] Such comments did not go down well with supporters living in Cardiff. See *SWE*, 31 August 1929, 11, 15 January 1932.

[37] Also see Jack Williams, '"One could literally have walked on the heads of the people congregated there": sport, the town and identity', in Keith Laybourn (ed.), *Social Conditions, Status and Community, 1860–c.1920* (Stroud, 1997), p. 133.

[38] *FE*, 5 May 1923.

average and the fixture clash was quickly blamed.[39] As the novelty of first-division soccer wore off by the mid-1920s, rugby internationals at the Arms Park or St Helen's do not seem to have been so vulnerable to clashes with association football matches. The rugby international was too embedded in Welsh culture to be seriously harmed by soccer. However, association attendances continued to fall when they clashed with rugby internationals. In 1924 only 12,000 saw Cardiff City (sitting high in the first division) play Arsenal on the same day as Wales met New Zealand before 50,000 at St Helen's in Swansea. By the 1930s the situation had stabilized, with clashes of typical club matches having a minimal effect on gates in either code. Rugby and soccer seemed to have developed their own set of regular followers while clubs were being more co-operative over fixture dates. By 1935 representatives of Swansea RFC were even appearing on the platform at a meeting to raise money for Swansea Town.[40] There did continue to be a considerable number of aficionados of both games in south Wales. As one writer put it, 'The Rhondda man is commonly bilingual; he also knows the two codes of football.'[41] Rugby and soccer had their own regular supporters, but many were more interested in seeing the most exciting and glamorous matches on offer, whichever the code.

When the 1922–3 season kicked off with Cardiff City entertaining Tottenham Hotspur before nearly 50,000, professional football seemed to have enraptured the locals:

> [T]he eye of the airman, had he come early to the match for a seat aloft, would have seen slow treading rivers of headwear, light hats, dark hats, men's hats dowdy or shiningly new, women's hats flower-decked and cherry weighted, caps of the Rhondda collier on holiday, flat topped blue 'tiles', and tall policemen . . . Here and there would be seen a group of workmen straight from the docks, to whom the calls of home and dinner had become microscopic before the looming importance of the 'Spurs' visit to the city.
>
> Small boys, ubiquitous and inevitable squirmed in everywhere, and somehow got the best places.

[39] *SWE*, 21, 28 January 1922.
[40] *SWEP*, 15 June 1935.
[41] However, the writer, in his attempts to paint the Rhondda as somewhere apart, did claim that rugby outrivalled soccer as the 'democratic' game. H. W. J. Edwards, *The Good Patch* (London, 1938), pp. 178, 181.

The clerkdom descended upon the district in its light-hearted thousands and the thraldom of ledgers was burst by excited debaters of the City's great prospect.

The wonderful thousands crowded the ground some time before the start of the game, and then one could observe how mixed a crowd indeed was this following of the Brown Ball.

Here and there was seen the white collar of a parson, minus his sermon voice and chaste eye.

Soldiers from the Barracks led the rest with snatches of song, catchy, if at times tending to the vulgar.

College students advertised their identity by strenuous, if vain, efforts to retain the becoming dignity of the 'coll. accent' . . . One saw a cripple being helped from the chair by old comrades, all of whom wore ex-services badges.

One smiled at the feverish scramble to the top of the advertising hoardings that surround the field, and one trembled also, for a slip and unsecure hand or two and . . . 'Midst all stood the policemen, busy and wonderfully disinterested.

Such was the crowd that invaded Ninian Park to-day, a crowd which cheered deafeningly when 22 men, cool-headed, took the field and kicked the leather outwards, and was as impressively silent when the sound died away, and the first breathless moments held sway.[42]

No longer was association football a minority sport struggling against a tide of rugby fanaticism. Cardiff City was so confident of its support in the early 1920s that it doubled the minimum entry price to some of its cup-ties to 2s. The club could afford considerable transfer fees like the £3,500 it paid Sheffield Wednesday for Scottish international Jimmy Blair in 1920 or the £2,500 it paid Swansea Town in 1924 for Welsh international winger Willie Davies. Some of the Football League's best players were employed at Ninian Park and soccer in south Wales could now claim to be on a par with the game in the rest of Britain. It had a developed pyramid of different levels from the inter-nationals it hosted, through to full-time professional clubs in the Football League and semi-professional teams in the Welsh and Southern Leagues. Underneath this was a multitude of junior clubs catering for the thousands of boys and men who wanted to play. Post-war developments, such as the publicity and added

[42] *SWE*, 2 September 1922.

excitement given to the game by cinema newsreels and the growth of pools betting, accentuated soccer's public profile and popularity. So too did the illegal (but widely tolerated) street betting that 'was one of the most distinctive features of English [and Welsh] town-life'.[43] Soccer, on a spectator and participatory level, was now the integral part of popular culture in south Wales that it was in England. Despite Edwardian fears, this was not achieved at the expense of rugby. The handling code may have lost its pre-eminence and the vitality that its club scene had enjoyed in the late nineteenth century, but it had settled at a new level. The two codes learnt to coexist, sometimes competing for spectators and players, but each having its own core of devoted advocates. Thus south Wales, like parts of northern England where rugby league was strong, had a popular sporting culture that genuinely embraced two winter sports. To the outside world, rugby may have been perceived as the game of south Wales but, to the people who lived there, their sporting culture was rich and varied.

The multifaceted nature of that sporting culture is illustrated by Benny Beynon. A regular with Swansea RFC, he briefly played for Swansea Town during the First World War and scored the winning goal in its famous victory over Blackburn Rovers in the 1915 FA Cup. To surprise and resentment in Welsh rugby circles, Beynon signed professional terms for Swansea Town in 1920, four days after winning his second Welsh rugby cap. The WFU refused to present him with the caps, indicating how its isolationism was not in tune with the sporting culture in which it operated. In 1922, Beynon further illustrated the diversity of that culture by quitting soccer to join Oldham's rugby league club.

Beynon was just one of a host of new heroes who were emerging to excite and inspire the south Wales sporting public. The dashing Charlie Brittan, who had joined Cardiff City from Spurs in 1913, was popular enough to be elected to the city council in 1919 on an ex-servicemen's ticket. He was applauded by the press for playing on election day instead of campaigning, probably safe in the knowledge that his performance on the pitch

---

[43] Ross McKibbin, *Classes and Cultures: England, 1918–1951* (Oxford, 1998), p. 372.

would win more votes than any speech he could make.[44] Brittan left Cardiff City in 1924, having lost his place in the first team. That year Swansea Town spent £1,280 on buying Cardiff-born Jack Fowler from Plymouth Argyle. Fowler had begun his career with Mardy in the Southern League and established a reputation as a versatile forward. In Swansea he achieved heroic status and was accorded his own version of a music-hall song ('Fow, fow, fow, fow, Fowler, score a little goal for me') by the Vetch Field faithful. He scored 102 goals in five years for the club and his failure to achieve a regular place in the national Welsh side was a cause of much frustration in west Glamorgan. William Hardy joined Cardiff City for £25 in 1911 from Heart of Midlothian. The club was short of cash, so Fred Stewart, the City manager, had to pay the transfer fee himself. Hardy began a business as a coal merchant, hoping that his football popularity and the plugs in match programmes would win him custom. He proved to be a halfback of supreme talent, and his prematurely bald head became something of an icon in Welsh football. His appearance on a newsreel at a Cardiff cinema was said to have caused the audience to cheer for ten minutes.[45] To City supporters, Hardy was a hero of their own kind, as one visiting reporter was told:

> 'Once he gave the ball such a one it hit me right in the heye, and me standing at back of enclosure. Snakes, that was a smack . . . I saw Hardy in the street a couple o' days after, and passed the time o' day but he didn't seem to see me.' His face grew wistful. 'Ah, he's one of the boys, is Hardy.'[46]

It was the exploits of such players, nearly all of whom were working men, that helped to cement the popularity of soccer. They gave the sport a human face which fans could empathize with, adulate and aspire to. Without such men, soccer could not have captured the hearts or imaginations of people across south Wales in such numbers. Sporting heroes are emblematic figures, representatives of wider experiences and values.[47] The maximum

---

[44] *FE*, 8 November 1919.
[45] *SWE*, 20 February 1922.
[46] *SWE*, 29 January 1924.
[47] H. F. Moorhouse, 'Shooting stars: footballers and working-class culture in twentieth-century Scotland', in Holt (ed.), *Sport and the Working Class*.

wage ensured that the stars of south Wales soccer remained working-class figures, very much in touch with their social and economic roots, rather than the dislocated heroes of the modern era.[48]

THE ECONOMIC BLIZZARD

By 1921 it was obvious that the post-war economic boom was subsiding in south Wales, and coal and rail strikes signalled tough times ahead. Unemployment was rising sharply and those out of work often did not have enough money for food, let alone entertainment. Many of those still in work were on short time or reduced wages. With watching soccer a relatively expensive leisure pursuit, gates began to fall.[49] As early as the 1921–2 season, unemployment and a coal dispute meant that Newport County's total league receipts were the lowest in the Football League outside the new third division north. Attendances at Rhondda clubs in the Welsh League never fully recovered from the blow of the 1921 coal strike.[50] Between 1921 and 1925 there was a series of brief economic revivals, but the structure of the south Wales economy was seriously flawed. It was heavily over-reliant on coal, and when problems re-emerged in the industry in 1925, the consequences were as disastrous for soccer as they were for the society of which it was part. By 1927, unemployment in Glamorgan stood at a devastating 24.1 per cent.[51] The smaller clubs collapsed and attendances tumbled across the region. There was a mass migration from south Wales as people left in search of a brighter future elsewhere – 50,000 people moved away from the Rhondda, while 27,000 left Merthyr. The majority of those who went were young males, the core sector in

---

[48] For an examination of the evolving place of soccer heroes, see Chas Critcher, 'Football since the war', in John Clarke et al. (eds.), *Working Class Culture: Studies in History and Theory* (London, 1979), pp. 161–84.

[49] See appendix A for Football League attendances.

[50] Simon Inglis, *League Football and the Men who Made it: The Official Centenary History of the Football League* (London, 1988), p. 127; *FE*, 1 February 1930.

[51] Colin Baber and Dennis Thomas, 'The Glamorgan economy, 1914–45', in Arthur H. John and Glanmor Williams (eds.), *Glamorgan County History*, vol. V: *Industrial Glamorgan* (Cardiff, 1980), p. 536.

society that watched soccer.[52] Half of Caerau AFC's shareholders had left the district by 1927.[53] Quite simply, many soccer
supporters uprooted in search of work.

In the final game of the 1923–4 season, the young Cardiff City
forward Len Davies missed a penalty that would have won his
club the league championship. Instead Huddersfield Town, level
on points, finished above Cardiff by a difference in goal average
of 0.024.[54] That season, Cardiff City had seventeen international
players on its books. From this point onwards it slipped into
gradual decline. The club reached the 1925 cup final but lost to
Sheffield United courtesy of a single deflected goal. Despite its
achievements, attendances were in decline as the impact of
unemployment in the Valleys began to hit home. The directors
now invested money in the ground rather than in players, but the
team was ageing. When it reached the cup final again in 1927 it
was already past its best. That season, the General Strike and
prolonged coal dispute had seen gates tumble further. In 1928,
Cardiff City sold three international players in two weeks to ease
its financial burden. This was not the action of a club out to win
at all costs, but rather one which had become aware that, with
falling attendances, it could no longer afford to compete seriously
in the transfer market. The FA Cup victory made it easier for the
club to execute such a policy, with the success-hungry supporters
satisfied for the time being at least. But, without new talent, the
club was living on borrowed time and, in 1930, it was relegated.
Its stay in the second division was short-lived and, in 1934, after
a period of severe financial problems, the club finished bottom of
the Football League.

Despite the relatively more prosperous conditions in west
Glamorgan, the optimism of Swansea Town's 1925 third-
division (south) championship was temporary. The club spent the
rest of the decade stagnating in mid-table and fighting for

---

[52] Of migrants from south Wales between 1921 and 1937, 71 per cent were aged
between fifteen and forty-five. John Davies, *A History of Wales* (London, 1993), p. 579;
Baber and Thomas, 'Glamorgan economy', pp. 540–1. For an examination of the causes
and experiences of migration see Andrew J. Chandler, 'The remaking of a working class:
migration from the south Wales coalfield to the new industry areas of the Midlands,
c.1920–40' (University of Wales, unpublished Ph.D. thesis, 1988).

[53] PRO, BT31/252422/162477.

[54] Teams on equal points were separated by goal average (goals scored divided by goal
conceded) rather than goal difference. Had Huddersfield Town won its last game 2–0
instead of 3–0, then Cardiff City would have been champions by 0.004 of a goal!

financial security, with gates in gradual decline. The enforced commitment to saving money rather than maximizing potential on the pitch was illustrated by the club's ambivalence towards employing a manager. The directors took eight months to replace Joe Bradshaw after he left in 1926, and no one held the position from 1931 to 1934. Even with such careful management, in 1935 the club was still more than £11,000 in debt and in danger of bankruptcy.[55]

Outside the Football League, the impact of the depression was cataclysmic. Caerphilly Town had a weekly outlay of nearly £100 in 1921, but an average income of only £50. The blame was placed upon the 'great trade depression in the coal-field'. Its plight was typical of that of the region's clubs in the Welsh and Southern Leagues. During the 1922–3 season poor gates meant that Ebbw Vale AFC lost £2,600 despite winning the Welsh section of the Southern League.[56] If clubs did try to save money by cutting down on the number and quality of players employed, performances on the pitch suffered. In 1922 Llanbradach AFC was relegated from the Welsh League's first division. The club's management blamed their refusal to enter the wage war and thus only pay players sensible rates. Even with this policy, the club lost £36 that season thanks to falling receipts, ascribed to the industrial depression.[57] The situation was not helped by the withdrawal of the reserve sides of Cardiff City, Newport County and Swansea Town from the Southern League, an act which had resulted in the remaining smaller clubs losing some of their most attractive and profitable fixtures.[58]

The financial strain was more than most clubs could cope with, and many went bankrupt or closed voluntarily. Abertillery Town, Caerphilly Town, Mardy and Ton Pentre all failed to complete the 1922–3 season. Porth AFC had folded by the beginning of the following season, while debts forced Llanelly AFC to close in 1925. Port Talbot AFC resigned from the Welsh League that year after the money spent on ground improvements had left it short of capital.[59] Pontypridd AFC's support collapsed

[55] *SWEP*, 15 June 1935.
[56] *SWE*, 21 October 1921, 11 July 1922.
[57] *SWE*, 18 July 1922.
[58] See, for example, Mid Rhondda's complaints in *SWE*, 8 April 1926.
[59] *SWE*, 9 January, 12 August 1925.

in the industrial turmoil of 1926 and the club folded with its debts unpaid. That year's six-month mining dispute left Mid Rhondda AFC unable to employ any professional players and forced to survive on gates of a few pounds. After the closure of so many of its neighbours, there were no remaining local derbies to generate enthusiasm and the club's plight deteriorated. By 1927, amidst rising unemployment, it was reduced to asking opponents for its share of the gate in advance, in order to pay its team's train fares. The bank's demand for repayment of the club's overdraft finally forced its closure in 1928.[60] Bridgend Town also folded that year, leaving Ebbw Vale AFC and Barry Town as the only Welsh clubs in the Southern League. By 1930 Ebbw Vale had decided to employ no professional players for the first time in thirty years. The club dropped out of the Southern League two years later because of the high travelling expenses incurred by playing in England.[61] In 1930 Barry Town was still considering Football League status but, as the press pointed out, this was quite unrealistic. Three years later, the club gave notice of its intention to quit the Southern and Welsh Leagues because it was in danger of going bankrupt. In 1937, it decided to concentrate on fielding local players instead of imported professionals.[62] Only eleven clubs entered the 1931 South Wales Senior Cup, and this included an amateur club, a works team, an unemployed side and a welfare club; such were the remnants of senior soccer in south Wales.[63] The FAW and the press were left looking back and lamenting the way many Welsh and Southern League clubs had tried to emulate Cardiff City's success by taking on too many players and paying too high wages.[64]

For the region's smallest Football League clubs, the depression was not much easier. 'Rampant unemployment' and bad weather during the popular Easter matches meant that it had not

---

[60] FAW minutes, 26 May 1926; *FE*, 13 March 1926. The directors had already tried to close Mid Rhondda, but their decision led to a renewed effort to save it. However, the efforts were to prove fruitless. Martin Johnes, 'Mushrooms, scandal and bankruptcy: the short life of Mid Rhondda FC', *The Local Historian*, 32, 1 (2002), 41–53.

[61] *FE*, 15 November 1930, 8 September 1928; *SWE*, 31 July 1928, 27 July 1932.

[62] *FE*, 18 January 1930; *SWE*, 14 January 1933; Jeff McInery, *The Linnets: An Illustrated History of Barry Town AFC* (Cardiff, 1993), pp. 30–41.

[63] SWMFA minutebook, 1930–1. The remaining entrants were the three Football League clubs, Merthyr Town, Aberaman, Penrhiwceiber and Ebbw Vale.

[64] For example, see *FE*, 25 January 1930.

always been clear that Merthyr Town would finish even the 1921–2 season.[65] Neither it, Aberdare Athletic nor Newport County enjoyed financial stability during the 1920s and all had to operate on tight budgets, unable and unwilling to invest in the players who could have brought promotion. Without the loans and efforts of their directors, the clubs would probably have closed. By 1924, Aberdare Athletic was losing £100 for every match it played and employing just sixteen players.[66] All three clubs tended to release most of their small squads over the summer to save on wages, and quickly sold any talented players they discovered. Such actions naturally had a negative impact on performances on the pitch, and each season became a struggle to escape the lower reaches of the table.

By the late 1920s, visiting clubs playing Merthyr Town and Aberdare Athletic found that their share of the gate often did not even cover travelling expenses. The cheque that one club received from Merthyr was so small that it was framed and hung in the dressing room rather than cashed.[67] In 1929 surprise was being expressed by one anonymous club official that, given the economic conditions, attendances in south Wales were still as high as they were.[68] By the 1929–30 season Merthyr Town's attendances were often barely a thousand, its average the worst of any club in the Football League and the lowest in its division for the third consecutive season. In June 1930 unemployment in the town stood at 50.1 per cent.[69] Initially, there was limited sympathy for the plight of the south Wales teams, with other clubs well aware that they could find themselves in a similar situation. Aberdare Athletic and Newport County were both re-elected to the Football League in 1923, as was Merthyr Town in 1925 and 1928. However, sympathy could only go so far, and as it became apparent that the depression in south Wales was more than a temporary downturn, economics took precedence. Mid Rhondda and Ebbw Vale's hopelessly ambitious applications, in 1925 and 1927 respectively, both failed to win a single vote. From 1927, all applicants to the Football League had to present

[65] *SWE*, 24 August 1922.
[66] *SWE*, 25 August 1924; *Aberdare Leader* (hereafter *AL*), 26 April 1924.
[67] *ME*, 24 May 1930.
[68] *FE*, 5 January 1929.
[69] *ME*, 11 January 1930; Tabner, *Through the Turnstiles*, pp. 82–4; Baber and Thomas, 'Glamorgan economy', p. 538.

their balance sheets and attendance details for inspection. Aberdare Athletic and Merthyr Town finally failed to secure re-election in 1927 and 1930 respectively.[70] In Merthyr's final season in the league, unable to afford to employ a manager, the club finished bottom of the table, conceding 135 goals in the process.

Watching senior football was not a cheap recreation. The Football League decreed that the minimum price at matches in its competition was 6d. before the war and 1s. after 1918 (including tax). To sit at a typical inter-war match cost between one and three shillings. In the Southern and Welsh Leagues entry prices for the popular banks were typically the 6d. minimum demanded by the league committees. In comparison, an inter-war packet of twenty cigarettes was a shilling and a pint of beer 8d., while entry to the cinema could be as cheap as 5d. in the coastal towns and 2d. in the Valleys. Greyhound races varied considerably in price but the cheapest tickets were sometimes as low as 2d.[71] Senior inter-war club rugby could be watched for 9d. and by the 1930s for as little as 3d. In 1932 a new rugby club at Merthyr charged the unemployed as little as 1d. for admission.[72] Thus, as economic conditions deteriorated, it was not surprising that soccer clubs often struggled to attract supporters in their former numbers.

Professional soccer operated within the context of an increasingly commercial and competitive popular culture which extended beyond contending with rugby union for fans and gate money. In 1926 the novelty of a rugby league international at Pontypridd caused a gate of 'only a few hundred' at a nearby Mid Rhondda match.[73] In the 1930s, the occasional broadcasting of football matches on the radio began to have an impact on

[70] Clubs that finished in the bottom two of divisions three north and south had to seek re-election. The 1930 election, which saw the expulsion of Merthyr Town, was the first time that the third divisions had recommended that one of their members not be re-elected. Cardiff City was forced to seek re-election in 1934, but its past record and comparatively healthy gates ensured that it received the maximum possible votes. Inglis, *League Football and the Men who Made it*, pp. 132, 135. Also see Matthew Taylor and John Coyle, 'The election of clubs to the Football League 1888–1939', *Sports Historian*, 19, 2 (1999), 1–24.

[71] David Berry, *Wales and Cinema: The First Hundred Years* (Cardiff, 1994), p. 119; BBC Wales, *All Our Lives: A People's History of Wales*, episode 17; *FE*, 27 August 1932.

[72] Philip Massey, 'Portrait of a mining town', *Fact*, 8 (November 1937), p. 48; *FE*, 1 October 1932.

[73] *FE*, 17 April 1926.

the attendances of smaller clubs.[74] It was not just traditional sports that affected soccer. The growth of greyhound racing, dances and, particularly, the cinema, all meant competition for the spare shillings of those in search of entertainment.

After 1928, while thousands would watch Merthyr Town train for free, the popular bank would be sparsely occupied on a Saturday.[75] In 1932, after two years of struggling in the Southern League, gates fell so low that the club decided to break league rules by reducing the entry fee to 2d. for the unemployed and 6d. for everyone else, whether they watched from the banks or grandstand. Attendances immediately rose from 200–300 to 3,000–4,000, and sometimes higher. Out of a crowd of 6,000 that watched the club play Bristol Rovers reserves, 4,000–5,000 were estimated to be unemployed. Merthyr was forced to abandon the 2d. fee after complaints from a neighbouring club which was concerned that it might lose fans, and intervention by the FAW, Southern and Welsh Leagues fearing a possible price war.[76] Gates collapsed again and, within two years, the club closed.

The press was sure that, in the larger towns at least, success could overcome the wider economic troubles. However, falling revenue meant that no Welsh club had the financial resources to build a winning side to test the theory. The occasional prominent match did certainly attract big attendances. A series of internationals at Ninian Park from 1933 onwards attracted crowds of over 40,000. Even in the economically dark years of 1929 to 1931, league derbies between Swansea Town and Cardiff City attracted crowds of over 30,000 at Ninian Park and 20,000 at the Vetch Field. While regular attendance was out of the question for those suffering economic hardship, the occasional luxury of a big match was not.[77] To save money for the admission, striking miners in 1921 walked ten miles to the South Wales Cup final between Ton Pentre and Bridgend, while others made a thirty-

---

[74] For example, see letter from G. Jones to SWMFA secretary, 6 April 1936, in SWMFA minutebook.

[75] Corrigan, *100 Years*, ch. 6.

[76] *FE*, 27 August, 17 September 1932; *SWE*, 19 August, 6 September 1932. The Welsh League did concede a 4d. entry fee for the unemployed and later allowed clubs under its jurisdiction to charge the out-of-work 3d.

[77] Although for the unemployed it could require much saving. See Massey, 'Portrait of a mining town', p. 75.

mile round-trip to a big match at Ninian Park.[78] For those out of work, soccer (and sport in general) offered a brief distraction from the drudgery of life on the dole. In 1931 one unemployed supporter told the press, 'The old woman gave me a bob, "Go and see the City", she said. "Better than 'anging round the 'ouse worrying about work that don't come." '[79] That the unemployed occasionally went to matches was seen by some as further evidence that their plight was being exaggerated. A member of the Merthyr Board of Guardians claimed that, in Aberdare, men had been paying to watch a game on the same day as they had drawn unemployment relief. He used this to argue that the relief was given out too freely.[80] In 1936 it was reported that at many Welsh League games (where the unemployed paid 4d. or 3d. admission by the mid-1930s[81]) 75 per cent of the spectators were out of work. Yet, in the 1930s, a crowd of over 200–300 was considered good for a typical Welsh League match outside the coastal towns.[82] Even with such cheap prices, regularly watching senior soccer was beyond the reach of many. The budgets of unemployed families show that they did not have enough money for food, let alone entertainment, and even single jobless men struggled to feed themselves. Watching professional soccer did not feature prominently in any of the surveys of the un-employed's lifestyles that took place during the 1930s in south Wales and other depressed areas of Britain.[83] In 1932, 33 per cent of unemployment in the Rhondda was long-term. Four years later the figure was 63 per cent.[84] With unemployment unlikely to be a temporary phenomenon, spending any financial reserves on going to a match was a difficult decision.

---

[78] *SWE*, 22 April 1921, 3 May 1921.

[79] *SWE*, 14 December 1931.

[80] *ME*, 23 February 1924.

[81] The tendency of working people to abuse lower entry prices for the unemployed probably contributed to the soccer authorities' reluctance to allow too many discount schemes. See letter in SWMFA minutebook to SWMFA secretary, 6 April 1936.

[82] For example, see *FE*, 6 October 1934, 4 April 1936.

[83] One survey reported that in Newport the unemployed did watch the local Football League club play. This was put down to the club's success in the competition, yet Newport County was struggling in the third division at the time and was certainly no more successful than Cardiff City, where no such trend was noted. Thus it is doubtful whether this means that the unemployed regularly watched professional football but it is a further indication that it was not unheard of, at least on an occasional basis. A. J. Lush, *The Young Adult in South Wales* (Cardiff, 1941), p. 77.

[84] Baber and Thomas, 'Glamorgan economy', p. 539.

This did not mean that the unemployed became distanced from the game. A 1937 book on the plight of Wales said that talk of Football League players dominated the conversation in un-employment clubs, while sport was one of the ways the local unemployed combated the feeling of uselessness brought on by being out of work.[85] As an official of one south Wales club said, to argue that the unemployed had lost interest in soccer was to do them a disservice.[86] For some unemployed men, their interest in soccer was maintained through the money that betting on the game promised. Be it the hope of winning a small sum or the earnings that running a sweepstake or pools scheme could bring, there was cash to be made by gambling on soccer. Betting in general was a popular pastime amongst the out-of-work that offered hope and excitement. Throughout the inter-war years, the press regularly reported that unemployed miners across south Wales had been prosecuted for running illegal gambling schemes. In 1928, police in Cymmer noted that there was a lot of poverty in the area, yet betting was on the increase.[87] A few individuals turned to more conventional crimes to raise the funds to attend matches. A 1936 survey of unemployed juveniles claimed that youths were pilfering to obtain money for their amusements. In 1921 three youths charged with housebreaking said they had done it to get money to go to a football match.[88] More common was for people to watch for free if they could. Newport County, Swansea Town and numerous smaller clubs complained that people were regularly watching games for nothing from nearby bridges, coal tips and houses. For the small clubs, surviving only through the sacrifices of committees and players, this was particularly galling.[89] As unemployment rose in

---

[85] Rhys Davies, *My Wales* (London, 1937), pp. 108, 115. Other surveys also noted that sport was an important topic of conversation amongst the unemployed. See, for example, Massey, 'Portrait of a mining town', p. 49.

[86] *FE*, 5 January 1929.

[87] *SWE*, 8 December 1928; Stephen G. Jones, *Workers at Play: A Social and Economic History of Leisure, 1918–39* (London, 1986), pp. 119–20. A 1937 survey of the unemployed in south Wales noted that many who did the pools had little interest in soccer. Lush, *The Young Adult in South Wales*, p. 77. Mark Clapson, *A Bit of a Flutter: Popular Gambling and English Society, c. 1823–1961* (Manchester, 1992), offers a wider history of betting in Britain.

[88] Gwynne Meara, *Juvenile Unemployment in South Wales* (Cardiff, 1936), p. 106; *SWE*, 5 October 1921. The judge said that it was a silly, boyish thing to do and that, while it was difficult to understand, it did illustrate the hold that sport had.

[89] See, for example, the complaints of Cilfynydd Welfare in *FE*, 19 March 1927. Of course, people still tried to watch for free even in more prosperous times.

the inter-war years, so too did attendances at matches in public parks where entry was free. In 1929 Aberaman of the Welsh League was said to struggle to attract attendances of around 100, while crowds of 2,000–3,000 were common at nearby junior matches.[90] Because of the shortage of pitches, matches were often played consecutively, meaning that for spectators there could be a whole afternoon of free entertainment. For some men on strike or on the dole, watching junior football became 'the main attraction of the week'.[91]

The period between the mid-1920s and the outbreak of the Second World War was not one of total decline for professional soccer in south Wales. Helped by the strength of the local tinplate industry and the domestic markets for anthracite coal, west Wales enjoyed a degree of economic comfort. In 1930, unemployment in south-west Wales stood at 8.3 per cent, while in the eastern coalfields the figure was over 20 per cent.[92] Consequently, Llanelly AFC could boast relatively healthy gates and some financial stability. The club had been re-formed in 1928 and was the only Welsh side to apply to join the Football League in the 1930s. It made its first application in 1929, and came close to being elected in 1932 and 1933. In the 1930–1 season, the club had an average attendance of 4,000, a similar figure to Newport County, which was located in a bigger town and played in the Football League. That season, while its peers were struggling financially, Llanelly made a healthy profit of £3,343.[93] Although the club's fortunes fluctuated through the 1930s, it undoubtedly benefited from the relative prosperity of its surroundings.

By the middle of the 1930s, economic conditions in the rest of south Wales were also beginning slowly to improve, particularly in commercially diverse Cardiff. Average attendances at the region's three remaining Football League clubs rose during the late 1930s. At Cardiff City and Newport County, this was accompanied by improved performances but, even at Swansea

[90] *FE*, 13 April 1929.

[91] Harry Presdee, 'Sporting days', in Anne Eyles, *In the Shadows of the Steelworks II* (Cardiff, 1995), p. 113.

[92] Baber and Thomas, 'Glamorgan economy', p. 537.

[93] *FE*, September 1931; *SWE*, 28 July 1931. Similarly, Llanelly RFC were one of the most successful rugby clubs in south Wales both on and off the pitch during the 1930s. Williams, *1905 and All That*, pp. 189–90.

Town, whose stagnation on the pitch continued, gates gradually improved. Cardiff City's gates were amongst the biggest outside the first division and larger than those of several clubs in the top flight itself. Although local unemployment still stood at 20.1 per cent, a 1937 marketing survey showed Cardiff to be amongst Britain's most prosperous cities.[94] In this improved economic climate, soccer began once again to demonstrate its popularity over rugby. In 1939 the *South Wales Echo* pointed out that, while Cardiff RFC would attract a crowd of between 4,000 and 7,000 for an attractive game, third-division Cardiff City regularly enjoyed crowds of between 20,000 and 30,000. The paper claimed that a similar disparity between the two codes existed in Swansea and Newport.[95] On 13 December 1937, the senior rugby and soccer clubs of Cardiff, Newport and Swansea all played at home. While only 7,000 watched the rugby matches, there were 44,000 at the soccer games.[96]

As the economy slowly improved, some smaller clubs began to re-form. However, the attempts of a few hopefuls were hampered by the debts left by their predecessors. In 1929, for example, moves to set up a new senior club in Port Talbot were refused permission by the soccer authorities unless the liabilities of the old Port Talbot Town club were accepted.[97] The clubs that did succeed in re-forming now operated on a significantly smaller scale than in the early 1920s and paid only nominal wages. Yet they still continued to struggle financially. A new Welsh League club at Porth had to survive on average gates of £5. Out of that sum, 30s. went for the use of the ground and a further £1 went on other expenses. This left very little for the players and the expense of away matches. To make matters worse, only two of the sixteen men on the committee that ran the club were in regular employment.[98] The club struggled on but failed to regain the stature its predecessor had enjoyed immediately after the Great War. In the 1937–8 season, Barry Town had an average gate of 1,533 and Aberdare Town around a thousand.[99] Both were mediocre sides in the Southern and Welsh

[94] Baber and Thomas, 'Glamorgan economy', p. 539; *Marketing Survey of the United Kingdom* (London, 1937).
[95] *SWE*, 28 January 1939. Similarly, see *FE*, 2 February 1935.
[96] Smith and Williams, *Fields of Praise*, p. 297.
[97] SWMFA minutes, 12 September 1929.
[98] *FE*, 18 January 1936.
[99] McInery, *Linnets*, p. 41; *FE*, 7 May 1938.

Leagues respectively and, for the mid-1920s onwards, this was probably typical for a standard match in one of the larger centres of population outside Cardiff, Swansea and Newport. Such gates were not large enough to support a fully-fledged professional club. Yet, even with the new caution, there were still fears that the old unrealistic ambitions would re-emerge. At the end of the 1936–7 season, the FAW again felt that it had to warn clubs against promising wages which they could not afford to pay.[100]

PLAYING PROFESSIONALLY

As for Welsh society as a whole, the inter-war years were a period of mixed fortunes for the professional footballer. For those players lucky enough to be in work, it was a time of comfort and opportunity. A maximum wage may have been in force but, at £8 a week for most of the inter-war period, it was a very healthy figure compared with the pay of other working-class professions. Of course, only the best players received the maximum, but even the 1930s average wage of £5 a week represented a comfortable living. Hence Ernie Curtis, a leading Cardiff City player, could say that he was unaffected by the depression.[101] Yet for some amateur and part-time players, the wages offered were no better than those paid in their existing skilled jobs. Thus, the offer of a full-time professional contract from even Cardiff City was not always accepted. Bill Jones, Southern League Barry Town's captain in the early 1930s, earned £3 a week for playing but also worked as a miner.[102] This ensured that he was better off than not simply his colleagues at the coalface but some full-time professionals too. Yet, when the fame, fun of playing and short hours that professional football could offer were added, it was an extremely attractive occupation. Roy Paul, a miner in the late 1930s and future Welsh international, dreamt of escaping a life underground through soccer. As the depression grew worse, the hopes placed in soccer were all the greater. As Paul put it, 'Soccer was the escape route from the dark dismal days of the 1930s. Only those who could sing, act or play soccer, had any

---

[100] FAW *Annual Report* 1936–7.
[101] Unbroadcast HTV interview with Ernie Curtis, 1987.
[102] McInery, *Linnets*, p. 34.

hope of getting into a better, brighter world where folks could eat three good meals a day.'[103] A professional player's wages may not have been on the same level as those of top actors, singers, or even boxers, but it represented notable wealth in the depressed mining valleys.

The number of jobs available to hopeful players was in decline as professional clubs went bankrupt or reduced their playing squads. Those who did find a club often faced difficult conditions and reduced wages. In the 1923–4 season, fourteen Aberdare Athletic players had to cope with playing four games in five days as the club, living 'from hand to mouth', struggled to meet its commitments in three leagues with a small squad.[104] During the 1922–3 season, professional players at poverty-stricken Bargoed AFC went for over seven months without being paid any wages. In 1922 Troedyrhiw, Porth, New Tredegar and Rhymney were all suspended by the SWMFA for failing to pay outstanding wages to their players.[105] With the suspended clubs no longer able to play matches, there was little hope that the players would ever get their wages. In 1928 a Barry Town player was jailed for obtaining assistance under the Poor Law through deception. His wages were 15s. a week when in the first-team and 10s. when out of it.[106] Unable to find any other work, his football earnings had simply not proved enough to live on.

By the late 1920s, the days of importing stars from England were over for all the south Wales clubs. Instead, they increasingly relied on surplus (and thus cheap) journeymen, or looked to local talent in the hope of discovering stars of the future, even if just to sell on for a profit. Near the end of the 1934–5 season, it was reported that as many as fourteen of the twenty-six players Cardiff City had used that season were Welsh. Amongst them was seventeen-year-old Reg Pugh. News of his impressive debut for Aberaman in the Welsh League spread quickly enough for him to turn out for Cardiff City just two days later; such was the club's desperation to secure new talent.[107] Pugh's early promise was never fulfilled. His form was erratic and he suffered severely

---

[103] Roy Paul, *A Red Dragon of Wales* (London, 1956), pp. 12, 14.
[104] *AL*, 26 April 1924.
[105] *ME*, 19 May 1923; *SWE*, 6 July 1922.
[106] *SWE*, 1 May 1928; McInery, *Linnets*, p. 24.
[107] *FE*, 6 April 1935; *SWE*, 25 September 1937. The nationality of players is explored in ch. 6.

from barracking from the Cardiff supporters. Like so many of his peers, the outbreak of war cut short his career. New talent was available, and English clubs increasingly began scouting the region to pick up the players whom local clubs had either missed or were unable to afford to employ. A Merthyr Town director complained in 1930 that south Wales had become a 'convenient and free football nursery' for English clubs. In 1938 Arsenal alone had fourteen Welsh players on its books.[108] Included in that number was Bryn Jones, at £14,000 the UK's most expensive player; he lived a comfortable life in London, despite failing to reproduce the form that had led to his huge transfer fee. Yet, for every Bryn Jones, there were many others who moved to England only to find themselves working as groundsmen and playing for a nursery side while the club which had tempted them away made up its mind whether to offer a contract or not.[109] Most did not make it and quietly returned brokenhearted to the pits or the dole queue.

Even for a player who did enjoy a successful professional career, life could be hard when his playing days were over, depression or no depression. Soccer tended to have deprived him of the chance of learning a trade, and often left him with painful injuries. After a period of being a relatively well-paid local celebrity, players in their thirties (or younger) suddenly found themselves out of work and unwanted. Working as a coach or manager was one option, but there were limited opportunities and positions were very insecure. It also took a certain type of temperament and an amount of luck to succeed.[110] The most popular alternative was to take on some form of licensed premises where their fame could attract custom. Here, players could live off their past glories, recounting old stories and retaining some popularity. After a brief and unsuccessful period as a coach, Jimmy Blair, formerly a back with Cardiff City in the 1920s, kept his Scottish international caps in a glass cabinet in the pub he kept in Cardiff. Such places could become a kind of living museum dedicated to a former hero. In his later years, Tom Farquharson was not tangibly better off for playing in goal

[108] *SWE*, 15 August 1930, 23 August 1938.

[109] For example, see Ron Burgess's account of his 1936 move to Tottenham Hotspur from south Wales in his *Football: My Life* (London, 1952), pp. 17–23.

[110] See Fishwick, *English Football*, p. 81.

for Cardiff City from 1922 until 1935. He may have escaped the political troubles in his native southern Ireland that had forced him to seek refuge in south Wales (though he continued to carry a revolver in his kit bag), but he still ended up practising his old trade of painting and decorating after retiring. For those with no trade to fall back on, the outlook was bleaker. This was graphically illustrated by Fred Keenor, captain of Cardiff's cup-winning side. After leaving senior soccer, he combined being player-manager at Tunbridge Wells with working as a poultry farmer. An obstinate character, he was not a success in management and resigned after disputes with his players. By 1937 he was seriously ill, unemployed and penniless. When the news became public, collections were held for him across Cardiff. To the shocked soccer public, his fate seemed to sum up the whole plight of the collapsing local game.[111] Keenor ended up a builder's store-keeper, a far cry from the day he lifted the FA Cup.

CONCLUSION

Supporters may have seen professional players as one of them, in contrast to the 'remote figures heard on radio or seen on the cinema screen',[112] but they were part of an increasingly commercialized leisure industry. At 1930s Arsenal in particular, with its sustained success, new tactics, film star connections and flair for publicity, the game had developed something of a new sophistication and an overtly commercial edge. Arsenal was unique but clubs across the rest of England and Wales hung on to the coat tails of its revolution. A Cardiff City player remembered an early meeting with Ben Watts Jones, a draper from Swansea who was appointed as the club's new manager in 1934:

> He took me on the pitch and told me that he intended to have advertising here and there, and things like that. I said to him: 'Don't you want to talk to me about football and what we can do on the pitch to get out of trouble?' I didn't have much time for him.[113]

---

[111] See Martin Johnes, 'Fred Keenor: A Welsh soccer hero', *Sports Historian*, 18, 1 (1998), 105–19.

[112] Malcolm Smith, *Democracy in Depression: Britain in the 1920s and 1930s* (Cardiff, 1998), p. 50.

[113] Ernie Curtis in Crooks, *Bluebirds*, p. 152.

Off-the-field commercialism was not the only modernization that the 1930s witnessed. By 1938, Cardiff City had split the position of trainer into two by employing a new player-coach and what, in essence, was the forerunner of a modern club physiotherapist. The latter's role was in the dressing room where he was responsible for massaging players' injuries, utilizing new techniques such as heat lamps. The players now spent twice-weekly sessions with the local educational authority's physical training instructor.[114] A year later, the club directors ceded control of team selection to the manager. The modern game was slowly being born.

Arsenal's successes and denudation of the provinces of local talent brought resentment in the north of England,[115] but it also illustrated the skewed nature of inter-war Britain. Unemployment and poverty stood alongside a new consumerism and wealth. The inevitable result was a leaning towards the English south and Midlands, and the rise of 'lucky' Arsenal, with its detractors and stars from the four corners of the UK, simply reflected that. Soccer in south Wales was at the receiving end of Britain's economic inequalities as its achievements of the early 1920s crumbled under the weight of overambition and declining attendances. But the game also illustrated the unity that helped Britain to avoid the extreme social tensions and political movements that economic dislocation brought on the Continent. For all its commercialization and economic problems, soccer had become part of a stable national culture that encapsulated British people's supposed humour, restraint and togetherness. The antagonism towards the game, generated by professionalism and the Great War, had subsided and, as Russell points out, soccer had assumed a place at the heart of the nation and represented something organic in the face of the invasion of the US culture of the movies.[116] But that nation was not just England. Wales too could claim its place, and its adoption of soccer and the behaviour of its crowds illustrated that:

> Now that South Wales is experiencing some of the enthusiasm for a Cup match, several papers describe Wales as 'mad' . . . Welsh enthusiasm is magnetic, and beyond that little criticism is possible . . . [T]he crowds on

[114] *SWE*, 27 July 1938; *FE*, 29 October 1938.
[115] Russell, *Football and the English*, p. 117.
[116] Ibid., pp. 118–23.

> Saturday were wonderful. British crowds, and the ease with which a handful of police manage them are the objects of wonder on the Continent. If you despaired of our ever getting back to pre-war days of respect for law and order, then after Saturday you must be converted.[117]

Indeed, through its expansion in south Wales, the very weight of soccer's claims to be a national institution was enhanced. When the 1927 FA Cup final became the first to be broadcast live on the wireless, south Wales soccer and south Wales itself were projected to the British people as part of a British cultural institution and, indeed, as part of Britain itself.

---

[117] *SWE*, 6 March 1922. The most powerful image that football provided of the orderliness of the people was the 1923 cup final at Wembley. Over 200,000 people packed into the new ground, spilling onto the pitch. Yet, deaths and the abandonment of the game were averted after a single mounted policeman and the appearance of the king supposedly dispersed the crowd. See Russell, *Football and the English*, pp. 120–1.

Figure 1. 'The ever spreading soccer movement', *South Wales Echo*, 29 March

Figure 2. 'Long live sport', *South Wales Echo and Express*, 17 October 1936

Figure 3.   'CARDIFF TO-DAY: No Monday morning feeling *this* week!',
Western Mail, 25 April 1927

Figure 4.   'Football starts today: Leaving them to it', *Weekly Mail and Cardiff
Times*, 30 August 1930.

III

RAG-BALLS, SCHOOLBOYS AND DISTRICT LEAGUES: THE WORLD OF AMATEUR SOCCER

I was just a wee lad when I played football for the first time. The pitch was the hard surface of Curre Street, Cwm, and the ball was a wad of rags tightly bound up with string. All the boys in the neighbourhood, big and small, joined, and no matter whether we played under association or rugby rules the thrills were fast and furious.

Ron Burgess, Tottenham Hotspur and Wales[1]

For every professional match that took place, there were countless games played in parks, on waste ground and in the streets. For every professional soccer hero, there were thousands of dreamers trying to recreate his deft dummies, crunching tackles and powerful shots. The amateur or junior game ranged from small town teams in the Welsh League's second division to kick-abouts on the streets with coats as goal posts.[2] Through this myriad of clubs, soccer was the leading physical pastime of a considerable proportion of the male population. Without this personal experience of the game, the thousands who flocked to see the professionals would never have emerged in the numbers that they did. Junior football was not just about playing. Its most important matches could attract crowds of several thousand who spilled onto the rough pitches in public parks, fields or mountainsides. Yet other games were highly localized events watched by just a handful of friends and family. This was the community at play. This chapter examines the world of junior soccer from the district leagues at its heart, to the street football that caused so many broken windows and so much residential anger.

---

[1] Burgess, *Football*, p. 9.
[2] Although 'junior soccer' is used here to refer to amateur clubs of all levels, the contemporary press was inconsistent in its use of the term, occasionally taking it to mean only schoolboy and youth games.

ON THE STREETS

The streets were the natural playground of children in urban working-class communities. With soccer (like other ball games) requiring neither fixed numbers, grass, goal posts nor even a proper football, it was a common sight on the streets of south Wales.[3] It may have been seen as 'unladylike', but girls played too when they could overcome the opposition of boys fearful of being seen as 'cissies' for playing with them.[4] Some games were planned with regular teams,[5] but others were disorganized and chaotic to the extent that they did not directly resemble either soccer or rugby. Not surprisingly, some adults viewed such games as a nuisance. Newspapers printed numerous letters complaining that street football was an obstruction, foul-mouthed, noisy, a hazard to windows and passers-by and, as road traffic increased, a danger to the lives of those participating. Worse still, some games took place on the Sabbath and unfortunate worshippers got their 'best clothes soiled with dirty footballs on the way to church'.[6]

Unruly and chaotic activities in public places were seen as a slight on civilized society and games of football were one of the most frequent street disturbances.[7] The future Labour MP George Thomas remembered playing football in the Rhondda with a tin and 'coats down on the ground in the street to mark goal posts with one boy on the look-out for Bobby Jones [the policeman]. If he caught us, and he was a good runner, he would give us a thump.'[8] Although some policemen were content with letting boys escape with a 'clip round the ear', the law did try to curb street football through prosecuting offenders. In 1920 in Aberdare, a 'battalion of youths' was said to appear in court each week charged with playing football in the street.[9] Although most

---

[3] Although stones and tins were sometimes used, balls were usually made from bundles of rags or newspapers. Many professionals claimed that playing with such small objects had developed their ball skills. Fishwick, *English Football*, pp. 5–6.

[4] For example, see I. R. Thomas, *Remember When: Memories of Yesteryear* (Abertillery, 1993), p. 122; Paul Thompson, *The Edwardians: The Remaking of British Society* (London, 1992 edn), p. 39.

[5] Charles Jones, interview with author.

[6] *SWE*, 24 April 1923.

[7] The regulation of public space is explored in the context of popular culture in Croll, *Civilizing the Urban*, pp. 87–103.

[8] George Thomas, *My Wales* (London, 1986), pp. 53–4.

[9] *SWE*, 5 May 1920.

Table 3.1

Number of under-sixteen-year-olds charged with playing football or bat-and-ball in the street in Cardiff[1]

	Number charged	Number convicted	Total number charged with any offence
1921	148	44	404
1922	216	151	447
1923	94	33	313
1924	93	54	426
1925	89	35	408
1927	108	40	405
1928	74	30	367
1929	82	33	418
1930	60	11	460
1932	41	8	352
1933	87	6	436

[1] Cardiff City Police *Annual Reports*. 1921 and 1922 refer only to football. Years selected according to available statistics.

perpetrators were discharged with a warning, the arrests involved made up a considerable proportion of all those of under-sixteen-year-olds (see table 3.1).

Even when fines were imposed, attempts to curb the games met with little success and sometimes contempt. The battles with the police entered into the lore of the street, resulting in a lingering resentment of authority amongst the victims.[10] The 1922 Cardiff City Police *Annual Report* declared that it was not directly concerned about 'the moral underlying tendency to use the street as a playground' but was, in prosecuting street football, reacting to the 'just' complaints of annoyed citizens. Many policemen and residents did turn a blind eye and, probably remembering their own childhoods, accepted that 'boys will be boys'.[11] Thus, the prosecutions were not the result of an authoritative attempt to control public places *per se*. Streets were accepted public domains, and although behaviour was expected

[10] Richard Holt, *Sport and the British: A Modern History* (Oxford, 1992 edn), p. 140.
[11] *SWE*, 13 April 1928. Also see, for example, Walter Haydn Davies, *The Right Place, The Right Time: Memories of Boyhood Days in a Welsh Mining Community* (Swansea, 1975 edn), pp. 114–15.

to conform to a standard that did not unduly inconvenience others, a degree of tolerance was displayed.

There are few references to street football on Saturdays, suggesting that the perpetrators may have been turning out for their local teams in organized leagues or attending professional matches.[12] Thus, those who played on the streets were not simply driven there by a lack of alternatives but were often just utilizing the nearest space. Even residents living near public parks could be troubled by games on their streets.[13] In 1925 a Barry magistrate complained that, in view of the number of open spaces with which the town was blessed, there was no need for games to take place in the street at all.[14] Table 3.1 shows that, in Cardiff at least, the number of convictions for street football tailed off through the inter-war years. Similarly, the frequency of letters to the press on the subject lessened. Although a more lenient attitude to the problem may have been adopted, this trend must also owe something to the continuing growth of the schoolboy game and the provision of public parks. While the latter did not meet demand, and were not even always used when available, there were increasing alternatives to playing in the street.

It was not just children who played football in the streets. Young adults played in the day and after work on any open space, be it a street, square or waste land, and often in 'anything but the team spirit'.[15] In 1934, 238 men over twenty-one were charged with playing games in the streets of Cardiff.[16] As juvenile unemployment rose, so too did the frequency of such games, as young men, with little to do, spent much of their time on the streets. Kicking some kind of ball around was a chance of entertainment and passing the time. The numbers involved could be

[12] One complaint specifically excluded Saturdays. *SWE*, 10 April 1928.
[13] For example, *SWE*, 23 March 1931. Some local authority-owned pitches did have rules forbidding their casual use. This meant that even where there were public parks in a town, they could not necessarily be used for games.
[14] Similar complaints were aired in Newport in 1920. *SWE*, 2 January 1925, 22 May 1920.
[15] Anon., *On Behalf of the South Wales Collier Boy* (Treorchy, 1929), p. 9.
[16] In 1935 the figure was 205 and in 1936, 203. Calculated from information in Cardiff City Police *Annual Reports*.

significant, as could occasionally be the violence.[17] The boister-
ous games of youths (or 'roughs' as they were described by one
angry letter writer[18]) were seen as more threatening than those of
boys. 'If there were elderly people in the way of the player
running for goal, down they had to go', was the complaint at a
meeting of the Pontypool Urban District Council in 1920, where
it was alleged that street football was causing 'rowdyism' in the
town, especially on Saturday nights.[19] Rising unemployment led
to increasing official concern about the number of youths
loitering on the streets and about public order in general. It was
difficult to do anything about the former but prosecuting their
football games was one way of attempting to restrain some of
their behavioural excesses. Thus, compared with prosecutions
against children, the number of adults charged and convicted
remained high in the 1930s.[20]

THE SCHOOLBOY GAME

It was in school that most boys first tasted organized soccer.
Organized games had been gradually introduced into elementary schools in the late nineteenth century but, despite official encouragement such as the 1902 Education Act, their adoption was
by no means wholesale and relied on the enthusiasm of individual teachers. Some Edwardian schools even assumed that
walking to school was sufficient exercise for pupils. Others dis-
trusted organized games because of their commercialization and
emphasis on winning, and instead preferred gymnastics and
drill.[21] At some schools, sports were orientated around the school

[17] One 'kickabout' game in Merthyr resulted in a participant being sentenced to one
month's hard labour for assaulting another player. *SWE*, 24 March 1922. The rough and
unruly nature of many of the street games suggests they represented an unorganized
continuation of the older traditions of folk football as much as an improvised version of
the modern sport. Richard Holt, 'Football and the urban way of life in nineteenth-
century Britain', in J. A. Mangan (ed.), *Pleasure, Profit, Proselytism: British Culture and Sport at
Home and Abroad, 1700–1914* (London, 1988), p. 71.
[18] *SWE*, 26 April 1928.
[19] *SWE*, 30 September 1920.
[20] In 1934, 100 of the 122 juveniles (under-twenty-ones) charged were dismissed, while
only twelve of the 238 men charged were discharged. Cardiff City Police *Annual Report*,
1934. A change in the way crime figures were recorded that year makes comparison with
the figures for the under-sixteens impossible.
[21] For example, Eugene Sully, 'Physical training and character', in T. Stephens (ed.),
Wales: Today and Tomorrow (Cardiff, 1907).

team and the best players, thus marginalizing the less talented or less enthusiastic pupils. At Landsdowne School in Cardiff, members of the school soccer team were taken to the park once a week for practice, but the rest of the school had to make do with a walk in the countryside.[22] In Edwardian schools where sports were actively encouraged, new concerns arose. In 1908, unease was expressed at Pengam County School that boys spent too much time talking about football. 'Games might be an excellent tonic,' said one speaker at a school function, 'but they could not live on tonics alone . . . the future of Wales was not in its heels but in its head.'[23]

The Welsh Schools Football Association (WSFA) was founded in 1912. Its objective was the 'mental, moral and physical development of schoolboys'.[24] Inter-war educational reports increasingly stressed the virtues of organized games, leading to a far wider encouragement of sport within schools. The poverty and poor nutrition that the depression was inflicting upon many south Wales children also accorded physical education an added importance. By 1930, organized sport was an integral part of the timetable in many schools, although girls were still largely neglected in the new agenda.[25] Yet the popularity and success of team sports remained dependent on the commitment of individual schoolmasters. Some took it very seriously, devoting up to three evenings a week to their budding young stars and even personally paying the teams' train fares to games or training sessions.[26] Such dedication and sacrifice were not just rooted in a belief in the moral and physical benefits of soccer. A love of the game and a pride in setting boys on their way to a professional career were more human motives.[27]

Alongside the rise of school sports was the adoption of soccer instead of rugby as the main winter game. Although rugby dominated such school sports as had existed at the turn of the

---

[22] Thomas, 'Physical education in Wales', pp. 117–39.
[23] *SWDN*, 2 April 1908.
[24] WSFA *Official Handbook*, 1933–4.
[25] Thomas, 'Physical education in Wales', p. 158.
[26] See Morlais Williams and Haydn Daniel, *Swansea Schools Football Association 75th Anniversary* (Swansea, 1989), pp. 6–36; *FE*, 24 December 1927.
[27] Several Welsh internationals credited some of their success to the encouragement and close interest of teachers in their abilities and careers. For example, Trevor Ford, *I Lead the Attack* (London, 1957), pp. 26–7; Jimmy Murphy, *Matt . . . United . . . and Me* (London, 1968), p. 19.

century in south Wales, soccer made rapid headway in the Edwardian period and the years immediately after the First World War. By 1910, the new Cardiff City directors were claiming that 80 per cent of the city's schoolboys played soccer.[28] In 1913, forty-five schools were affiliated to the WSFA. Ten years later there were nearly 300, and twenty-seven affiliated leagues.[29] During the First World War, schoolboy rugby had ceased along with the senior game, which allowed soccer to become established in some schools. Also important was the growing number of teachers in south Wales who had attended the training colleges in Carmarthen and Bangor which had strong soccer traditions.[30] Leagues, cups and internationals all added to the attraction and development of the school game for both boys and teachers.[31] Soccer also gained support from the belief that it was a safer game for children because it involved less physical contact than rugby.[32] Rugby enthusiasts, already worried about the growth of professional soccer, began to express concern that boys were not having the opportunity to play the handling code. In an attempt to stem its growth in schools, they decried the evils of professionalism and soccer's lack of patriotism during the war.[33] Such animosity spilt over into several local authorities. In 1920 Newport's elementary education committee made a grant to the local schools' rugby league but was adamant in its refusal to do so to the local schools' soccer league. Only after pressure from the ratepayers' association was there an eventual change of heart.[34]

By the mid-1920s, disdain for soccer's associations with professionalism and gambling led many secondary and grammar schools to revert to rugby. The growth of league and cup competitions had also raised fears that school soccer was too fixated with winning rather than the traditional Corinthian

---

[28] *SWDN*, 5 May 1910.
[29] *SWE*, 7 July 1923.
[30] Smith and Williams, *Fields of Praise*, pp. 139, 233; Lile and Farmer, 'Early development', p. 200.
[31] Wales's first schoolboy international was held in 1907, while leagues in Cardiff and Swansea dated back to the 1890s.
[32] See *SWE*, 10 December 1920.
[33] See Smith and Williams, *Fields of Praise*, p. 233.
[34] Thomas, 'Physical education in Wales', pp. 414–15.

values.[35] The WFU actively encouraged schools to take up rugby again through letters of persuasion, financial grants and, in 1923, the belated formation of the Welsh Secondary Schools Rugby Union. By the 1930s, nearly every secondary school in south Wales played rugby as its main winter sport.[36] Yet schoolboy soccer retained its dominance in elementary schools and many older boys continued to play the code outside school. The WSFA, essentially an elementary school organization, still had over 300 affiliated schools in the 1938–9 season, a figure comparable with the early 1920s.[37]

The schoolboy game could be a source of considerable local pride and entertainment. In 1921, 11,000 people watched a midweek match between Aberdare and Caerau schoolboys. A year later in Ebbw Vale, 16,000 watched the local schoolboys play a team from West Ham.[38] It was in Swansea that pride in the schoolboy game was strongest. In the 1930s and 1940s a succession of players of immense talent was educated in the town's schools, where soccer continued to exert a hold, even at secondary level. Most notably, Trevor Ford, John and Mel Charles, Cliff Jones, Ivor and Len Allchurch and Jack Kelsey all went on to become international stars. Swansea schoolboys won the English schools shield in 1939 before 20,000 at the Vetch, a crowd nearly 10,000 higher than Swansea Town's average that season, and the mayor gave the victorious boys an official civic reception. The feat was repeated another three times in the years immediately after the Second World War.

Many schools had neither the facilities nor the willing teachers to provide an extensive sports programme. This meant that many boys' clubs were organized by individual adults or even by the children themselves. Money was raised for equipment through door-to-door collections or enterprises such as selling jam jars or collecting empty beer bottles. Such independence not

[35] See, for example, W. J. Hoare, 'Schoolboy rugby football', address delivered to meeting of teachers interested in school sports, at the Margate conference of the NUT, 1938. Reproduced in the appendix of Carl French, 'The history of the Welsh Schools Rugby Union, 1903–39' (University of Wales, unpublished M.Ed. thesis, 1991).

[36] Smith and Williams, *Fields of Praise*, pp. 240–3; French, 'Welsh Schools Rugby Union', pp. 93, 101. The switch to rugby was mirrored in schools in England, where fears about the ethics of a professional game had also increased. James Walvin, *The People's Game: The History of Football Revisited* (London, 1994 edn), p. 120.

[37] WSFA *Official Handbook*, 1938–9.

[38] *SWE*, 27 April 1921, 6 May 1922.

only annoyed residents, who found themselves plagued by the 'young beggars',[39] but was also a cause of concern for those who saw sports as having a social function:

> In the case of a youth working in cramped, unnatural conditions out of the sunlight, and living such a confined existence at home, the matter of physical recreation must have a prominent place. We have to encourage and control it rather than hand it over to undesirables . . . The control . . . of many of our physical recreations has either passed into the wrong hands and been prostituted accordingly, or our boys have been left to play their games in their own way, and 'dirty play', the winning of cups and medals at any price, the laying of protests and the clever avoidance of rules . . . [become] the main features.[40]

That boys' teams often changed in the tempting surroundings of public houses further developed fears about the way football was being run.[41] Thus, youth organizations were encouraged to take a more active role in physical recreation, so as to ensure that games were played and administered in the right spirit. Rising unemployment intensified concern about the pastimes indulged in by youths. Providing the opportunity of playing organized soccer was seen as a means of helping to ensure that they did not fall into unhealthy physical and moral habits. The Scouts, like many other youth organizations, ran regular soccer competitions in south Wales to develop individuals' self-control and 'foster a spirit of brotherhood' between competing troops, although there was some concern that football might become the only motive for the existence of troops. Moral concerns also contributed to ex-schoolboy leagues being set up for youths not yet old or developed enough to play in adult competitions. Teams were usually run by youth clubs or religious institutions under the guidance of concerned adults, keen to instil certain standards of conduct and discipline. Typical was the Merthyr headmaster who set up a side for his former pupils in 1921, because so many of them were unemployed. He was insistent that the team be well behaved, win or lose.[42]

---

[39] *FE*, 22 October 1934.

[40] Anon., *South Wales Collier Boy*, p. 13. Such ruthless tactics were a feature of junior soccer at all levels.

[41] For example, see the comments of a Swansea Corporation education subcommittee in *SWE*, 7 December 1921.

[42] *SWE*, 8 January 1920; *ME*, 1 October 1921.

DISTRICT LEAGUES AND LOCAL CLUBS

Between the schoolboy and professional games lay a complex web of junior clubs playing in town, valley, city and county leagues across south Wales. Founded in 1904, the Swansea and District League had twenty-three clubs by 1907, and seventy-seven clubs and 2,445 registered players by 1911, making it the largest league in south Wales.[43] By 1926, there were twenty-one leagues, 700–800 clubs and over 20,000 players under the jurisdiction of the SWMFA, the vast majority of which were junior organizations.[44] Ted Robbins, secretary of the FAW, proudly claimed in 1933 that 'there is scarcely a town, hamlet or village in Wales that is without a soccer team'.[45] By 1938, the 134 teams in the Cardiff and District League (founded in 1897) made it the third biggest league of its kind in Britain.[46] This spiralling growth in localized teams probably accounted for the apparent decline in street football in the 1920s.[47] In comparison with such numbers, junior rugby in south Wales was insignificant. In 1921, the Ministry of Health noted that

> Football is almost the only outdoor game that is now indulged in to any considerable extent in the South Wales valleys, and it is to be feared that only a very small proportion of the total male population take any part therein beyond that of spectators.[48]

Despite the impressive number of registered players, playing any sport was still a minority activity.

Most junior clubs were based upon a locality (ranging from street to town according to the league), but there were also teams based at churches, public houses, places of work and, particularly in the industrial Valleys, working men's institutes and welfare halls. The junior leagues were rooted in, and a reflection of, the complex social networks of male urban life. Richard Holt sees junior clubs as a formalization of local friendships and social

---

[43] *SWDN*, 7 January 1907, 17 July 1911.
[44] SWMFA *Annual Report*, 1925–6.
[45] Quoted in Corrigan, *100 Years*, ch. 6.
[46] Jenkins, 'Football in Cardiff', p. 41.
[47] McKibbin, *Classes and Cultures*, p. 340.
[48] Ministry of Health, *Report of the South Wales Regional Survey Committee* (London, 1921), p. 59.

Table 3.2
Team names in the Cardiff and District League[1]

	1924–5	1934–5
Place-name in Cardiff	20	38
Place-name outside Cardiff	2	10
Religious – Nonconformist	5	1
– Other	14	6
Works team	9	26
Private institution	6	11
'Cardiff' as prefix	4	3
Miscellaneous	5	4
Total clubs	65	99

[1] Cardiff & District Football League, *Official Handbooks*; *Western Mail Cardiff Directories*. The category 'private institution' consists of institutes, welfare halls, political clubs, sports clubs and old boys' clubs. NB. In 1924–5 other clubs did enter the league, but only those listed in the league handbook are featured.

Table 3.3
Headquarters of clubs in Cardiff and Barry District Leagues[1]

League	Cardiff & District		Barry and District	
Season of observation	1924–5		1926–7	
	A	B	A	B
Private address	8	–	2	–
Religious	16	14	3	2
Institute/welfare/political hall	8	3	6	3
Public house/hotel	7	–	5	1
Workplace	3	3	4	3
On ground	8	–	5	–
Not listed	15	–	3	–
Total clubs	65		28	

Key   A: Listed headquarters of clubs
         B: Clubs with names corresponding to their headquarters

[1] Cardiff & District Football League, *Official Handbooks*; Barry & District Association Football League, *Official Handbooks*. These two seasons have been chosen on the basis that handbooks for other years rarely give complete information on clubs' headquarters.

relationships that had often existed since childhood.[49] As one player said of his 1920s club, 'I just sort of drifted into it you know. We were all kids together sort of thing. Got to know each and started playing like. We used to play on the tithe fields and that's how we got together and formed a team.'[50] Where institutions were used by a club as a meeting place and changing-room, there was rarely any official link or material assistance. Hence, as in England,[51] teams actually named after pubs were rare, and many clubs who used them as bases did not list them as their official headquarters. Other clubs developed links with institutions purely to ensure they had somewhere to meet. A group of Cardiff friends chose Splott Labour Amateurs as the name for their team because they had intended to use the local Labour Party hall as a clubroom. When it became apparent that they would have to join the party in order to use the hall, the arrangement was dropped. Yet the club retained the name despite having no connections with the Labour Party.[52] Some clubs chose glamorous names, often inspired by professional teams, such as Park Villa or Ely Hotspur. Naming the club after a district helped to give it and its members a sense of grandeur and importance, a feeling of representing their area, even if the reality was quite different. Several clubs often shared a district's name and would be largely unknown outside their own social network, which supplied them with small bands of followers comprising friends and family.[53] With many clubs dependent on individuals rather than institutions, they were often transient and short-lived. They would disappear as players got married or moved on, with new clubs, composed of the next generation of unmarried men, springing up in their place.[54] Only eleven of the sixty-five teams listed in the Cardiff and District League handbook in the 1924–5 season were still there ten years later. In the

[49] Holt, *Sport and the British*, p. 154.
[50] Ivor Harris, interview with author.
[51] Jack Williams, 'Churches, sport and identities in the north, 1900–39', in Jeff Hill and Jack Williams (eds.), *Sport and Identity in the North of England* (Keele, 1996), p. 120.
[52] E. J. Jenkins, *The Splott I Remember* (Cowbridge, 1983), p. 19.
[53] See *FE*, 17 November 1934.
[54] Jenkins, *Splott I Remember*, p. 19.

Barry and District League, only two of the twenty-eight clubs in the 1926–7 season had been members five years earlier.[55]

In the higher divisions of local leagues, there were more established and organized clubs. Fairoak AFC of Cardiff, founded in 1912, was running three teams by 1938, playing friendlies in England and touring each Easter.[56] Some established clubs were officially connected to, and named after, the various institutes, working men's clubs and welfare halls which offered their members everything from adult education to another drinking haunt. The formation of a soccer team was a natural extension of the social and recreational activities of such institutions and offered the players vocal and financial support and a degree of prestige that marked them out from the multitude of their peers. In 1910, Splott Baptist AFC of Cardiff could boast D. A. Thomas MP as its president and Lord Ninian Crichton Stuart and the deputy lord mayor as patrons.[57] This was a club that must have liked to see itself as superior to the public house teams it played. Prestige was at the heart of an argument that erupted in 1913 over the name Cardiff Amateurs. A group of former players from Canton Parish Church AFC set up a new team calling itself Cardiff Amateurs, with plans to tour France and play in the local league. There were objections from other Cardiff sides who claimed that the new club was not representative of the best amateurs in the city and would bring no credit to the name.[58] Some of the smallest teams may have seen their name as a matter of convenience or glamour, but to others it was an important statement of whom they represented. In the Valleys, the local welfare or working men's institute often owned the only local pitches available. Thus, affiliation to such an institution promised stability and access to a playing field. Some clubs outgrew the institutions that had spawned them and developed an infrastructure of their own. In 1914, for example, Canton Baptists AFC renamed itself Cardiff Bohemians.[59] The

---

[55] The demands of some leagues' regulations also contributed to the transient nature of these small clubs. A fine for an improperly registered player would frequently be a fatal blow to a team, although it would often reappear later under a different name, having done a disappearing act to avoid impossible financial responsibilities. See, for example, SWMFA minutes, 4 August 1932.

[56] Jenkins, 'Football in Cardiff', p. 46.

[57] *SWDN*, 6 August 1910.

[58] *SWDN*, 10–12 September 1913.

[59] *SWDN*, 25 May 1914.

successful team had firmly established itself and its reputation, and no longer had much in common with the chapel and the congregation from which it had originally grown.

By the 1930s, after a number of senior clubs closed because of financial difficulties, several leading junior clubs moved up into the second division of the Welsh League. Joining the lower echelons of the senior game may have brought greater prestige, but it also meant greater expenses and a financial struggle. Thus few junior clubs held such lofty ambitions. Perhaps the most notable of the large junior clubs in south Wales was Cardiff Corinthians. Founded in 1898 as an offshoot of a local cricket club, it tried to carry on the traditional amateur values of Victorian sport that its name evoked. Such ethics meant the club did not play competitive soccer until 1904, but by 1924 it had its own ground and had risen to the heights of the first division of the Welsh League. At one point in the 1930s, Cardiff Corinthians was running as many as five different teams. Other teams thought its players had a somewhat aloof attitude.[60] The club, however, suffered from continual financial difficulties, despite having a significant number of middle-class patrons and players. It typified the junior clubs that had outgrown their origins but never developed enough support to compete successfully in the world of senior soccer. By the late 1930s, Cardiff Corinthians had begun to concentrate on young players and in 1939 effectively became a nursery club for Cardiff City.

Junior soccer offered physical and emotional rewards. As Holt points out,

> Being in a team was to be 'one of the lads'; it gave warmth, simple shared values and objectives, and an endless source of banter. Tearing around, hurling yourself into tackles, sliding through the mud, and just pushing yourself through a hard and exhausting match was supremely worthwhile because it bound you to your side.[61]

Many of the working men's institutions were large and unwieldy organizations, and the creation of 'sub-clubs' (such as soccer teams) was a way of breaking down large memberships into

---

[60] Arthur Slade, 'Cardiff Corinthians AFC', *The Cardiff Spectator*, 2, 13 (April 1961); Ivor Harris, interview; Jenkins, 'Football in Cardiff', ch. 5.
[61] Holt, *Sport and the British*, p. 155.

smaller, more sociable groups.[62] The Monmouthshire League saw its clubs as a way of fostering 'the spirit of comradeship' so that 'friendship would grow not only on the football field but off it' too.[63] To one junior player from Cardiff, one of the game's attractions was the way it enabled him to meet people and make friends from all over the city.[64] Soccer also offered a social arena where one was judged on talent rather than occupation, thus enabling some to overcome temporarily the perceived stigma of unemployment. A 1937 survey of young unemployed adults in south Wales found that membership of sports clubs was popular because of the opportunity it provided of being part of a team.[65] Soccer thus offered not just fun and games but also self-esteem and a sense of purpose and of belonging.

Clubs played too vital a role in many lives to lie dormant outside the soccer season, and some began to meet in the summer to play baseball or cricket or even to swim. A small minority of junior clubs were supremely ambitious, even using the press to advertise for talented new players, but for others the social contact was more important, and there was less emphasis on winning. Clubs could sustain heavy defeats week in, week out without losing too much heart. An appeal by Penarth Road Juniors for players in 1936 stated that anyone able to kick a football would be welcomed with open arms.[66] Keeping the club going was more important to its young members than securing quality players. The larger clubs did not limit their activities to soccer alone and organized social occasions such as end-of-season dinners and fund-raising dances. As well as enhancing the social bonds within a club, such events helped to bring females into what was often a man's world. Women not only participated in junior soccer's social occasions but they also watched their male friends and family play and were responsible for much of the game's supporting organization. Washing the kit was a traditionally female role but at some junior clubs women actually held official positions such as that of treasurer. In 1930, the *South Wales Echo* claimed that the participation of women, both as members and organizers, had been the financial salvation of

[62] Ibid., p. 156.
[63] *SWE*, 27 July 1926.
[64] Ivor Harris, interview.
[65] Lush, *Young Adult in South Wales*, p.77.
[66] *SWE*, 4 September 1936.

many Monmouthshire clubs.[67] Off-the-pitch needs also ensured that men who were too old to play could remain actively involved as coaches or administrators should they so wish. The involvement of women and older men ensured that some clubs were genuine parts of local neighbourhoods, networks and communities that reaffirmed their togetherness.

A club known as the Cardiff All Blacks, formed in the late 1930s and based in the docks area where many of its members worked, was particularly important in this. The club was comprised of black players and it played charity matches across south Wales. Had it competed in the often heated atmosphere of leagues and cups then trouble might have been inevitable but, by playing for charity, it no doubt hoped to promote racial tolerance. The club certainly enjoyed prominent and sympathetic press coverage.[68] Its matches outside Cardiff, sometimes followed by a special dance, offered a rare and welcome opportunity for the black population in that area to meet up and publicly take pride in their colour.[69] Similarly, in the 1920s, an annual match was held between Jews from Swansea and Cardiff which was followed by a social evening.[70] The games offered the Jewish community an opportunity to meet peers outside the restrictions and restraints of a religious gathering.

Given that clubs were an integral part of life for many people, it was natural that wider social tensions spilt over into junior soccer. This is clearly illustrated by the treatment that police teams received. Consistent failures to solve the unemployment of the inter-war years resulted in a growing animosity towards the

---

[67] *SWE*, 27 March 1930.

[68] The contemporary racial attitudes of whites tended to mean a reluctance for close physical contact with the black population. A Cardiff cricket side, largely made up of West Indian immigrants, always had to travel far out of the district to get a game. Even then, their appearance would be greeted with a degree of surprise and shock. K. L. Little, *Negroes in Britain: A Study of Racial Relations in English Society* (London, 1947), pp. 42, 105, 140. For evidence of racial tensions when black players did take part in local competitive games see Ian Pincombe, '"Out of Rexville": G. F. Lovell and the south Wales confectionery industry, c.1830–1940' (University of Wales, unpublished Ph.D. thesis, 2000), p. 221. Wales was actually the first of the home nations to award an international cap to a member of its black communities. John Edward Parris, born near Chepstow of West Indian parents, gained his one and only cap in 1932, while playing for Bradford Park Avenue, which he had joined from his home-town club. Davies and Garland, *Welsh International Soccer Players*, p. 158. For a history of black players in Britain, see Phil Vasili, *Colouring over the White Line: The History of Black Footballers in Britain* (Edinburgh, 2000).

[69] See *SWE*, 8 April 1939.

[70] See, for example, *SWE*, 18 April 1922.

traditional sources of authority. The police were the most visible and thus potent symbol of this authority, and their role in strikes, before and after the First World War, increased the animosity. Police soccer teams suffered because of this hostility. In Cardiff, it was reported that they were constantly verbally abused by spectators who shouted 'Murder 'em' and the like. In Swansea, such behaviour was said to be emulated by the opposing players and encouraged by the crowd, who 'applaud[ed] any rough play against the police club'.[71] A similar situation existed in rugby, but the sport's more physical nature meant that the potential danger for police players was more serious. This may have been behind the official encouragement of soccer at the expense of rugby in the south Wales forces.[72] During the 1934–5 season, the Cardiff police soccer team suddenly withdrew from the local district league in which it had enjoyed much playing success. Its motives were unclear but may be explained by the treatment its players were receiving from other clubs and spectators.

The police were not the only social outcasts to suffer in soccer. Matches between Catholic and Protestant teams in Merthyr, a town where the Irish were often discriminated against, were particularly prone to fighting and ill feeling amongst spectators.[73] During the 1926 miners' strike, a Bargoed Juniors player was barracked by a section of the crowd who believed him to be a blackleg. The club secretary said that the player denied the accusation and implied that he would not have been selected had it been true.[74] In contrast, soccer also offered a way of lessening tensions that arose out of industrial disputes. Matches between strikers and police were a feature of most industrial disputes in the region. They were seen as a way of reducing wider tensions and symbolic of a wider communal solidarity that rose above the present conflict.[75] Troops stationed in the Rhondda after the

[71] *SWE*, 6 February 1934; *Sporting News*, 1 December 1928.

[72] One policeman, who had badly beaten a miner with his baton during the 1925 anthracite strike, was subsequently so severely injured in a rugby match that he was crippled for life. Williams, *1905 and All That*, p. 187; Gordon West, *A Century on the Beat: A History of 100 Years of Police Rugby Football in the South Wales Constabulary Area* (Cardiff, 1992), pp. 8–9, 42, 93.

[73] Charles Jones and W.R. King, interviews with author. See Paul O'Leary, *Immigration and Integration: The Irish in Wales, 1798–1922* (Cardiff, 2000), for a wider account of Irish Catholics in Wales.

[74] *SWE*, 19 October 1926.

[75] For example, see ' "Lock ups" v. "Lock outs" ' in *SWE*, 14 April 1921; Fishwick, *English Football*, pp. 15, 138.

riots of 1910 played regular matches against not only local junior sides but also semi-professional sides and, by all accounts, they were reasonably talented players.[76] Such contact helped to ease the tensions that haunted the area in the aftermath of the dispute and its violence.

It was in junior soccer that the most frequent and serious crowd disturbances occurred. Bad language and assaults on players, referees and fellow spectators were not uncommon throughout south Wales. Most were isolated incidents but some did escalate into mass brawls and led to the abandonment of matches.[77] Nor were some of the players much better behaved, often beginning disturbances, indulging in rough fouls or even leaving the pitch if they disagreed with a decision. Matches usually took place on open grounds with no police present, while spectators often knew, or were related to, the players, and were closely associated with the clubs involved. Thus they were 'at home' and reacted in a way that was the norm in male working-class culture. Play was hard and physical like work, but it was not dangerous, and the authority of the referee was accepted if it was fair. But when someone overstepped the mark, then to interfere or retaliate was deemed acceptable. As Fishwick points out, spectators and players saw no clear-cut distinction between play and the wider experience of life.[78] The harsh cautions and bans meted out show that the game's administrators were not always so understanding, but they were anxious to ensure that the game was deemed respectable.[79] The excesses of working-class culture were never universally acceptable amongst those in traditional positions of authority and responsibility. From the 1927–8 season to the mid-1930s, the annual reports of the SWMFA claimed that misconduct amongst players was on the increase, although few incidents were of a serious nature. In the 1931–2 season it

[76] For example, see *Rhondda Leader*, 14 January, 11 February 1911.
[77] For one of the more extreme examples, see *SWE*, 27 May 1937, when, amidst free fights between players and spectators, one player allegedly tried to strangle the referee.
[78] This paragraph draws upon Fishwick, *English Football*, pp. 20–1, and W. R. King, interview.
[79] In 1923, the Cardiff and District League handed out severe punishments to impress on young players that the game must be played in the right spirit. One player was suspended *sine die* for simply using 'foul language' to a referee. See unaccredited press clipping in SWMFA minutes. The SWMFA encouraged clubs themselves to expel 'undesirable' players. See, for example, SWMFA *Annual Report*, 1934–5.

stated that there were cases in one in every forty matches.[80] However, many were little more than arguments or swearing, and it would be foolish to suggest that junior soccer was a hotbed of immoral and unruly behaviour. Instead, the games, like life, occasionally overheated into a clash of swearwords or a few fists.

Clubs needed somewhere to play, but not all were lucky enough to find a piece of wasteland on the edge of town to rent from a local farmer. By the late 1930s, half the clubs in the Cardiff and District League had private grounds, with the remaining sixty-odd clubs sharing twenty-one public pitches between them.[81] South Wales's larger municipal authorities had been providing recreational facilities since the 1860s in the interests of public health and to discourage more disreputable activities. Pitches were marked out in public parks for soccer, rugby and, in the summer, cricket and baseball. Yet park soccer, with its fights and bad language, was not always the most respectable of leisure activities and deprived others of space and peace-and-quiet in public parks. In 1925 the Swansea Corporation investigated fears that playing fields were pushing the public out of parks.[82] Thus, compared with expenditure on public parks, baths and cultural facilities, municipal provision of pitches was limited.[83] With rugby also competing for space in public parks, supply was outstripped by demand.[84] In 1924 there were just thirty-five public playing pitches in Cardiff to be split between the two codes. However, with soccer alone having over ninety teams in the Cardiff and District League, twenty-two in the Cardiff schools league and eighteen in the ex-schoolboys league, this was hardly sufficient, even allowing for those clubs with private pitches.[85] Several matches had to be played consecutively on the same pitch and, in winter, the last would often not finish until after dark. Such shortages frequently caused

[80] SWMFA *Annual Report*, 1931–2. While the report did not distinguish between junior and senior games, most clubs under its jurisdiction were junior sides.
[81] *FE*, 28 August 1937; *SWE*, 14 August 1937.
[82] *SWE*, 23 September 1925.
[83] See Raymond J. Stroud, 'The landscape of popular recreation in Newport, Monmouthshire, 1888–1914' (University of Wales, unpublished MA thesis, 1993), ch. 2.
[84] Accusations of bias against both rugby and soccer were commonly thrown at local authorities and other owners of pitches. In Nantyglo and Blaina it was alleged that clubs of both codes had been indulging in 'cheap stunts', such as making councillors vice-presidents, in order to secure use of the local park. *WM*, 6 March 1922.
[85] Cardiff Corporation, Parks, Open Spaces and Burial Lands Committee minutes, 12 February 1924; *FE*, 8 September 1923.

backlogs in fixtures across south Wales and prevented some interested people from playing at all.[86] By the mid-1930s, overuse had caused many Cardiff park pitches to deteriorate into dangerous mud baths that discouraged skilful play. Injuries led clubs to refuse to use certain pitches. In 1938, the Cardiff and District League went so far as to ban the use of two particular pitches. They were little more than a thin layer of earth over concrete and often littered with sharp refuse.[87] Nets may have been 'a luxury', goalposts may have had to be carried to the ground (and even then would not necessarily fit the slots), changing facilities may have been limited to the biggest parks, and council bureaucracy may have had to be negotiated with to obtain a playing permit, but such municipal pitches were vital to ensuring the junior game could exist at all.

In 1921 a Ministry of Health survey on the region reported that the 'extent of land available in the way of public parks and recreational grounds outside the seaboard towns is almost negligible'.[88] Even in Barry in 1923, thirty clubs had to share just six pitches between them. The hitherto successful club, Caerphilly Albions, was forced to disband in 1921 after failing to secure a ground to play on.[89] It was in the mining Valleys, where there was a lack of suitable flat ground, that the situation was worst. The welfare schemes funded by coal companies did provide playing fields, but they were often monopolized by the largest local teams and inaccessible to the public.[90] In 1936 it was reported that there were around twelve playing fields in the Rhondda, but 120 teams. Some clubs were left to play on small, uneven and grassless pitches built on refuse, coal tips or just patches on the mountainside. Black Diamond AFC of Edmondston had a pitch which was 'solid rock in some places and a quagmire in others'. As the coal companies utilized more and more flat land for coal tips, including areas they had previously allowed local clubs to use, the pitch shortage grew worse. In October 1925, Rhondda League matches from the previous season had still not been completed because of the lack of playing fields.[91]

---

[86] *SWE*, 1 December 1938.
[87] *SWE*, 24 December 1936, 9 October 1937, 10 September 1938; Cardiff Corporation, Parks etc. Committee minutes, 4 October 1933.
[88] Ministry of Health, *South Wales Regional Survey*, p. 58.
[89] *FE*, 21 April 1923, 27 August 1921.
[90] See, for example, Ministry of Health, *South Wales Regional Survey*, p. 59.
[91] *FE*, 29 August 1936, 6 September 1919, 3 October 1925; *SWE*, 3 October 1989.

During the inter-war period, wider pressure for public playing fields developed as rising unemployment and poverty raised concerns about the physical well-being of the region's youth.[92] Providing public pitches was also a way of finding work for the local unemployed and discouraging street games. Yet the supply of any municipal recreation was never a priority for local authorities in the 1920s, and any imposition on the rates was politically controversial. Sport could only ever play a small part in remedying the region's health problems, and better housing was a more important and effective solution. In 1935, part of a public playing field in Ely in Cardiff was actually given over to a housing development.[93] By the mid-1930s, there was a new impetus in the campaigns for more playing fields. The deteriorating political situation in central Europe renewed fears about the fitness of the nation, and a national memorial scheme for George V, based upon the creation of more playing fields, was set up in 1936. In Cardiff, these new concerns and the increased publicity given to the poor and sometimes dangerous pitches in the city led the corporation to repair old fields and begin an extensive programme of providing new public pitches, helped by grants from the National Playing Fields Association and the National Fitness Council.[94] While Hitler's activities led to new concerns about playing-field shortages, they also created a new problem. Land was needed for military buildings and defences, and playing fields were ideal for the purpose. The Splott district in Cardiff alone lost four football grounds to the military in 1938.[95]

---

[92] See, for example, Ministry of Health, *South Wales Regional Survey*, pp. 58–9.

[93] Cardiff Corporation, Parks etc. Committee minutes, 15 March 1935.

[94] By 1938, the number of public soccer pitches in Cardiff had increased to forty. In contrast, in Manchester in the same year, there were 201 football pitches. The new programme was to benefit football, cricket, hockey, swimming and baseball. The National Playing Fields Association had already made grants of £6,000 to help purchase new fields in Monmouthshire, and the SWMFA credited it and mining welfare schemes with helping to combat the playing field shortage in the 1930s. Thomas, 'Physical education in Wales', p. 162; Stephen G. Jones, 'Working-class sport in Manchester between the wars', in Holt (ed.), *Sport and the Working Class*, p. 78; *SWE*, 18 October, 13, 17 December 1938, 4 October 1935; Jenkins, 'Football in Cardiff', p. 47; SWMFA *Annual Report*, 1930–1 and minutes, 23 July 1932.

[95] *SWE*, 1 October 1938; Jenkins, 'Football in Cardiff', p. 46.

RELIGION, WORKERS AND ECONOMICS

Religious bodies in England were integral providers of junior soccer.[96] Although never as common as in England, thanks to the dominance of socially conservative Nonconformity, teams based at religious institutions were also important in inter-war south Wales (see table 3.2). Interdenominational Sunday school leagues were formed across the region in the early 1920s, and church leagues were set up in Barry and Aberdare.[97] In 1924, most junior clubs in the Monmouthshire Eastern Valley League were run by either churches or chapels. By 1930, the Cardiff Sunday School League had twenty sides, fifteen of which appear to have been based at Nonconformist institutions.[98] The fact that at least some chapels were now actively embracing soccer was perhaps the final recognition of the social acceptability of the sport in south Wales. Religious influence could also be found in the upper echelons of the game. In the mid-1920s, the Revd E. R. Davies, vicar of Cyfarthfa in Merthyr, was chairman of the Merthyr and District League, a member of the FAW and SWMFA councils and a Merthyr Town director. He saw soccer as a way of ensuring boys played fairly throughout life. The Cardiff Sunday School League's refusal to allow teams to meet or change in licensed premises similarly suggests a determination to promote moral lessons through the game.[99] Running teams also offered an ideal opportunity for securing younger congregations and, by insisting that registered players regularly attend services, the game was used to try to reverse the trend of an increasingly secular youth.[100] To what extent soccer actually drew boys to religion itself is unclear, but many did join churches

---

[96] Williams, 'Churches, sport and identities'.

[97] Intriguingly, interdenominational clubs were also known. In 1924, Church Village Amalgamated Church AFC was set up. Its players had to be certified members of any church. SWMFA minutes, 6 November 1924.

[98] FE, 16 February 1924; SWE, 9 May 1930.

[99] Unaccredited press clippings in SWMFA minutes, 1927; Jenkins, 'Football in Cardiff', p. 196. Such attempts were not always successful, as the disciplinary proceedings against church sides for bad or foul behaviour show. See, for example, SWMFA minutes, 7 December 1907.

[100] Players in the Merthyr Sunday School League were required to attend at least two services of any denomination a month. SWE, 22 August 1923. The existence of a soccer club at one church was noted as part of a general progressive policy which had been successful at building up a young congregation. Anon., South Wales Collier Boy, p. 11.

or chapels simply for an opportunity to play in competitions.[101] As in England, the gradual decline of organized religion went hand in hand with a decline in soccer clubs and leagues with religious affiliations.[102] The Merthyr Sunday School League was forced to merge with the local welfare league in 1923. Its clubs tried to retain a rule that players must attend services but were forced to drop the idea by the new league which viewed it as 'propaganda'. By the 1937–8 season, the Cardiff Sunday School League was down to ten members and even those clubs still in existence had problems fielding eleven players.[103]

Table 3.2 shows that in Cardiff, as in England, there was a growth in the number of clubs representing places of work as the number of church-based teams declined.[104] In south Wales during the early 1920s, there were leagues for workers in the railways, docks, trams, civil service and collieries, but by the 1930s most works teams had turned to competing in the local district leagues instead. Some teams received no help from their bosses, but other employers encouraged and supported works soccer in order to foster better industrial relations, ensure the fitness of employees (and thus productivity) and obtain publicity for a company.[105] But soccer could also bring pride and honour, and companies were keen to foster the game for this less sinister reason. Thus firms were prepared to reward successful teams. In 1933, for example, British Ropes Ltd promised its team a special dinner should they win their division of the Cardiff and District League. In the Valleys, clubs affiliated to places of work were less common, and teams officially associated with mining companies were rare. The local colliery company in Abertridwr did purchase a ground for a local club but was not involved in its administration in any other capacity.[106] Instead of directly sponsoring sport through works teams, as happened in other industries, colliery companies financially supported welfare schemes

---

[101] This even led to some boys swapping denominations on occasions. See Jenkins, 'Football in Cardiff', pp. 195–6.

[102] Fishwick, *English Football*, p. 12; Williams, 'Churches, sport and identities', p. 115. It was usually league subscriptions that spelt the death of religious teams with falling membership.

[103] The Sunday School League still had over 600 registered players. *ME*, 12 May 1923; *SWE*, 22 August 1923; Jenkins, 'Football in Cardiff', pp. 199–200.

[104] Williams, 'Churches, sport and identities', p. 124.

[105] Fishwick, *English Football*, p. 13.

[106] *FE*, 7 January 1933, 2 September 1922.

and institutes. What these institutions did with their resources was up to their members, but most supported sport to varying extents.

Some companies had ambitious plans for their teams that went far beyond any attempt to manipulate their employees. Lovell's, a Newport confectionery manufacturer, turned its club, Lovell's Athletic, into a significant force in Welsh soccer. At times Lovell's Athletic was running four different teams and was more like a senior club than a works outfit. In 1923 the club was asked to resign from the South Wales Amateur League because it had professional players on its books. When it (successfully) applied to join the Welsh League in 1924, Newport County feared that its attendances would suffer and threatened to resign should its neighbour be admitted. In 1930, there were (denied) rumours that an employee who played for Newport County was told that he must transfer to the works club or lose his job.[107] The height of the depression brought a greater sense of proportion to the club. Henceforth it limited its activities to the Welsh League and began to help rather than to rival Newport County, with some players regularly turning out for both clubs during the 1930s.[108] The club could not have rivalled Newport County even had it wanted to. Irrespective of any success, the club was seen as representing a company rather than the town in which it was based. It had thus struggled to attract enough support to become financially self-sufficient even when doing well on the pitch. Lovell's were not the only works side which, with the security and stability of backing from a company, managed to advance in the soccer world. By the mid-1930s vacancies in the first division of the Welsh League caused by senior clubs folding had been filled by works teams.[109] Yet such teams were always the exception, and most works clubs operated alongside the institute, pub and church sides in the district leagues.

---

[107] Newport County did not carry out its threat. Lovell's also, this time unsuccessfully, applied to join the Southern League. *SWE*, 20 June, 28 July 1924, 31 August 1923, 22 January 1930. For more information on the Lovell's company, see Pincombe, 'Out of Rexville'. For the soccer club, see Dave Twydell, *More Defunct FC: Club Histories and Statistics* (Harefield, 1990).

[108] Tony Ambrosen, *The Ironsides: A Lifetime in the League: A Who's Who of Newport County, 1912–89* (Harefield, 1991), pp. 64, 89; *SWE*, 14 February 1933.

[109] In 1937, in addition to Lovell's Athletic, teams from Tredomen works and Gelli colliery were playing in the Welsh League's senior division.

Another important component of junior soccer in the large towns was the Wednesday and Thursday leagues which were set up to cater for men who worked on Saturday afternoons and wanted to play on their own half-day. The pre-1914 and early 1920s leagues were amalgams of sides based on geographical areas, teams from the service industries and works teams. As unemployment rose, the character of the competitions changed because out-of-work men, with enforced time on their hands, established Wednesday league clubs. By 1932, the Cardiff Wednesday League had changed so much from its original purpose that it was considering allowing professionals to play in its senior division. The changes were not universally popular, and a year later there was talk of the league insisting that only genuine 'Wednesdayites' (those whose only free afternoon was Wednesday) play. This idea was attacked in the press with arguments that, with high unemployment, there was a moral obligation to cater for all players. As the economic situation slowly improved, many Cardiff clubs had problems fielding sides as unemployed members found jobs which left them unable to play on Wednesday afternoons.[110]

Despite the growing dominance of the Labour movement in local politics, its role in junior soccer was limited. Trade unionists and other Labour activists in Edwardian south Wales (and England) did not see sport as a potential vehicle in their struggle and made no effort to appropriate the growth of soccer. Wheeler argues that the existing English sport network was perceived as being democratically run, thus lessening the need for workers to control it.[111] This seems true of south Wales before and after the First World War, and opponents of Communist-run sport reminded the working class that they already had their say in the running of junior soccer.[112] Although knights, former army officers and local JPs often held honorary positions on district leagues, club representatives dominated the controlling committees, thus ensuring that the junior game was relatively democratic. Apart from shortages of playing fields, junior soccer

[110] *SWE*, 14 September 1929, 28 June 1932, 13 June 1933, 23 November 1935.
[111] R. F. Wheeler, 'Organized sport and organized labour: the workers' sports movement', *Journal of Contemporary History*, 3, 2 (1978), p. 205. This was in contrast to Germany, where there was a strong socialist sports movement. See Arnd Krüger and James Riordan (eds.), *The Story of Worker Sport* (Leeds, 1996).
[112] *Rhondda Gazette* (hereafter *RG*), 24 March 1928.

suffered only from arguments over ineligible players, occasional pitch brawls and fixture backlogs. All clubs were keen to solve these problems and they could hardly be blamed on the administrators. Even the suspension of clubs for failing to pay subscriptions does not seem to have caused much resentment, partly no doubt because an erring club could just re-form under a different name. Thus, junior soccer was run relatively successfully by largely democratic committees, and the growing labour movement had no need to become involved. Instead it concentrated its energies on the more important battles elsewhere.

Clubs desirous of establishing leagues firmly under the control of the working class risked alienation and the principle does not appear to have been strong enough for them to chance this. When, in 1928, local representatives of the Communist-orientated British Workers' Sports Federation (BWSF) suggested to the Rhondda Amateur League and its clubs that they should affiliate and sever links with soccer's ruling authorities, there was little positive interest and some hostile opposition.[113] The local Communist team, like other clubs based on left-wing political bodies in different leagues, continued to play in the competition. Despite the existence of Communist sympathies in the Rhondda, the BWSF did not make widespread progress in south Wales. It had a number of branches and clubs in the Rhondda (one of which the press rather condescendingly described as playing good football in spite of their political views) and a small workers' league, but in no way did it rival the established junior soccer institutions.[114] In 1930 a match at Tonypandy between the south Wales and London BWSFs did attract a crowd of 3,000 and stimulated public awareness of the movement. That year, there were also plans for a team from the Soviet Union to play a match at Porth against a local representative BWSF side, which the organizers ambitiously hoped would attract a crowd of 15,000–20,000. In the end the Soviets were refused visas by the Labour government, and a game was played against a side of

---

[113] *FE*, 24 March 1928; *RG*, 24 March 1928; unaccredited press clipping in SWMFA minutes.
[114] *FE*, 14 November 1925; *SWE*, 17 April 1930; Stephen G. Jones, 'The British Workers' Sports Federation, 1923–35', in Krüger and Riordan (eds.), *Story of Worker Sport*, p. 111.

English Communists instead before just 500 spectators.[115] The leader of the Young Communist League in Merthyr in the late 1930s, who was a keen soccer fan, said that, although he knew of the BWSF, the idea of a workers' sports body was never raised or thought of in his organization. They were wholly absorbed with 'fighting to live'.[116] Communism had little to offer the world of junior soccer. An extensive league system with satisfactory resources already existed, and the BWSF could offer nothing to rival that. The Rhondda's Communist sympathies won the BWSF no more support than it enjoyed in other depressed areas. Much of the appeal of the far left in the mining valleys was the human relevance of its leaders rather than their ideological messages.[117] For most people such radical politics were a possible answer to economic and social problems rather than an all-embracing ethos that could underpin all aspects of life, including those that already worked. Hence, leisure and politics remained, for the majority, separate ideological spheres.[118] As a result, the BWSF was nothing more than a marginal organization whose argument, that sport was part of the capitalist stranglehold on society, went largely unheard or ignored.

Yet soccer suffered in the depression like so much of south Wales society. It may have been run relatively democratically, but the junior game was not an autonomous working-class pursuit. Clubs had to pay for travel, referees' expenses and league and cup subscriptions, ensuring that money was a constant consideration. Since most teams played on open grounds where no admission fees could be charged, hats were passed around the crowd during games to ask for donations. Clubs had to survive on this money, together with what they could raise from fund-raising events and the subscriptions of members and players. Consequently, not all soccer enthusiasts could even afford to join a club. A 1937 survey showed many of the unemployed in south Wales were being held back from playing

---

[115] *Daily Worker*, 5, 8 April 1930; *WM*, 28 April 1930; *SWE*, 17–26 April 1930.
[116] W. R. King, interview.
[117] Chris Williams, *Democratic Rhondda: Politics and Society, 1885–1951* (Cardiff, 1996), p. 208.
[118] In 1923 the resolution of a Pontypridd Labour soccer club to wish the local Labour Party candidate good luck in the forthcoming general election was defeated by a single vote at a meeting of the Pontypridd League. It was resolved that in future politics should not be discussed. Pontypridd Association Football League minutes, 4 December 1923.

sport by monetary factors. In Cardiff, only 14 per cent of its sample were members of sports clubs, in Newport the figure was 9 per cent and in Pontypridd, 10 per cent. For many, being involved in soccer meant a sacrifice such as forgoing cigarettes, or even walking an eighteen-mile round-trip to play a match because the train was too expensive. Money was so short at one club that its members had to buy the components of a ball separately and assemble it themselves. During the 1926 coal dispute, Kenfig Hill AFC lost the majority of its players who were miners, but then regained them when they returned to work. Other clubs suffered as their unemployed players joined the exodus of men leaving south Wales in search of work. Once they were established in England, forming a soccer club did offer a way for men from south Wales to stay in touch or make contact with each other. Men, for example, from the Ton Pentre area who moved to London, set up Brixton Welsh AFC.[119]

With some clubs in the Rhondda having as many as 75 per cent of their members out of work, it was inevitable that many clubs closed.[120] As early as 1922, the *South Wales Echo* was calling it a 'miracle' that any clubs below the first division of the Newport and District League were able to survive at all because of the economic conditions.[121] Reports of league committee meetings were often dominated by the expulsion of clubs for failing to pay their subscriptions. Declining membership caused the Barry and District League to fall from five divisions in 1924 to three in 1927, while the 1928–9 season alone saw a quarter of the clubs in the Newport and District League fail to complete their fixtures because of financial problems. At the beginning of the 1929–30 season, there were only four clubs in the Abergavenny League that were willing to continue. Such problems caused some leagues to fold. The number affiliated to the SWMFA fell from twenty-one in 1926 to twelve in 1938.[122] League subscription prices were leading to the peculiar situation where some clubs were keen to compete in the lowest division possible because fees were cheaper there. In the 1925–6 season

[119] Lush, *Young Adult in South Wales*, pp. 76–7; *SWE*, 5 January 1935, 4 August 1934, 21 December 1933, 21 January 1937; *FE*, 27 November 1926.
[120] *SWE*, 4 August 1934.
[121] *SWE*, 18 March 1922.
[122] *FE*, 27 August 1927; *SWE*, 9 May 1929, 27 September 1930; SWMFA *Annual Reports*.

this reached farcical levels in the Rhondda Amateur League. A reorganization led to forty applications for the third division but only four for the second division. Clubs would even try to switch districts *en masse* if a neighbouring league had lower subscriptions.[123] Costs led some leagues to merge, while others switched to smaller, and thus cheaper, geographic areas. The result was arguments over jurisdiction between different authorities within an increasingly complex and overlapping network of competitions.[124] Some clubs gained through men using their enforced leisure time to labour on ground improvement schemes,[125] but, on the whole, the depression was as problematic for soccer as it was for the rest of society.

'AMAZON FOOTBALLERS'

It was not just men who played soccer. Before 1914, there were very occasional women's matches in south Wales, but it was the First World War that brought an increase in the popularity of women's soccer as both a spectator and participatory sport.[126] The demands of the war effort had brought new levels of female emancipation and this, together with the money matches raised for charity, gave the women's game a lease of life in England.[127] Interest in south Wales was stimulated by these developments, and clubs were formed in Cardiff, Swansea, Merthyr and Llanelli during and after the conflict. However, those who wanted to play still faced considerable problems and women's soccer remained very much a peripheral activity. A 1921 Ministry of Health report on south Wales noted that 'adult females do not as a rule indulge in [outdoor] games at all'.[128] Photographic evidence suggests that the players were mostly teenagers, but even finding a club could be difficult for anyone

[123] *FE*, 5 September 1925; *SWE*, 26 August 1929.
[124] See, for example, *SWE*, 25 January 1929; SWMFA *Annual Report*, 1928–9.
[125] E. E. Edwards, *Echoes of Rhymney* (Newport, 1974 edn), p. 86.
[126] Cardiff played host to the British Ladies Football Club as early as 1895. There was a 3,000 attendance at the game, in which the goalkeepers were men. Lile and Farmer, 'Early development', p. 203.
[127] John Williams and Jackie Woodhouse, 'Can play, will play? Women and football in Britain', in John Williams and Stephen Wagg (eds.), *British Football and Social Change: Getting into Europe* (Leicester, 1991), pp. 90–3.
[128] Ministry of Health, *South Wales Regional Survey*, p. 58.

interested, as letters of complaint to the press testified.[129] For females in the industrial Valleys, there were even fewer opportunities, as gender roles were more rigid. Married women everywhere were constrained by the demands of looking after a family and a home, and, even had they had the time, a more relaxing recreation would have probably held greater appeal for most.

The clubs that did exist had to fight against the prejudices of both sexes. Soccer was regarded as a man's game and female players were derided, or at best patronized, by the press. Both supporters and opponents saw female football as part of a wider change in the status of women but, to its adversaries, this was a matter of horror:

> In my opinion there are plenty of pastimes for girls without indulging in such masculine games as football and I don't think any really nice girls would play it. I am sorry to say, many girls today, in 'trying to keep with the times' as they call it, are losing all sense of decency. Modesty and womanliness are a woman's greatest charms and I am sure there is nothing womanly about a girl dressed in knicker-bockers kicking a ball about. Equally bad is the sight of girls dressed in tight bathing suits walking the beach and posing before cameras as we see them so much today. I am utterly disgusted with them. Vera.[130]

Faced with such opposition, much of women's soccer remained a humorous spectacle rather than a serious sport. Many female teams ended up just playing novelty matches against teams of men, who were handicapped by their advanced age, having their hands tied behind their backs or similar.[131] Both novelty and more serious teams remained localized, and the Welsh women's game did not share in the popular boom that Dick, Kerr's Ladies and other English teams enjoyed during the immediate post-war years. Nonetheless, in 1921, Kerr's played in Cardiff and Swansea before 18,000 and 25,000 spectators respectively.[132] Such teams have been described as essentially show-business

---

[129] For example, see *SWE*, 21 September 1920.
[130] *SWE*, 23 September 1920. Also see 'Should women play football?' and the ensuing debate in the letters pages in *SWE*, 15–25 September 1920.
[131] See, for example, *SWE*, 10 May 1921.
[132] Gail J. Newsham, *In a League of their Own! The Dick, Kerr's Ladies Football Team* (London, 1994), p. 48.

outfits,[133] and Welsh audiences probably saw women's games in the same light. Yet this should not devalue the role of women's soccer for its players. The spectacle and the charitable cause may have drawn the spectators but the matches provided interested women with their only opportunity of playing football.

The English soccer authorities shared the moral objections to women playing. In 1921, despite (or perhaps because of) the large crowds watching Dick, Kerr's and others, the FA banned any club under its jurisdiction from allowing its ground to be used for women's matches. The FAW was not quite so stringent on the matter and granted permission in 1921 for 'ladies' clubs' to play charity matches across south Wales. However, a year later, the association followed the FA's line and took the decision that, in the 'interest of the game', ladies' matches should not be allowed on Welsh grounds. For the rest of the decade, women's soccer was almost dormant in England and south Wales. Yet, by 1931 the FAW's resolve had weakened, and permission was given for a women's charity match at Llanelli, although it was stated that this was to be an exception.[134] But social needs began to take priority, and the 1930s saw an increasing number of charity matches involving Welsh women's teams and visiting sides from England. Although many of the games took place on grounds outside the FAW's jurisdiction, the association's stance had been reluctantly relaxed, with permission being given for specific games. South Wales even hosted women's internationals involving Great Britain and England sides playing France, possibly because of the FAW's more lenient approach.[135] It was not uncommon for women's games in the 1930s to attract crowds of several thousand.[136] More serious matches had largely replaced the comedy style of the early 1920s, but teams were still limited to playing in aid of charity. Many sides were raised only for a specific match but there were some established clubs, such as the Newport sweet manufacturers Lovell's which ran a team for its younger female employees. However, the FAW was still not happy. Not all matches were granted permission and, in

[133] Fishwick, *English Football*, p. 17.
[134] FAW minutes 1921, 3 March 1922, 9 September 1931.
[135] England v. France in Pontypool, 1935, and Great Britain v. France in Pontypridd, 1937. Both matches were in aid of charity. *SWE*, 18 July 1935, 20 July 1937.
[136] For example, a crowd of 5,000 watched Cardiff Women play Lovell's Women in Newport in 1932. *SWE*, 12 October 1932.

1938, the secretary of the FAW claimed that soccer was 'a man's game and women don't look well playing it'.[137] In 1939 the association claimed that an excessive proportion of receipts was being taken up as expenses at women's charity matches and it reiterated its ban.[138]

Conclusion

Junior soccer was intensely competitive: winning was important. The habit of 'pot hunting', where teams entered competitions beyond their area in search of glory, typified this attitude.[139] But win or lose, for many men and boys, playing soccer was a source of considerable physical and emotional reward. For the unemployed in particular, it offered a rare opportunity to feel 'somebody'.[140] Sport was thus seen as a way of maintaining the spirits and optimism of those out of work, as well as regaining the physical fitness that enforced idleness had undermined.[141] Although there was no official state policy of utilizing sport to help those on the dole, concerned individuals, local institutions and the out-of-work themselves set up teams, leagues and cups for the unemployed. Soccer not only provided some relief from poverty and unemployment, it also provided fund-raising opportunities for charities and other voluntary groups. As the needs of south Wales grew, benefit games and competitions, particularly cups in aid of local hospitals, became an integral part of junior soccer. Indeed, the SWMFA on a number of occasions expressed concern that the competitions were interfering with the running and popularity of established cups and leagues.[142] Other help for the community was less official. At a 1921 cup match in Ynysddu, the gatemen secretly let local men on strike in for free.[143] Thus, the junior game offered more than just individual rewards. It played its part in helping a working-class society keep

---

[137] Quoted in Newsham, *Dick, Kerr's*, p. 93.
[138] FAW minutes, 29 August 1939.
[139] For example, see *WM*, 22 July 1929.
[140] Eyles, *Shadow of the Steelworks*, p. 60.
[141] See, for example, South Wales and Monmouthshire Council of Social Service, *A Social Approach to Unemployment in South Wales* (Cardiff, 1935), pp. 30–3.
[142] See, for example, SWMFA *Annual Report*, 1935–6.
[143] The two gatemen ended up being charged with trying to evade the entertainment tax. *SWE*, 26 August 1921.

its humour, fitness and finances afloat. Yet soccer did not enfranchise the underprivileged. Working-class culture was not autonomous. To play, men required money, space and time that were not always available. Women, meanwhile, required a change in social and material conditions that was even more elusive.

Junior soccer was more than just a working-class game, and clubs like Cardiff Corinthians ensured that soccer enjoyed a broad appeal. Indeed, it was probably the major participatory sport of south Wales, 'the game of the masses and the classes', as the FAW secretary claimed.[144] Rugby may still have thought of itself as the national game, but just a glance at the multitude of local leagues reveals that soccer was bigger in terms of participation. Junior soccer was always secondary to the professional game, and matches were often cancelled if they coincided with an important game for the local senior club. Indeed, the popularity of senior soccer did much to stimulate interest in the junior game. Nonetheless, the junior game played its part in helping cohere an often fragmented society, be it through matches which pitted strikers against police, or by the bringing together of communities, struggling under the burden of unemployment, behind a local team. Fights and arguments, be they physical or verbal, may have been relatively regular but so were they in wider society. Most importantly, the junior game helped to articulate the life and consciousness of a community. Whether it be through characters who insisted on playing in their flat caps, fiery women who poked visiting goalkeepers with broomsticks, the dashing star player who caught the eye of the girls, or simply the fun of playing and watching with friends and family, junior soccer was a game of the local community.[145] Even if it only offered a distraction from the problems and routine of daily existence, the junior game's social function was important, and to many it was an integral part of life.

[144] Quoted in Corrigan, *100 Years*, ch. 6.
[145] Miscellaneous interviews with author.

IV

'THE GREAT HOARSE CROWD': SUPPORTERS AND SPECTATORS

> The Saturday afternoons specially made for Cardiff City,
> The avalanche of hands and feet to Ninian Park,
> The clamour and the roar, disputed goal, play up the blues,
> The brass band at half-time, *Abide with Me* and *Sospan Fach*.
> The pigeons released and sweeping north and east and west,
> The beer bottles waving, the mascot vendors,
> And then the returning crowd, the great hoarse crowd,
> Surging back to city streets for ale and chops and tarts.
> And in the winter evening Tiger Bay *was* Tiger Bay,
> And the moon rose over the Severn Sea.
>
> Idris Davies, *Gwalia Deserta*, part XXXIII, 1938[1]

Without supporters, professional soccer would be soulless, a game without life or colour. Their shillings financed the clubs and their voices fed the spectacle that was match day. The man (and woman and child) on the 'bob bank' was as much a part of the game as the players on the pitch. In return, soccer offered its fans excitement, entertainment and escape from 'this lesser life, from work, wages, rent, doles, sick pay, insurance cards, nagging wives, ailing children, bad bosses [and] idle workmen'. Following professional soccer was a communal experience; it provided a shared emotional and social satisfaction and a sense of belonging as you escaped with 'your mates and your neighbours, with half the town'.[2] Even amongst the local people not at the match, there were many who would want to know how 'City' or 'the Swans' got on. The experience of being there was not always positive. Matches were lost and drawn and the open banks could be uncomfortable and wet. Most supporters had played the game at some point in their lives.[3] They appreciated the talents on display but were quick to criticize if performances did not live up to expectations. Soccer was a sport of mixed and varied emotions.

---

[1] Islwyn Jenkins (ed.), *The Collected Poems of Idris Davies* (Llandysul, 1980 edn), p. 46.
[2] Priestley, *Good Companions*, pp. 13–14.
[3] Richard Holt and Tony Mason, *Sport in Britain, 1945–2000* (Oxford, 2000), p. 1.

A SEA OF CLOTH CAPS

Although there is an absence of firm quantitative evidence, historians have interpreted English soccer crowds in this period as being dominated by the skilled working class or 'decent workaday folk'.[4] There is little to suggest that the same was not also true of south Wales. A visitor to Ninian Park's 'bob bank' noted that all around him were 'highly respectable members of the football loving proletariat – faithful fellows all, if a trifle too emotional'.[5] Photographs of the area's popular banks show a sea of the flat caps that characterized working-class male dress and disguised differences of age and region.[6] Most notably, football crowds in south Wales were often characterized by large numbers of miners; a group who, Holt and Mason argue, were perhaps the sport's most loyal followers.[7] In 1926 the press estimated that they made up as much as 90 per cent of Mid Rhondda United's support.[8] To the anger of colliery companies, some miners would leave work early, or even not turn up at all, in order to watch matches.[9] Such was the importance of miners to soccer, that kick-off times in the Welsh League (and sometimes in the Football League) were often co-ordinated with shifts at local collieries. Such arrangements were not possible in winter's shorter hours of daylight and, thus, to secure earlier Saturday finishes, longer midweek shifts were organized in some collieries. Merthyr Town officials urged the adoption of such practices in

[4] See Mason, *Association Football*, ch. 5; Fishwick, *English Football*, ch. 3.
[5] *SWE*, 29 January 1924.
[6] Smith, *Democracy in a Depression*, p. 50.
[7] Holt and Mason, *Sport in Britain*, p. 3.
[8] *FE*, 18 September 1926. In 1923, 87.2 per cent of insured workers in the Rhondda–Pontypridd district were employed in the coal industry. Baber and Thomas, 'Glamorgan economy', p. 538.
[9] *SWE*, 17 September 1924; *FE*, 8 November 1919. Miners were not the only workers unable to watch matches because of the time of their shifts. In 1921, the Cambrian Wagon Company issued summonses to twenty employees who had missed work to watch a mid-week Cardiff City match. The company explained that in the past when men wanted time off to watch a game they appointed a deputation to wait on the management, who then closed the works in accordance with the wishes of the men. However, large numbers of workers, who did not want to see the match, had begun to complain because shutdowns meant they lost wages, and this time the works remained open. The company eventually withdrew the summonses in order to prevent any bad feeling. In 1922 the postmen's union in Cardiff asked for Saturday afternoons off to allow members to attend games. The union suggested earlier deliveries instead. The Chamber of Trade refused, saying that, although they were sportsmen, they thought business should come before pleasure. *SWE*, 23 March 1921, 16 October 1922.

their area, but local miners feared that if they willingly worked longer hours it might give employers an excuse to return to the eight-hour day.[10] As economic conditions and industrial relations deteriorated, the arrangements that did exist collapsed, longer Saturday hours were worked generally and, with jobs being insecure, men were less willing to take time off voluntarily to watch games.[11] The SWMFA and FAW therefore made various approaches to mining companies asking for shorter Saturday working hours.[12] Some new arrangements were secured but, in the unstable economic climate, they did not last. Thus working practices and unemployment in the coal districts may have gradually reduced the numbers of miners who attended matches, but they remained an integral part of soccer crowds throughout the inter-war years. The reporter who wrote, in 1936, that the 'Welsh collier is still a 100 per cent sportsman, with perhaps a greater loyalty to soccer than any other pastime', may have been romanticising but there was some foundation to his sentiments.[13]

Research on England suggests that the majority of soccer spectators were males between their late teens and fifties.[14] Younger boys did attend games, on their own or with their fathers, and were a regular sight at the front of the popular banks where they could safely secure a view.[15] Yet, although football was a staple of schoolyard conversation, many interested boys did not regularly watch professional matches because they were either playing themselves or could not afford the admission fee. Ron Burgess, brought up in Cwm and a post-war Welsh international, wrote that when, in 1934 aged seventeen, he was asked to go for a trial at Tottenham Hotspur, he had never seen a professional match because he had always been too busy playing the game.[16] At the other end of the age spectrum was a

[10] *SWE*, 2 January 1923, 12 February 1924.
[11] *SWE*, 14 January 1927. As spring 1930 approached, Merthyr Town hoped that the increasingly lighter evenings would ease its financial problems, since the bulk of its supporters were miners unable to get away for early kick-offs. *SWE*, 14 January 1930.
[12] SWMFA minutes, 28 June 1934; *WM*, 29 August 1934; FAW minutes, 29 December 1937.
[13] *SWE*, 23 July 1936.
[14] Fishwick, *English Football*, p. 56; Mason, *Association Football*, p. 158.
[15] To attain such positions, boys either had to arrive early or be passed down over the heads of the crowd. A series of complaints to the press led to Cardiff City creating a boys' enclosure. *SWE*, 30 August, 1, 3 September 1921.
[16] Burgess, *Football*, p. 17. At a match between Wales and Scotland at Ninian Park in 1933, many boys were stranded outside, unable to afford entry, after they discovered that the admission price was 6*d*., not the advertised 4*d*. *SWE*, 7 October 1933.

sprinkling of elderly supporters who did not mind standing for two hours. Newport County could boast an eighty-six-year-old supporter who never missed a match, while a man in his nineties was a regular on Cardiff City's 'bob bank'.[17] Such individuals were uncommon enough to be the subject of press attention but are evidence that soccer attracted fans of all ages.

For many married working-class women, the burden of motherhood and running a household denied them the opportunity to watch soccer or, indeed, regularly take part in many other leisure pursuits. Compared with the comforts of the increasingly popular cinema, soccer, with its standing in uncomfortable conditions for long periods, probably held little appeal for many working-class women anyway.[18] Increased press references to female supporters suggest that the number of women attending matches in England and Wales did rise after the First World War.[19] Although, in the mining districts, women were very much under-represented,[20] in the more socially diverse coastal towns, young single women in employment, girlfriends and middle-class wives did attend games. Cardiff City could even boast a seventy-five-year-old female fan who rarely missed a home match.[21] The greatest number of women were to be found in the comfort of the stands, but females also stood on the popular banks, often unaccompanied, although not always happily given the overcrowding.[22] The potential crush did discourage some interested women from attending, be it on their own or with their partners. One correspondent argued that many men would like to take their wives, but as this would mean

[17] *SWE*, 26 July 1932, 7 November 1936, 29 August 1938.
[18] For the popularity of the cinema with working-class women, see Deirdre Beddoe, *Back To Home and Duty: Women between the Wars, 1918–1939* (London, 1989), pp. 115–17.
[19] Several south Wales letter writers noted the trend. For example, *SWE*, 29 August, 3 September 1922. See Eric Dunning, Patrick Murphy and John Williams, *The Roots of Football Hooliganism: An Historical and Sociological Study* (London, 1988), pp. 99–101, for a similar argument for England, although, as Russell points out, there is little hard evidence for an increased number of women at inter-war matches. Russell, *Football and the English*, p. 99.
[20] Nonetheless, Ebbw Vale AFC did have a ladies' supporters' club, and women were also very active in the Merthyr Town supporters' club. *ME*, 11 August 1925; Charles Jones, interview. See Chris Williams, *Capitalism, Community and Conflict: The South Wales Coalfield, 1898–1947* (Cardiff, 1998), pp. 62–9, for the life of women in the coalfield.
[21] *SWE*, 19 January 1939.
[22] See, for example, *SWE*, 1 September 1921, 12, 18 January 1923.

using the expensive stands, they went on their own instead.[23] Cardiff City, in an effort to help female spectators (and increase revenue), decided in 1923 to allow women to stand in the boys' enclosure if they so wished.[24]

In 1938, a Cardiff City match programme told its male readers that they were not

> the one and only critic of our national game. The Ladies, who attend in large numbers, are well-versed in the finer points of soccer and we raise our hats in sincere acknowledgement at their fervour. Ladies present, we must stick to Parliamentary language in watching the game. Afterwards we feel all the better for the curb.[25]

While some females, on their own admission, did not understand the game, there were others who were impassioned enough to write letters to the press on team selection and were as keen fans as any man.[26] There is some evidence from England that individual male fans resented female interest in soccer.[27] In south Wales, there is nothing to suggest that such feelings were particularly common. A male supporter thought 'all concerned like to see the ladies present', while one woman, who watched games on the Ninian Park popular bank, said that her sex were always shown the 'greatest courtesy' by male spectators.[28]

The number of women at matches probably owed something to the spread of the wireless and the football pools. Encouraged by the dream of a big win, one in five pools coupons were filled in by women.[29] While this did not necessarily mean that they were actively interested in the game, it must have stimulated their awareness of it, especially since choosing random numbers was not the best route to winning. Middle-class women, who often spent long hours listening to the radio, could have had their

---

[23] *SWE*, 1, 3 September 1921.
[24] One female supporter argued that women should be allowed in the back of the boys' enclosure so that their hats would no longer obscure men's views! *SWE*, 12 January 1923.
[25] Cardiff City, *Official Programme and Journal*, 31 December 1938.
[26] For example, *SWE*, 24 February 1922, 7 September 1933, 8 December 1934.
[27] Fishwick, *English Football*, p. 58.
[28] One letter to the local press, however, did suggest that ex-soldiers should not give up their seats at matches to sports-loving women. *SWE*, 29 August 1922, 18 January 1923, 24 November 1920.
[29] Clapson, *Bit of a Flutter*, p. 174.

interest in the sport developed by hearing soccer discussions, or even commentaries of games, just as their interest in other topics was stimulated by the wireless.[30] One inter-war Merthyr Town fan's interest in the game began with her attending matches because they were one of the few opportunities she had of being with her boyfriend. Similarly, a female Lovell's Athletic fan started going to matches to avoid being separated from her husband.[31] Thus, soccer may have been a predominantly male activity but women were getting more involved, especially in the years before marriage, just as they were in many traditionally male facets of life. Indeed, had the practical constraints that dogged the lives of many women been removed, it is reasonable to suggest that they would have been there in even greater numbers. This recognition of the role of soccer in the lives of at least some women is an indication of the need to question conventional assumptions and narratives about gender roles. Working-class women's lives were not simply the stuff of motherhood, home and burden, and their involvement in soccer marked the game's incorporation into mainstream popular culture.

From time to time, reporters would remark on the cosmo-politan character of soccer crowds.[32] At a time of rising class tensions, the press dwelt upon any evidence of social cohesion and was eager to point out that both the middle classes and workers watched soccer. The existence of stands charging a 3s. entrance fee suggests that affluent people must have attended in reasonable numbers, even if they were always a small minority compared with the thousands standing on the popular banks. In 1920, Ninian Park had a capacity of around 50,000, but only 3,000 covered seats. In 1938–9, 5 per cent of Cardiff City's average crowd were season ticket holders.[33] Given that season tickets usually cost men £1 to £3 in the inter-war years, soccer was clearly not the preserve of the working class alone. Grandstand tickets for the 1922 cup-tie between Cardiff City

[30] See Beddoe, *Back to Home and Duty*, pp. 129–31, for an examination of the impact of the wireless on women's interests, as well as their involvement in the pools, and Fishwick, *English Football*, ch. 5; Russell, *Football and the English*, pp. 106–7, for a discussion of soccer and the radio.

[31] Pincombe, 'Out of Rexville', p. 223.

[32] For example, *FE*, 17 January 1925.

[33] Calculated from information in Tabner, *Through the Turnstiles*, pp. 93, 149.

and Tottenham cost as much as 10*s*. 6*d*., while the demand for Swansea Town's FA Cup match against Arsenal in 1926 was so great that the club could charge 10*s*. to sit in the gangways of the stands.[34] Of course, not all the people purchasing expensive tickets for an occasional big match were necessarily wealthy. Less well-off fans were willing to pay more than normal to ensure that they did not miss out, but the cost of the most expensive tickets was beyond the reach of all but a minority. The increasing volume of motor traffic at matches was a mark of the new consumerism of the 1930s and further evidence of the existence of a financially comfortable group of supporters. There were enough cars parked on the roads outside Ninian Park at a 1933 international to cause a traffic jam, scenes of general chaos and a public rift between the Cardiff police and FAW.[35] As early as 1921, there was enough traffic at big matches for it to be profitable for individuals and companies to run private car parks, and the Cardiff Corporation was running a car park on all match days by 1937. The existence of relatively affluent fans ensured soccer's place in the entrepreneurial leisure industry.

THE SPECTATORIAL EXPERIENCE

Historians have made much of the excitement and escapism that supporters contributed to and enjoyed.[36] But the match-day experience varied significantly according to one's vantage point in the ground and the size of the crowd. Securing a view on the packed banks was not always easy, and many had to content themselves with an occasional glimpse of play caught through a sea of heads and hats. Even the war-disabled at the front could not be guaranteed a view thanks to the policemen standing in front of them. The sheer numbers standing on the popular banks could cause a pronounced crush, sometimes even breaking the barriers at the front. Swansea's Vetch Field, in particular, was too small for the club's biggest matches, and the crowds that spilled off its North Bank had to be allowed to sit on the

[34] *SWE*, 23 February 1922, 5 March 1926.
[35] *SWE*, 5, 6, 11, 17 October 1933. The FAW blamed police mismanagement and found itself with a very heavy bill for policing an international the following year.
[36] See Fishwick, *English Football*, pp. 59–61.

touchline to watch such games. Clubs were not aware exactly of what their ground capacities were, and the decision when to close the gates was often a haphazard guess. Even when the gates were shut it was not uncommon for people to break or sneak into a ground. Once the game had begun, a goal or near-miss would produce surges forward, thus increasing the crush. The observation, 'The net result of that goal was that my collar was torn from my neck, and my parting was entirely ruined', was amongst the least serious of the potential dangers. Even the swaying of a singing crowd could result in hazardous situations.[37] The following letter summed up the experience of many in such conditions:

> To me it appeared the world had congregated to see this match. I am not very tall, about five foot two, and in the crowd that was in the ground, I can assure you, the view of hats and heads was simply wonderful. The feeling of having my ribs staved was not so wonderful . . . There were about 10,000 too many people in the ground on Saturday and it is a wonder that there were not a lot more causalities than there were. We are human beings not sardines and I hope that in future the directors will bear this in mind. VERY MUCH CRUSHED.[38]

At big matches, ambulance men were kept busy as men, women and children fainted in the crush.[39] In 1911, at the end of a match at Ton Pentre, iron fencing gave way in the general rush to leave the ground. A number of men fell into the river below and sustained head injuries.[40] It was by luck rather than judgement that serious accidents were not commonplace at big matches. In 1932 the chief constable of Cardiff police stated that Ninian Park was not safe for more than 25,000 spectators. Yet it had, in the past, held twice that number. Safety at the ground was such a concern that one local MP brought it up in

---

[37] *SWE*, 29 January 1924. See *Sporting News*, 31 January 1925, for the dangerous effect of a crowd swaying whilst singing.
[38] *SWE*, 28 February 1923.
[39] For a typical example of the problems of a large crowd, see the report on Swansea Town v. Arsenal in the 1926 FA Cup sixth round in *Sporting News*, 6 March 1926.
[40] *SWDN*, 13 March 1911.

Parliament.[41] Some of the problems could have been avoided since there were often empty spaces at the ends of banks while people were being crushed in the middle. Although the police and stewards would try to distribute the crowd evenly, it was not an easy task, with people often putting a good view before personal safety. Flag poles, advertising hoardings, roofs of stands and houses were all scaled at times (occasionally with injurious consequences) by people trying to see the game or avoid the crush.[42] Even those who sat in the stands sometimes suffered from the inadequacy of crowd management. In the chaos of a 50,000 crowd at a 1938 international at Ninian Park, hundreds of people with stand tickets found themselves unable to gain entry to the ground since their places had already been taken.[43]

The popular banks were simply open mounds of earth and ash. Thus, watching a match in the rain meant getting a drenching and standing in mud. The situation was especially bad at Ninian Park, where the popular bank was an ash-covered rubbish tip. Rain sometimes washed away the covering, leaving spectators standing on a pile of refuse. Even grandstands were not fully protected from the elements. Leaking roofs and open sides exposed to the wind meant that sitting could be an equally unpleasant experience at some grounds.[44] Thus, it was no wonder that rain could easily ruin a gate. In 1937, an anticipated 30,000 crowd for an important league game at Ninian Park was halved by heavy rain. On a rainy Saturday afternoon in 1931, a crowd of just 2,000 saw struggling Cardiff City play Queen's Park Rangers. It was reported that there was not a single person standing on the 'bob bank'.[45]

The poor condition of many grounds meant that, even with fine weather or a small crowd, attending a match could be

---

[41] *SWA*, 15 February 1932. Consequently, the Home Office wrote to the FAW on the matter. The association simply said that it would try to ensure that the ground authorities took the suggestions into consideration. Despite periodic police concern, the attitude of clubs, football authorities and the government towards safety at football matches was essentially complacent across the UK. See Martin Johnes, ' "Heads in the sand": football, politics and crowd disasters', paper given at BSSH annual conference, University of Liverpool, 2000. Cardiff City actually used the danger of excessive crowds as an excuse to raise the minimum price of entry to a 1922 cup-tie. The club said it hoped to reduce the size of the crowd, and thus the danger, by raising the prices. *SWE*, 22 February 1922.
[42] See, for example, *FE*, 2 February 1924, and *SWE*, 31 January 1925.
[43] *SWE*, 25 October 1938.
[44] *SWE*, 4 February 1925, 4, 7 February 1928.
[45] *FE*, 4 December 1937, 14 November 1931.

frustrating. In the mid-1930s, Newport County's Somerton Park had big dips in its popular bank which made it very difficult for people to see properly.[46] At Ninian Park, 'bob-bankers' complained of having to stand on 'coke, ashes, corned beef cans, buckets and any old thing'. There were also 'huge lumps of slag' on the bank and an 'evil smell' from the refuse below. To add to the discomfort, the crowds could throw up clouds of dust. After attending an international at the ground, one collier claimed that the conditions had left him almost as dirty as when he came up from the pit. Improvements were gradually made but the bank was not terraced until 1938.[47] Toilet facilities were also limited, and even had they been more numerous, leaving a dense crowd in order to reach them would have been difficult. Many men did not bother and utilized rolled-up newspaper and the floor, which made standing at the bottom of the bank a particularly unpleasant experience. Such 'scenes of indecency' shocked one visitor enough to write to the press, calling for action from the directors or even the police. These habits must have reinforced the male predominance of the popular banks, and in 1913 more supervision was called for at Ninian Park in the interest of female spectators.[48] That people continually endured the poor condition of grounds says much about the attraction of soccer. Thousands arrived over an hour early in 'driving rain' for an important cup match at Ninian Park in 1920.[49] Some people evidently thought soccer was worth a soaking.

The hold that soccer could have over people was clearest on the days of important league or cup games. Such occasions became a holiday to be enjoyed by all, including those not normally interested in the game. In 1912, a derby between Aberdare and Merthyr Town was turned into a carnivalesque event with a large procession of Merthyr supporters, mostly miners on strike and many in fancy dress, making the journey to Aberdare on foot with a band at their head.[50] The match provided an excuse for some festivity during the hardships of the coal dispute. By the inter-war years, the demand for tickets for

[46] *SWE*, 13 August 1936.
[47] *SWE*, 1, 5 September 1920; *FE*, 24 October 1936.
[48] *SWE*, 23 October 1920; *SWDN*, 12 August 1913.
[49] *FE*, 10 January 1920.
[50] *SWDN*, 28–30 March 1912.

such matches could be enormous. Queues would form early in the morning, sometimes with people even sleeping outside a ground to ensure admittance.[51] Six hundred people turned up for a small whist drive in Cardiff in 1927 where the prize was three tickets for the cup final.[52] The crowds at such high-profile games were notably more cosmopolitan than usual. This was especially true at away matches in England, which had the added expense of travel. The *Western Mail* described the crowds that travelled from south Wales to the 1925 FA Cup final:

> It was a wonderful cosmopolitan train that started the first Welsh Cup final invasion of Wembley. There were professional men and ladies of leisure, shop girls, clerks, miners, artisans, seafarers and labourers, all equal and all happy on the common level of patriotism for the city and its association football team. Just the same equality of sport and of enthusiasm that carried Britain shoulder to shoulder through the nasty patches of the Great War.[53]

Again, the press was using soccer to stress the benefits of social unity. Prominent games attracted groups of people who would never attend an everyday league match. They were turning out more for a social affair and an excursion than a game of soccer. This was especially true of females of all classes whose numbers increased significantly at big matches. Men took their partners for a big day out, with even many miners bringing their 'hearts' best beloved'.[54] A London evening newspaper, noting the number of female Cardiff City supporters arriving for the 1927 cup final, exclaimed that 'The girls have come to town!'[55] Many of the women did not go to the match at all but rather took advantage of the opportunity to visit the city. The *Western Mail* estimated that possibly half the people that travelled to London for the 1927 cup final were more interested in seeing the capital's sights than the game. The press helped out by publishing guides of what to do in London. Music halls and theatres were all

---

[51] For example, in 1921, despite the rain, little parties of people were reported to have slept outside Ninian Park and in nearby doorways the night before a big FA Cup match. *SWE*, 4 March 1921.

[52] W. M. Rogers, *Camp ar Gamp* (Pontypridd, 1969), p. 19.

[53] *WM*, 25 April 1925.

[54] *SWE*, 27 August 1921.

[55] Quoted in *WM*, 27 April 1925.

booked up well in advance of the final as people took in all the opportunities of the trip.[56] From the beginning of the train journey there to the stories told afterwards, the whole occasion was a memorable experience of which the game was only a part.

The expense of such a fun-laden trip was obvious, and people would economize where possible, with some even sleeping rough in parks. Such was the attraction of a FA Cup final, that even when a Welsh team was not involved, groups from south Wales would save through the year and travel to the game in the same way as they made annual excursions to the seaside. As early as 1913, the GWR was running a special train from the region to London for the match.[57] It was not just games outside Wales that offered an opportunity for a big day out. Women from the Valleys also sometimes travelled with their partners to games in the coastal towns and went shopping while their men were at the match.[58] Soccer could also offer the opportunity to escape from the whole industrial and urban environment. Miners travelling by charabanc to Cardiff City's 1927 FA Cup semi-final in Wolverhampton stopped off in the Malvern hills to take in the fresh air.[59]

Even run-of-the-mill games could have a holiday quality to them. As with the seaside excursion, alcohol was closely associated with the match-day experience and it was not uncommon to see men drunk at matches.[60] On big match-days, local public houses would apply for an extension to licensing hours so that people could go straight there after the game.[61] In 1925, the day after a prominent match in Swansea, a magistrate expressed some surprise that he had no cases of drunkenness over which to preside.[62] The fact that many people drank at and after matches was another arrow, alongside professionalism and barracking, for

---

[56] *SWE*, 21, 25 April 1925; *WM*, 25 April 1927. Such days out in London were also a feature of northern clubs' appearances in FA Cup finals. See Jeff Hill, 'Rite of spring: cup finals and community in the north of England', in Hill and Williams (eds.), *Sport and Identity*.

[57] *SWDN*, 14 April 1913.

[58] See, for example, *SWE*, 8 October 1934.

[59] *WM*, 28 March 1927.

[60] Boys would collect and sell the empty beer bottles left at the end of matches at Ninian Park. See *SWE*, 29 January 1924. For the seaside, see John K. Walton, *The British Seaside: Holidays and Resorts in the Twentieth Century* (Manchester, 2000).

[61] Such applications were often granted in order to relieve the potential congestion in the city centre. For example, see *SWE*, 10 March 1920.

[62] *SWE*, 4 May 1925.

the bow of the game's opponents, as is apparent from the following letter to the *South Wales Echo*:

> We are drawing very close to the football season, when old and young get
> infected with a disease known as football fever. We shall see crowds from
> all directions making their way to Ninian Park to hoot and brawl like a lot
> of wild savages. As a sport football is very fine, but to think of the
> thousands that go simply to watch 22 men kick a ball about makes one
> wonder how these football enthusiasts get any sense of responsibility. What
> is our future generation going to be like? Not only is football the danger. As
> soon as a match is finished a great number of football supporters make
> headway for a public house to disgrace themselves and the country they
> live in. I trust the day will come when professional football and public
> houses will be a thing of the past. PRO BONO PUBLICO, Cardiff.[63]

People could turn a game into a whole day and night's entertainment. This was especially true for supporters from the Valleys,
for whom a match provided an excuse for a night on the town.
Such drink-fuelled nights led to fights and business for prosti-
tutes. *Gwalia Deserta*, Idris Davies's 1938 poem, refers to supporters visiting Tiger Bay, Cardiff's notorious docks, for 'ale and
chops and tarts' after matches at Ninian Park. This meant
trouble for the local black population: 'they didn't like the
coloureds . . . It was very nasty, used to have big fights sometimes. Every time there'd be a football match or anything – when
they'd come down on a holiday there's sure to be a row before
they go back.'[64] Indulgent nights were not dependent on soccer
but they did help mould the game into working-class culture by
providing the excuse for groups of men to travel to town and
enjoy themselves in its anonymity.

For many supporters, soccer's attraction ran deeper than a fun
day out, and the sport was an integral and routine part of their
lives. Such people would go to games with the same group of
friends and stand on the same part of the bank. These were the
supporters who made up a club's core following, who would turn
up no matter what the conditions or recent results. In times of
austerity, they were the loyal but bitter few: 'Barren banks and

---

[63] *SWE*, 20 August 1925.
[64] Harriet Vincent, interview quoted in Thompson, *The Edwardians*, p. 100. For some
Merthyr supporters, a match in Aberdare was even an opportunity for some shoplifting.
Charles Jones, interview.

empty stands told their own story, whilst the faithful few who did attend seemed so resigned to defeat that they were as cold in their vocal support as the weather.'[65] This was not a pheno-menon unique to soccer or even to sport. A 1937 survey of young people in south Wales reported that many devotees of the cinema went even when they knew the film was of poor quality. Attendance had become a matter of routine.[66] Just as some people would knowingly go and see a bad film, others would go to a match expecting a poor game. Routine and stability were important factors in people's lives, particularly during the uncertainty of the depression. For those in work, soccer could be an extension of the routines and camaraderie of the workplace; for the unemployed it could be an attempt to recapture some form of structure in their lives.

Yet the hold of soccer on such people's lives was stronger than routine visits to the cinema. They followed the game with a ferocious interest and devotion, even if they did not regularly attend matches. If the first team was playing away, people would congregate outside newspaper offices or attend reserve matches to find out the score before that evening's newspapers ap-peared.[67] Supporters were keen for every scrap of information they could acquire about their teams. They developed an en-cyclopaedic knowledge about the game, which many used in elaborate betting systems. 'Citizen' of the *South Wales Echo* claimed that he was plagued with inquiries after he announced anonymous potential signings. Supporters had their own strong opinions on their team, and letters about team selection were a common feature of all the popular newspapers. Some letters received, but not published, by the press were so caustic that they were felt to be libellous. Letter-writing fans' recipes for success for Cardiff City included converting the team to vegetarianism and exorcizing its bad luck through voodooism. One supporter went as far as contacting a player himself and asking him to sign for the club.[68] Then, as now, every supporter knew best and was not afraid of voicing his opinion.

[65] Newport County v. Charlton Athletic, attendance 2,401. *FE*, 12 January 1929.
[66] Lush, *Young Adult in South Wales*, pp. 80–1. Neither was the cinema always a passive escape, with audiences cheering and jeering the heroes and villains. *All our Lives* (BBC Wales, 1994–6), episode 17.
[67] *SWE*, 10 March 1923.
[68] *SWE*, 8 December 1932, April 1938, 20 August 1921.

SUPPORTERS, CULTURE AND IDENTITY

Fishwick explains this football obsession by means of the existence of a soccer subculture in which people grew up and lived. Working-class males would be surrounded by soccer throughout their lives, making at least an awareness of the game inevitable. Soccer could certainly dominate the talk of the workplace and pub; not to have an opinion on the local team was to be an outsider.[69] The degree of devotion to the game and to any particular club obviously varied from the extremes discussed to a simple awareness of the local club's fortunes. For many fans, active support was determined by their club's fortunes and the time and money at their disposal. The dramatic decline in Cardiff City's attendances as the club slipped down the divisions in the late 1920s is clear evidence of the attraction of a winning team and quality opposition. As one City supporter put it, 'Pay envelopes are small for the majority of valleyites, and the money we spend in pleasure has to be distributed to bring the greatest possible benefit.' An appeal for bigger attendances from the directors of second-division Cardiff City in 1930 brought a barrage of letters claiming that the crowds would return when the soccer improved.[70] A strong promotion bid in the 1937–8 season gave third-division Cardiff City an average attendance of over 20,000, a figure higher than two first-division clubs. This was after six poor seasons where the average had languished around the 8,000 mark. Even the promise of improvement through the purchase of new players was said to sustain attendances.[71] Contemporary criticisms of crowds only being interested in winning teams may have been somewhat harsh (and were meant to be so), but there was an element of truth in them. The same players that spectators hailed as heroes a week earlier could become the subject of discontent after a poor result.[72] However, even when their club was doing badly and supporters had stopped attending matches, their interest remained strong. The sporting press was still bought and results continued to be studied

[69] Fishwick, *English Football*, p. 55; Richard Hoggart, *The Uses of Literacy* (Harmondsworth, 1957), p. 108.
[70] *SWE*, 2 April 1938, 10 September 1930.
[71] *FE*, 22 October 1932.
[72] *ME*, 2 February 1924.

carefully. A hint of a revival and the crowds, finances permitting, returned to matches. A string of wins in 1932 saw Cardiff City's gates double in a month.[73]

The subculture that perpetuated this interest was not isolated. The growth of soccer in the region in the years before and after the First World War was too rapid to be explained simply by the kind of socialization that Fishwick suggests. Many of the thousands who started watching soccer had grown up in a sporting world of rugby. Soccer's rapid establishment was primarily down to the playing achievements of the clubs, the resultant extensive press coverage and rugby's stagnation. A population hungry for success and celebration, particularly after the horrors of war, did not need to have been brought up in a soccer culture to flock to its matches and revel in its achievements and victories. Once established, no doubt there was a process of socialization that ensured the game's popularity continued to grow, but even then soccer was not a distinct subculture. Along with rugby, it was part of a sporting culture, which, along with other leisure forms, work, family and religion, belonged to a wider, diverse and rich pattern of working-class cultures. As McKibbin argues of England, there was 'no common culture, rather a set of overlapping cultures'.[74] Both soccer and rugby did have their own committed supporters; individuals had their preferences and some were even violently loyal to their chosen code.[75] But most working-class sports-lovers appreciated both codes, and their respective subcultures had no distinct boundaries. The greater complexity of the world of cups and leagues meant that club soccer had a more prominent everyday role in the wider sporting culture than rugby did. With no competitions to offer celebration and success, club rugby could never attract the widespread devotion that was a part of club soccer. It was an appreciation of the common appeal of the two codes that was at the heart of the rugby fraternity's Edwardian concerns at the rise of soccer. The large number of Edwardian supporters who transferred their match-day allegiances to the dribbling codes confirmed the

[73] *FE*, 12 March 1932.
[74] McKibbin, *Classes and Cultures*, p. 527.
[75] An argument on a train between two colliers on the relative merits of soccer and rugby led to the rugby fan ramming the other's head through a window. *SWE*, 23 July 1923.

shared audience. In competitive working-class communities, people celebrated the achievements of all local successes, and soccer was just one component of the complex society in which people lived and worked.

Behaviour at soccer matches was shaped by the values of this wider society and culture. Swearing was commonplace on the popular banks, and there were also occasional unruly and sometimes violent scenes. Barracking, whether crude, unruly or not, was disapproved of by the game's authorities but was commonplace enough for reminders that 'referees are only human' to be regular features of match programmes.[76] Most incidents of actual disorder were little more than verbal exchanges or aggressive posturing by youths, and were simply sparked by disputed incidents during matches. When actual violence did occur it was limited to isolated assaults on referees, players or rival fans inside or outside grounds. Before the First World War, there were more serious incidents where referees and players found themselves followed home or on the end of a volley of stones and mud. But these were the infrequent actions of small groups of usually young men, or 'lewd fellows of the baser sort', as one reporter put it.[77] They were not a signal that grounds were under the 'dominance of the roughs'.[78] The intended consequence seems to have been more humiliation than harm. Like conflicts between street gangs, trouble was 'to a large extent ritualized and involved customary constraints that prevented serious injury'.[79] For the victims, the incidents may have been frightening, but it was certainly not their normal experience at a soccer match.

Working-class society was deeply competitive and slights that endangered the chance of winning were keenly felt. In such cases of injustice, be it a bad refereeing decision or a starvation wage, retaliation was justifiable within the wider cultural context. Eric Hobsbawm has argued that a belief in fairness and the readiness to fight for just treatment were central characteristics of the

[76] For example, Aberdare v. Bargoed match programme, 2 September 1920.

[77] *WM*, 15 October 1910.

[78] As is suggested in the work of Dunning et al. In particular, see their *Roots of Football Hooliganism*. Their methodology and conclusions have been much debated. For a discussion related to south Wales and a more in-depth view of football hooliganism in the region, see Martin Johnes, 'Hooligans and barrackers: soccer and crowd disorder in south Wales, c.1906–39', *Soccer and Society*, 1, 2 (2000), 19–35.

[79] Stephen Humphries, *Hooligans or Rebels? An Oral History of Working-Class Childhood and Youth, 1889–1939* (Oxford, 1981), p. 189.

British working class.[80] Furthermore, the working class believed in righting perceived wrongs in its own way, even if this meant breaking the law. Thus remonstrating, verbally or physically, with a poor referee drew upon the same set of values as attacks on blackleg labour during strikes. Behaviour at soccer matches was not only an escape from the constraints of everyday life but an extension of that life. In this context, it is unsurprising that disorder was also a feature of more 'respectable' working-class pastimes. In particular, judges at musical competitions could find themselves assaulted if spectators disagreed with their decisions. Just as in sport, such remonstration 'was rooted in popular notions of legitimacy'.[81]

The frequency of disorderly incidents in soccer in south Wales declined from the mid-1920s owing to a number of factors. The number of matches fell as the depression led to the closure of many clubs, more police were present at more developed grounds, and society in general appears to have witnessed a decline in disorderly behaviour. In the years before and after the First World War, crowd disorder was never seen as a significant problem, while actual violence related specifically to soccer rather than drink was rare. Incidents largely took place inside grounds or later that night in working-class pubs which were hidden from the public eye, thus helping them to avoid moral and physical condemnation and suppression. Given the politically laced public-order problems of industrial disputes in the region, soccer crowds seemed comfortingly well-behaved. In this context, even at its height, disorder in soccer did not seem a problem and was, thus, not treated particularly seriously by the press. Although there were the occasional uses of phrases such as 'hooligan' and 'disgusting scenes', reports of incidents were often hidden at the bottom of the match reports. Even the stoning and attempted dismounting of a policeman on horseback outside Ninian Park in 1923 was reported with the humorous title, 'Police share cup tie thrills'.[82] As Mason points out of Edwardian and Victorian disorderliness, incidents seem to have had no significance or

[80] Hobsbawm, *Worlds of Labour: Further Studies in the History of Labour* (London, 1984), p. 191.

[81] Indeed, parallels were sometimes drawn between the rowdiness of musical and football audiences. Williams, *Valleys of Song*, pp. 131, 173–8, quotation from p. 176.

[82] *SWE*, 26 February 1923.

impact outside the footballing context in which they took place.[83] Disorder was simply an extension of the general rowdiness elsewhere in society and never on the scale of the disorder in contemporary industrial disputes or indeed modern soccer violence. As Fishwick concluded of England, for all the passion of crowds, 'enthusiasm was not incompatible with restraint'.[84]

As well as being shaped by the values of south Wales's wider working-class society, soccer offered a sense of identity within that society. Supporting a club accorded people a sense of belonging which could be as much a part of a person's identity as his sense of community, class or nationality. For marginalized sections of society, such as ethnic minorities, following soccer could be a rare opportunity to feel part of the wider local community.[85] Supporters wore badges, rosettes, ribbons and scarves which proclaimed their allegiance to a club. They made placards which implored their team to 'play up!' Such overt displays of loyalty were far more prominent and important when supporters followed their teams to away matches. Here, they were not on their own territory and were eager to make themselves seen and heard. Of course, such antics were light-hearted, but underlying the behaviour was a declaration of a genuine sense of attachment to a club. Patrick Joyce argues that working people had a spectrum of collective identities, such as neighbourhood, workplace, class, religion, town, region and nation, that were often cross-cutting or contradictory. From this fusion of different loyalties they derived shared values.[86] As Huggins notes, sport was 'a major vehicle in producing the populist discourses in which these are identified'.[87] With clubs acting as potent representatives of towns and communities, supporting a team was one such collective identity for football fans. Yet, for the most loyal supporters, the identity was more complex than this. Their team's ground acted as a second home, within which they stood on the same spot on the popular banks every fortnight sur-

[83] Mason, *Association Football*, p. 167.
[84] Fishwick, *English Football*, p. 65.
[85] In 1936 the *Echo* published a cartoon depicting Arabic, Chinese and European members of the local community at an international match at Ninian Park under the title 'Long live sport'. *SWE*, 17 October 1936 (see Figure 2).
[86] Patrick Joyce, *Visions of the People: Industrial England and the Question of Class, 1848–1914* (Cambridge, 1991).
[87] Mike Huggins, 'Second-class citizens? English middle-class culture and sport, 1850–1910: a reconsideration', *International Journal of the History of Sport*, 17, 1 (2000), p. 18.

rounded by the same people.[88] Devoted supporters had an affinity that went beyond just the team and encompassed their part of the ground and the other people who stood there.

The sense of a collective identity amongst those on the popular banks is illustrated through the frequent use of pseudonyms such as 'bob banker' or 'bobbite' when writing to the press. Many such fans would continue to stand on the banks in bad weather, despite the fact that, at some grounds, they could watch the match under shelter for the same price. During the 1920s there was resentment over the money being spent on stands at Ninian Park while the popular banks were left in a critical state. This left some 'bob bankers' feeling they were being 'crowded like sheep' into an increasingly restricted part of the ground.[89] In 1923, the price of admission to a new stand at Ninian Park was a source of further discontent on the banks:

> We notice with some surprise that the 'poor' patrons of 'the City' who have hitherto been able to afford a three shilling seat in the concrete stand have been given relief in the shape of a reduction of eight pence in the price, whereas supporters who can only afford one shilling, and that sometimes at great personal sacrifice, have received no consideration in this direction.[90]

It was not just the 'bob bankers' who felt that clubs gave preferential treatment to other sections of supporters. Before some stand prices were cut, the cost of entry to the new stands built at Ninian Park in the 1920s brought complaints from those who preferred to sit, some of whom wryly noted that the bank prices were remaining the same.[91] The discontented could, of course, watch matches for only a shilling but their reluctance to do so indicates that there was a certain sense of detachment from those who stood on the popular banks. Supporters may have been united by their loyalty to their club but within their number there were different factions with their own identities.

The popular banks, being the cheapest part of grounds, were largely inhabited by the working class, while the more expensive stands were probably patronized by the middle classes. However,

---

[88] This is explored in John Bale, *Sport, Space and the City* (London, 1993), pp. 68–70.
[89] *SWE*, 26 August 1921.
[90] *SWE*, 23 August 1923.
[91] *SWE*, 24, 26 August 1921.

the divisions between supporters were not indicative of a decisive sense of class difference. At a 1920 match between Cardiff City and Swansea Town, there was a rush from the queue for the grandstand to the popular bank after news spread that there were no seats left.[92] Seeing this eagerly anticipated derby was more important than remaining separated from the 'bob bankers'. Further evidence of a common cause could be seen at reserve games where those sitting in the stands would often signal the score of the away first-team to the masses on the banks.[93] The banks and stands could not even be clearly delineated along class lines. Season tickets were available for the popular banks, which, at a cost of £1, must have been bought by people with greater financial resources than the average worker. The petty bourgeoisie were concerned with demonstrating their status in life, but they were often closer in their sporting tastes to the urban culture of the workers than to the more aloof and amateurist pursuits of the wealthy middle class.[94] Soccer did witness minor class tensions amongst its fans but they were also united by their support of their club.

'THE BIRD THAT LAYS THE GOLDEN EGG'

Devoted supporters often felt that the directors who ran their clubs did not share their commitment. Some saw directors as only there for their egos, while others thought them out of touch:

> The true position with the [Cardiff] City at the moment has nothing to do with the players but concerns the management, and I'm afraid that unless they consider a little more of the wishes of the supporters they will kill the bird that lays the golden egg. If the directors would mingle with the crowd, instead of being perched like tin gods in their reserved stands, they would find that what I say is true.[95]

[92] *SWE*, 7 February 1920.

[93] It was reported at the Vetch Field that the popular bank's cheers, when it heard the first team was winning, often confused the players on the pitch. *FE*, 18 September 1926.

[94] Geoffrey Crossick (ed.), *The Lower Middle Class in Britain* (London, 1977); Huggins, 'Second-class citizens?', pp. 15–6, 29. This is not to suggest that there were no fans amongst the more comfortable middle class. As ch. 5 argues, an appreciation of soccer was a major reason for directors' involvement in the game.

[95] Charles Jones, interview; supporter's letter in *SWE*, 3 December 1927.

Had the directors come down from the stands they would have been told that what supporters wanted was a winning team. For Cardiff City, the 1920s were largely a decade of progress and achievement, but a string of poor results would see letters in the press criticizing team selection. However, given the club's rapid climb to the first division, the board felt it was doing its primary job reasonably well and refused to enter into public discussion about whom it chose to play. With the bad runs being short-lived, the criticisms never gathered momentum, thus ensuring that the directors' silent approach was never subjected to intense public scrutiny.

On non-team matters, directorates could not be so aloof. Supporters, and in particular the 'bob bankers', saw themselves as the financial backbone of a club; it was their shillings that kept clubs alive. They thus felt that directors had certain obligations towards them which extended beyond supplying a winning team. In 1922 Cardiff City decided to double the price of admission to the popular bank for a match against Tottenham Hotspur. The *Echo* was 'overwhelmed' by letters of protest from supporters who felt let down and exploited.[96] Fans felt that to be asked for more money at a time of economic hardship was a betrayal by the club they financially and emotionally supported. Boards tried to answer such criticism and explain their decisions. They may have regarded team matters as an internal matter, but accusations of inflating prices could not be ignored. It was a subject that was obviously the business of supporters, and to treat it in any other way would have risked alienating them and even the wider community. Yet success remained the key to a harmonious relationship and, if the team was winning, then complaints about prices and the condition of the ground were soon forgotten.

When reasonable levels of success on the pitch were not forthcoming, supporters tended to hold the directors responsible. They, after all, picked the team and released money for signing players. Even as managers assumed more authority over team selection during the 1930s, directors still tended to be criticized for not providing enough money for players or for failing to hand over full control to soccer men.[97] When paid soccer men failed to

---

[96] In particular, see *SWE*, 23, 24 February 1922.
[97] See, for example, *FE*, 10 March 1934.

perform as expected, they too could expect jeers or even abuse from the banks. Many supporters felt entirely justified in criticizing any mistake, just as the spectators themselves, often skilled workers, would expect to be reprimanded if they let standards slip in their own jobs. As one correspondent put it,

> I have often been to Ninian Park but in the same spirit as I go to the Empire or theatre, namely, to be entertained by men who are paid to give me value for my money, and if the performance is poor I consider I am fully entitled to grouse.[98]

Yet if the players were simply not good enough, the fault lay with the men who employed them. They may have been criticized in the heat of the match, but to supporters they were ultimately ordinary men. In 1938 the Newport County players signed a letter of confidence in the club's board and management.[99] Their opinion was obviously thought to carry more weight than any excuse the directors could give. Similarly, the popular and well-respected Fred Stewart, a merchant by trade and Cardiff City secretary-manager during the 1920s, often spoke up for his directorate when it was under pressure. Managers were often ex-players, working men and, by the nature of their job, charismatic figures. In contrast, directors were something of a remote, middle-class and often anonymous clique. They thus represented a more detached and impersonal target than the men on the field or the manager.

The actual extent of success expected by supporters varied significantly. The followers of smaller clubs, such as Aberdare Athletic or Merthyr Town, never realistically expected their teams to achieve anything significant, and their rise to the Football League was, in many ways, success enough. Once there, mediocrity was anticipated and, amidst some complaints, tolerated. Similarly, throughout Newport County's 1938–9 third-division (south) championship season, many supporters were waiting for the bubble to burst and the team to fall from the top of the table.[100] The fortunes of local rivals had a significant impact on the expectations of supporters. While towns such as

[98] *SWE*, 10 October 1925.
[99] *SWE*, 30 November 1938.
[100] *SWA*, 15 April 1939.

Merthyr or Newport did not see themselves on a par with Cardiff, Swansea did, and thus its soccer supporters were not happy at being in the shadow of their neighbour's successes. The 1921–2 season was one of third-division mid-table obscurity for Swansea Town. Meanwhile, Cardiff City reached the FA Cup quarter-finals and finished fourth in the first division. A local newspaper called it Swansea Town's most disappointing year ever. At the club's AGM, frustration came to a head, and the board was forced to resign, restructure and then offer its members for re-election.[101] Had Cardiff City not done so well, the failures would have been more tolerable.

The wider economic climate also affected the level of expectancy amongst supporters. As the depression sank to new depths after 1929, there was a gritty realism in the attitude of the supporters in both Swansea and Cardiff. Attendances and playing standards plummeted, but supporters did not publicly blame the directors. Cardiff City's relegation from the first division saw criticism of the directorate but no more than the usual individuals' gripes over team selection. Not until the club began to struggle in the third division, just three to four years after the Wembley triumph, did the condemnation gather pace. It then quickly subsided when the extent of the club's debts was finally made public (see chapter 5). South Wales suffered quietly and with dignity in the depression, and placed most of the blame beyond its borders in both the sporting and the wider worlds. For Swansea Town supporters, this general feeling of pessimism continued through the 1930s, and they seem to have accepted the club's almost annual struggle against relegation from the second division. Apart from one isolated attempt to get another supporters' representative on the board, the authority of the directors was never challenged in the way it was in 1922. The club's stagnation must have been made more tolerable for supporters by the knowledge that the club was, at least, the highest-placed Welsh team in the Football League. At Aberdare and Merthyr, this pessimism entered supporters' views of their clubs earlier. For the clubs and their supporters, the optimism of elevation to the Football League was quickly replaced by a grim battle for economic survival. In 1924, when accusations of

---

[101] *Sporting News*, 1 July 1922; Farmer, *Swansea City*, pp. 48–9.

mismanagement erupted at Aberdare Athletic, the directors
successfully defended their position by pointing towards the
club's poor financial position and falling gate receipts.[102] The two
towns suffered during the depression to a far worse degree than
Cardiff or Swansea; the decline of their soccer clubs was merely
one element in the collapse of their societies. Given the scale of
the economic depression, supporters could hardly blame the
directors for failing to give them winning teams.[103]

The mid and late 1930s was a period of mediocrity, frustration
and disappointment for Cardiff City. The team continually failed
to live up to early-season promise and seemed doomed to a life
of inconsistency in the third division. Gradually, frustrated
supporters no longer saw the depression alone as the cause.[104] By
the late 1930s, with economic conditions improving in the
coastal towns and some prudent management by the directors,
the club achieved financial stability. In 1938, it could even
announce its biggest-ever profit. This, together with Newport
County's improved fortunes, led to renewed frustration at the
club's apparent reluctance to buy new players, despite obvious
weaknesses in the team.[105] Failure to turn strong starts into
promotion in two successive seasons resulted in talk of match
boycotts and open anger at the directors' prudence. The press
evoked memories and expectations by printing cartoons of the
ghosts of past achievements looking over Ninian Park and the
current side.[106] With glories so recent and a renewed financial
stability, supporters expected renewed success, and that put
public pressure on the board. Animosity towards the directors
was increased because of their long delays in letting H. H.
Merrett, one of Britain's leading coal and shipping magnates
who was offering to invest £14,000 in the club, join their
number.[107] The criticism voiced in supporters' letters did not fall

---

[102] See *AL*, 19 April–10 May 1924.

[103] In 1929, one reporter tried to place the blame for Merthyr Town's situation on the
team and the sale of players rather than the depression, but he was an isolated voice.
SWE, 11 April 1929.

[104] See, for example, *FE*, 10 February 1934.

[105] *FE*, 27 August 1938; *SWE*, 25 August, 19 October 1938.

[106] Fred Keenor, Cardiff City's captain in the late 1920s, was usually used by the press
as a personal and potent symbol of these former glories. See Johnes, 'Fred Keenor'.

[107] Merrett wanted control of the club in return for his money; hence the directors'
reluctance to cede power after all their hard work in keeping it afloat. Under Merrett's
chairmanship, the club returned to the first division in 1952.

on deaf ears, and the directors responded in the 1939 close season by signing ten new players, appointing a new manager and, as was the case at Newport County, giving him complete control over team affairs.

It is tempting to see the tensions between predominantly working-class supporters and middle-class directors in terms of class. The inter-war period saw a marked increase in working-class consciousness in south Wales as the economy deteriorated, the legacy of the war turned sour and the Labour Party replaced the Liberal consensus. A number of fans certainly saw class as an issue in their grievances over admission prices. After the price rises for the 1922 match against Tottenham, some letters of complaint from Ninian Park 'bob bankers' made it clear that they saw themselves as workers suffering in the economic downturn:

> If the City is to maintain the good feeling of its supporters, it would be wise to give all classes an opportunity to see the match, because, after all, the working man is the backbone and stay of the club. It is a pity that the directors should confuse and misconstrue sport for greed, and remember the story of the magical goose. If the directors cater only for the rich they will find that class deserting them in times of trouble. WORKING SPORT.[108]

However, such overt class-based antagonism was not representative, and most complainants merely felt that they were being treated harshly by a club of which they were an integral part. They argued that, in a time of unemployment and economic uncertainty, it was unfair to deny some loyal supporters the opportunity to attend matches. Class was not the direct cause of tensions but rather the underlying basis of economic inequalities from which the problems arose. It may have contributed to feelings of separation from directors, but this did not automatically make fans hostile to the boards, as the relative harmony in times of success illustrates. Class was largely an economic and contextual issue rather than a lens through which people viewed all aspects of their lives.

If fans were unhappy with internal affairs at their club, one option was to organize themselves into supporters' clubs. Yet

---

[108] *SWE*, 23 February 1922.

such organizations were primarily concerned with raising money for the parent club rather than representing fans' interests. In England, such fund-raising was usually neither appreciated nor fully rewarded by the professional clubs.[109] In south Wales, given the economic difficulties experienced by many clubs, supporters' fund-raising was so important that most enjoyed close relationships with directors. This was clearest at Newport County, where the supporters' club played such a vital role in raising funds that, by the 1930s, it was increasingly assuming an official role at the club. It took charge of the match programme and refreshments, set up a scheme to help supporters buy season tickets in instalments and hired out cushions to spectators in the stands. In 1933, it even proposed to set up and run an 'A' team for the club and, to encourage the purchase of players, offered to pay half the wages of any new signing for six weeks.[110] Yet, for all its work, the supporters' club did not challenge the directors' right to run Newport County or try to influence the composition of the team. It maintained that the players were the responsibility of the manager and directors, and criticized those who wrote to the press commenting on team selection.[111]

The supporters' clubs of most other teams were not so generous, and successfully demanded places on the board in return for their fund-raising. Such demands indicated how supporters saw themselves as stakeholders in a club who deserved recognition and a voice in return for their organized efforts. Because the funds that fans raised were so vital to clubs, directorates could not afford to refuse such requests in times of financial difficulty. In 1921 Caerphilly Town had only been able to have its suspension by the FAW lifted after its supporters' club paid off some of its debts.[112] Cardiff City, where there was never a strong and organized supporters' club, was the only

[109] Rogan Taylor, *Football and its Fans: Supporters and their Relations with the Game, 1885–1985* (Leicester, 1992).
[110] *SWE*, 16 August 1932, 8 November 1938, 14 June 1937, 14 February 1933; *FE*, 23 December 1933.
[111] *SWE*, 14 February 1933. In England, many supporters' clubs were run by respectable members of the middle class and acted as moral guardians of crowd behaviour as well as raising funds. Taylor, *Football and its Fans*. In south Wales, local dignitaries were certainly involved in supporters' clubs (a mayor of Newport was chairman of the Newport County supporters' club during the mid-1930s), but there is no evidence of any sustained programme of trying to influence crowd behaviour.
[112] *SWE*, 21 October 1921.

professional team in south Wales which did not at one time or another grant supporter representation on its board. At Mid Rhondda in 1925, a meeting of supporters expressed dissatisfaction with the club's administration and then elected a new management committee meaning that, for a short period, there were actually two groups claiming the right to run the club.[113] Other supporters' clubs assumed temporary control of their team during financial crises to assure that it did not go bankrupt, but financial realities meant that such takeovers were short-lived. Soccer was an unprofitable business and this meant that running a club was beyond the means of the typical working-class fan. Yet, if his team was winning and financially secure, then the question of ownership and representation never arose. For all the emotional ownership that supporters felt towards their teams, they were primarily interested in what happened on the field.

CONCLUSION

By the mid-1920s, watching professional soccer was a regular pastime of a huge number of working-class males across south Wales and the rest of Britain. During the 1937–8 season, attendances in the Football League totalled 31.5 million. Many more who stayed away because of money, time or other more pressing interests, still kept an eye on the results, bought an evening sports paper or even went to watch the team train. Clubs occupied central positions in the lives of committed supporters, acting as an overriding passion and an integral part of their identity. As Holt put it, supporters were as much members as customers of clubs.[114] Fans did not simply go elsewhere if the product was not to their liking. When all was not well on the pitch and the club had (or was believed to have) money, supporters felt let down, and directors incurred their wrath. They had expectations of varying levels of success and expected to be treated fairly in return for their shillings. Others were less obsessed and committed, their attendance at matches being governed by factors such as the weather, transport and, in

---

[113] *SWE*, 23 July 1925.
[114] Holt, *Sport and the British*, p. 165.

particular, the recent fortunes of their team. Nor was the game the preserve of the male worker alone. In the stands, and to a lesser extent on the banks, were a small number of women and middle-class men. At a glamorous game like a cup-tie, a more socially cosmopolitan crowd would join soccer's regular devotees. Such occasions had a holiday-like quality: a day of escape, fun and, frequently, drinking. Soccer 'brought sunshine and excitement into the black valleys of South Wales'.[115] The miners of those valleys were devoted enough to the game to attend matches straight from work, without bothering to wash first. The attraction of such merriments and the excitement of even routine matches ensured that soccer became a prominent part of local popular culture. Its gossip and happenings became staples of male conversation in the pub and workplace. Even those initially not interested would have had problems not becoming versed in the fortunes of the local teams and then may have even been tempted to savour them for themselves.

It was such evidence of social unity and stability that led soccer (and sport in general) to be seen as a social healer. Different classes were united by their support for a club while soccer crowds offered an example of the orderliness and good humour of the masses. The game was both criticized and celebrated for taking men's minds off the bigger struggles in life.[116] Yet soccer and society's wider conflicts existed alongside each other. The striking miners who flocked to matches in 1921 did not lose their determination in their battle for better wages. The struggles of the football field and life did not detract from each other in the minds of those involved. Class tensions and injustices were too prevalent in south Wales society to be nullified or forgotten because of a mere game. Soccer (like all sports) offered a relief from these wider conflicts, not an alternative to them or a site on which to continue the struggle.

Russell argues that it 'is inconceivable that something which drew the time, energy and money of so many people did not have ideological repercussions for some of them'. He maintains that football, as one of those things that working men did, helped

---

[115] Paul, *Red Dragon*, p. 12.
[116] The sporting attitudes of the left, which on the whole tended to ignore the sphere of leisure in its philosophy and rhetoric, are examined in Chris Waters, *British Socialists and the Politics of Popular Culture, 1884–1914* (Manchester, 1990).

to generate 'a consciousness of class rather than class consciousness'.[117] When tensions arose in soccer circles it was inevitable that questions of class would arise, but they were depoliticized and never a central issue.[118] The predominantly working-class 'bob banks' may sometimes have felt mistreated, just as they felt wronged by society and the government, but the issues were contextualized by those involved. Class was a complex product of numerable interacting and indistinct facets of people's lives. Sport was just one agent in the conscious ascription of people's sense of class, but others, like work and community, were more powerful. Soccer may have contributed to people's sense of being part of the working class but, ultimately, assertions like 'the football ground has been an important arena within which individuals can learn lessons about social and political roles and identities which are then carried "back" into other aspects of daily life' are speculation.[119] If such crossovers did take place then their form is lost to the historian, but they were probably limited to legitimizing and reinforcing existing values. A sense of class neither precluded a sense of other identities nor dictated all aspects of an individual's behaviour. Class consciousness sometimes influenced supporters' relations with directors, but it did not preclude a sense of a common cause with them or with middle-class fans. Class was just one identity amongst many that the working class possessed.

---

[117] Russell, *Football and the English*, pp. 114, 72.
[118] McKibbin makes a similar depoliticized case for other socio-cultural expressions of class difference. McKibbin, *Classes and Cultures*, p. 528.
[119] Russell, *Football and the English*, p. 237.

V

'PART AND PARCEL OF THE TOWN': PROFESSIONAL FOOTBALL AND CIVIC IDENTITIES

[S]upporters, who have a right to expect the directors to maintain the club at a high standard, are getting disgruntled. The retort to this from some of the officials who are responsible for the upkeep of the club is that they have no use for supporters who do not know how to accept defeat, and who are not satisfied with anything less than a winning side. They are perfectly justified in taking this attitude, but when they express opinions to the effect that because it is they whose money is at stake in running the club, the 'man in the street' has no right to criticise them upon their methods of team control, they err and they err badly. They must not lose sight of the fact that they have accepted a responsibility – the reward of which maybe no more than prominence in the football world – to build up and maintain a first-class club at Cardiff . . . but the reputation of Cardiff City belongs not to a small select body. The club has become something of a national institution . . . it would be a blow to the game in Wales if the distinction of having a first division club in the Principality was lost . . . It is Cardiff's duty to the Principality to guard the distinction . . .

South Wales Football Echo, 11 December 1926

Whatever the retorts of directors under pressure, soccer clubs were not regarded as private institutions. For individuals in the towns of south Wales, many of them communities that had exploded into being in the last quarter of the nineteenth century, sport offered a route to developing and clarifying a collective identity amidst the diversity and heterogeneity of urban life. As Holt points out, by 'supporting a club and assembling with thousands of others like himself a man could assert a kind of membership of the city, the heart of which was physically and emotionally his for the afternoon'.[1] When those clubs were successful they acted as an advertisement for their town, placing it on the national map and engendering a heightened sense of pride amongst those who lived there. Even when it failed to deliver victories, professional soccer occupied an important place

[1] Holt, 'Football and the urban way of life', p. 81.

in the civic culture and life of a town. Teams' nicknames are an apt illustration of how clubs were seen as representatives of a town. Clubs were often nicknamed after some special feature or industry of the town. Hence, Merthyr were the Romans, Aberaman the Tinplaters, Newport the Ironsides and Caerphilly Town the Jackdaws, after the birds in its famous castle. In a region dominated by mining, no club could claim a special tie to the coal industry and none had a nickname that referred to it. Hence, the Rhondda teams Treharris and Ton Pentre were nicknamed the All Whites and the Bull Dogs respectively. Mid Rhondda AFC's nickname, the Mushrooms, was derived from its near-overnight foundation and suggested an image of rapid growth that symbolized the Rhondda Valleys' whole history. It gave the team a unique identity that fitted in with the tradition of its surrounding community. Professional soccer clubs were 'part and parcel' of their towns.[2]

Clubs played on the idea that they served a civic function and represented the community in order to attract support and patronage. Yet professional soccer was also a business and, as such, required directors, shareholders and equity. The scale of the senior clubs may have varied dramatically, from the city clubs, with their large squads of professional players and thousands of supporters, to the small-town teams with players turning up after work to play for a few shillings before small crowds in rudimentary grounds, but each had to be solvent to survive. This chapter examines civic authorities' and supporters' ideas about civic identities and how they viewed clubs as community institutions. The tension between such ideals and the financial realities of the professional game is a recurring theme. It begins by exploring the club directors who, despite the financial and time commitments they made to the game, have been figures of some derision at the hands of both contemporaries and historians.[3]

[2] *FE*, 12 January 1935.
[3] Russell, *Football and the English*, p. 44; McKibbin, *Classes and Cultures*, p. 348.

THE CLUB DIRECTORS

The Edwardian age was one of enterprise in south Wales. Many industries were generating sizeable profits and the crowds that watched soccer suggested that handsome returns could be made there too. This inevitably drew entrepreneurs to the sport. Yet no existing or prospective club could afford to agree to demands such as those made in 1913 by an advocate of a second professional team in Cardiff. He wanted 15 per cent of the proposed club's gross gate in return for his investment.[4] Without non-profit-driven backing, the idea came to nothing. Despite their often large crowds, clubs had unstable incomes and high costs and overheads. Any profits were eaten by investment in the team and ground. FA rules forbade directors from holding any sort of salaried position at their clubs, while dividends were limited and rarely paid anyway. What teams needed were patrons willing to put their hands in their pockets, and not ones who sought pecuniary gain. Over the summer months, when clubs had no income, directors at clubs of all sizes were frequently left personally to guarantee or pay the bills. In 1926, members of the Mid Rhondda AFC directorate found themselves harassed by court summons and in danger of losing their homes over the club's debts. A local colliery manager and a former mining chief chemist were actually declared bankrupt because of financial guarantees they had signed on behalf of the club while serving as directors there. Swansea Town director, Benjamin Watts Jones, saw his tailoring business fold amidst rumours that he had neglected it because of commitment to his club.[5]

In 1932, two working-class Newport County directors, who had pawned their houses to help the club, resigned saying, 'we have learnt from experience that directing a professional club is not a workman's pastime.'[6] The club only had working-class directors because, from 1921 until 1932, it leased its ground from a local iron manufacturer's workmen's committee, which demanded that it have a majority on the board. Smaller teams in the industrial Valleys also had occasional working-class directors. When Mid Rhondda AFC was formed in 1912, its board

[4] *SWDN*, 3 April 1913.
[5] *SWE*, 8 April 1926, 22 August 1925, 16 October 1928; Farmer, *Swansea City*, p. 48.
[6] *SWA*, 17 February 1932.

consisted of three licensed victuallers, a schoolmaster, an accountant, an ironfounder and a colliery weighman, a reflection of the cross-section of small tradesmen and workers' representatives who provided the coalfield's civic leadership.[7] But in south Wales and England, the typical soccer club director was a professional man or the owner of a small local business.[8] These were men of the same status as those who dominated the Liberal associations, chapels and other traditional institutions of Edwardian community life in south Wales or, as McKibbin puts it, 'characteristic of the interwar provincial middle classes'.[9] During the inter-war years, as the Labour Party replaced the Liberals as the dominant force in the region's politics, the power of the local middle class subsided. Nonetheless, it continued to participate in the cultural life of south Wales and middle-class individuals remained integral figures in the region's professional soccer clubs.

Before the First World War, south Wales's rich élite had been reluctant to help clubs by providing them with land. But, as soccer gradually established itself as an important part of the local community, the élite began to provide symbolic assistance. In 1923, Swansea Town's largest shareholder was the MP, industrialist and baronet, Sir Alfred Mond.[10] Yet that was the limit of his involvement in the club. The earl of Plymouth, a large local landowner, became president of Cardiff City and invited the players to dinner at his castle every pre-season. However, he was not a shareholder in the club and, in 1921, refused to become a guarantor on a new lease for Ninian Park.[11] Coalowners rarely lived in the areas they dominated economically and their involvement in community projects tended to be limited to charitable donations and public appearances.[12] The coal magnate D. A. Thomas bought shares in Cardiff City, Mid Rhondda AFC and Merthyr Town but was not actively involved in any of the clubs. Like his industrial interests, his patronage of soccer was spread across the region.

[7] PRO, BT31/20937/124400.
[8] See appendix B; Fishwick, *English Football*, p. 29; Mason, *Association Football*, ch. 2; Vamplew, *Pay Up*, ch. 10.
[9] McKibbin, *Classes and Cultures*, p. 348.
[10] Swansea Town Annual Return, 1923.
[11] *SWDN*, 12 August 1913; Cardiff Corporation, Parks etc. Committee minutes, 19 April 1921.
[12] E. D. Lewis, *The Rhondda Valleys* (Cardiff, 1963 edn), p. 218.

There was no monolithic élite class, and some owners of smaller companies, with strong links with particular towns, did have a closer involvement with the local soccer club. W. R. Lysaght owned a Newport ironworks and, after the First World War, became the main financial backer and president of Newport County. It was he who gave the club's ground to a committee from his ironworks. Without his financial support through the inter-war years, Newport County could not have survived. He made substantial donations, paid for new stands and kept the club afloat. Yet he too had no daily role in its running, and at no time did he try to influence the club directorate's decision-making. He was a paternal but democratic benefactor, interested in the welfare and entertainment of his workers but without wishing to control them. William Llewelyn, a colliery owner, was instrumental in the setting up of Aberdare Athletic after the First World War. He supplied the initial capital, purchased the ground, helped to find players other work and sat on the board of directors. However, he too began to then take a more backseat role. By the end of the 1923–4 season, he and his family had put £16,000 into Aberdare Athletic, but he still gave away all his shares on condition that they were distributed among a number of people to avoid one person being able to dictate to the club.[13] Once Llewelyn was in the background, Aberdare Athletic fell into the more traditional hands of small local business and professional men whose sacrifices and commitments often ensured that smaller professional soccer clubs could exist at all.

SERVING THE TOWN

Despite their financial commitments to the game, directors were not 'wealthy men', as a player pointed out of Cardiff City.[14] For many, the motive for their sacrifices was a love of the sport and personal gratification. A 1923 who's who of Aberdare Athletic directors emphasized their involvement and interest in the game itself.[15] Telling the public that they had captained their school team was not just to prove to supporters that they knew about

[13] SWE, 7 May 1924; AL, 10 May 1924.
[14] Ernie Curtis, in Crooks, Cardiff City, p. 151.
[15] Aberdare Athletic supporters' club handbook, 1923–4, pp. 25–7.

soccer; it was also a statement of which the directors were probably genuinely proud. Not having had the talent to become a professional player, being a director was the next best thing. One Newport County board member claimed that some directors were just in it for the publicity and the best seat in the stand, while the press added the free half-time whisky to the list.[16] The Cardiff City directors, who railed off a large portion of the centre stand for the use of their personal entourage, were described by one of their players as 'a boozy lot'.[17] Yet, whatever the fun and prestige of sitting on a board, personal gratification alone was not enough to compensate for the time and finance that professional clubs could require. Sitting on a board might bring the odd contract or free advertising for one's business, but such indirect gains are unlikely to have been sufficient to draw men to the financial risks and costs of running a club.[18] Indeed, many directors shunned publicity, preferring to leave the public face of the club's administration to the manager, who could also take the criticism should things go wrong.[19] Cardiff City's expenditure of £4,000 on new players during the summer of 1936 was made possible through the help of one director who insisted on remaining anonymous.[20] Whether or not the 'brutal and unwarrantable attack . . . by half-a-dozen roughs' on a Cardiff City director in 1921 had anything to do with his footballing duties is unclear, but it, like noisy demonstrations outside club offices, was an indication that the position was not just one of perks and status.[21]

---

[16] *South Wales Football Express*, 19 October 1929.

[17] Ernie Curtis, in Crooks, *Cardiff City*, p. 151; *SWE*, 9 September 1921.

[18] One Edwardian Cardiff City director won a contract for his building firm to construct a new stand for the club. Another director at the club owned a hotel and advertised it as 'the footballer's hotel'.

[19] This resulted in some public and acrimonious fallings-out between managers and directors at smaller clubs. In 1924, for example, the Aberdare Athletic manager Frank Bradshaw accused directors of leaving the daily running of the club to him while trying to exclude him from board meetings. The chairman hit back saying that it was surprising that town men like the directors were being attacked while Bradshaw, who had been in the area eight months, was given support. He claimed that Bradshaw was leaving because the club was not good enough for him and that his wife did not like the town. Ideals of civic loyalty were obviously thought to carry some weight with the public. *AL*, 26 April, 4, 10 May 1924.

[20] *SWE*, 30 June 1936.

[21] Cardiff City match programme quoted in Lloyd, *C'mon City*, p. 68. In 1934 a group of young men gathered around the Newport County directors' room at the end of a match to complain aggressively about team selection. *SWA*, 19 November 1934.

In 1925, when Evan Morris, a former Mid Rhondda AFC director and chief chemist with a local coal company, was asked by a judge why he had signed a guarantee on a stand over which he was being sued, he replied, 'I thought as things were so bad locally, and owing to the unrest, it would be wise to have an antidote such as sport and music to keep the people quiet.' The judge asked him if he meant against Bolshevism, to which he replied, 'Hardly that but I still think that if things got better people will support me.' Morris may not have thought there was a Communist threat, but he saw soccer as a way of reducing the social tensions that were building up in the deteriorating economic climate. He also claimed that he was not alone in his thinking.[22] Marxist interpretations of professional sport see it as a tool with which the ruling classes diverted the attention of the masses from their economic slavery. This is a simplistic interpretation that assumes a common and coherent purpose amongst sport's and society's governing class. The working classes were not mindless consumers of a mass culture, and there is no evidence to suggest that soccer actually contributed to their subordination.[23] Yet, as the case of Evan Morris illustrates, such thoughts, even if not explicitly articulated, were not unknown in the minds of directors. McKibbin points to the intensity of middle-class consciousness in inter-war England. Social tensions and antagonisms were prevalent despite the relative tranquillity of Britain in a contemporary European context.[24] In this light, Morris must have been aware that his statement would probably have won him some sympathy with the judge. This does not mean that he was not telling the truth but rather that social unity was unlikely to have been his primary motive for involvement in the club.

At the meeting to launch Aberdare Athletic, the colliery owner and club director, William Llewelyn, said that he thought it more essential to look after the welfare of people between fifteen and thirty than the welfare of children. This was the age group that made up much of his workforce. Providing them with 'healthy

---

[22] *SWE*, 22 August 1925.
[23] See Jones, *Workers at Play*, pp. 81–6. For a neo-Marxist interpretation of sport, see John Hargreaves, *Sport, Power and Culture: A Social and Historical Analysis of Popular Sports in Britain* (London, 1987 edn).
[24] McKibbin, *Classes and Cultures*, p. 529.

recreation' may have contributed to their well-being and con-
tentment, but this does not necessarily indicate dominant
political undertones; his motive was as much moralistic and
paternal. Llewelyn also saw the club as a way of helping to keep
men out of pubs and making the town 'a place worthy to live
in'.[25] Professional soccer may have had the supposed purpose of
distracting the attention of the masses from less morally uplifting
activities, or even from political thoughts, but there is no
evidence to suggest that this was ever anything more than a
marginal motive for the involvement of directors.[26] Nonetheless,
the reluctance of Lysaght at Newport County and eventually
Llewelyn at Aberdare, to become directly involved in their clubs
may have been political. With their position as major local
employers already exposing them to class-ridden hostility, it was
wise to avoid any possible further conflict that could arise out of
a close association with a failing team.

In 1913, the Swansea Town directorate declared in an appeal
for new shareholders, 'Our only desire is to provide Swansea
with a team worthy of a town of such importance.'[27] Professional
clubs were imbued with notions of civic identity. The English
leagues ensured that the club and town would gain recognition
on a wider stage while matches generated trade for local businesses. Directors of professional soccer clubs liked to see themselves as patrons and servants of their town and community. It
was no coincidence that many were also local councillors; such
individuals were at the forefront of civic life and felt it their duty
to be so. The occasional director may have resented the losses he
sustained in soccer,[28] but most felt a sense of duty to club and
community that meant they were willing to sustain the losses that
overly ambitious clubs made in the unstable south Wales inter-
war economy. That sense of duty was evident in the retiring
Llanelly AFC chairman who, in 1924, offered to cancel £3,500

[25] *AL*, 17 April 1920.
[26] For an examination of the invalidity of social control interpretations for other
activities of coalowners, see Williams, 'Capitalists and coalowners', pp. 124–5.
[27] *SWDP*, 17 April 1913.
[28] At Newport County in the late 1930s there was a prolonged argument between the
club and its former chairman over money invested by him. He ended up threatening to
sue the club to recover his money. *SWE*, 14–19 September 1936, 18 November,
16 December 1938.

owed to him on condition that the new directors could put the club on a sound financial footing.[29]

No matter how genuine the commitment of such men to their community, such rhetoric could not be divorced from soccer's commercial context. Appealing to a sense of civic duty was a useful ruse in trying to raise financial support:

> [T]he Directors wish to make it clear that the issue of shares about to be made is not one which is intended to appeal to the speculative investor; the only material object of the company is to promote Association Football in the District of Newport and this issue is intended and will only appeal to the sporting members of the public who desire that the Newport County AFC shall continue to exist as a Member of the English Football League, to Employers of labour in Newport and District who desire to support a form of entertainment which attracts a large number of their employees and to all engaged in trade who recognise that first class Association Football not only brings thousands of visitors to the Borough but that a successful 'Newport County' Team means a free and nation-wide advertisement for the Town.[30]

Some clubs tried to attract investment with more paternal sentiments. The Llanelly AFC prospectus appealed for the 'financial and general support of parents, employers and others who are interested in the physical welfare of the youths' of the district.[31] Clubs' shareholders were certainly not drawn by any avaricious motives, with most tending to be local supporters holding just a handful of token shares. At Mid Rhondda, nearly half the club's shareholders were working-class, but they owned just under a third of the shares.[32] In 1911, only four of Merthyr Town's ninety-nine shareholders lived outside the modern town. Of those, only a brewery company from Pontypool came from further than three miles away.[33] Certain types of companies valued the publicity and visitors that professional soccer brought to a town and were thus common investors in clubs. Newport

---

[29] *SWE*, 24 May 1924, 20 August 1927. A year earlier he had paid off the club's debts of around £6,000.
[30] Newport County AFC Ltd, *Share Issue Prospectus*, 1937.
[31] PRO, BT31/20801/123192.
[32] Calculated from information in PRO, BT31/20937/124400. Eight per cent of Swansea Town's and 12 per cent of Cardiff City's 1923 shareholders can be classified as working-class. Company registers, Companies House, Cardiff. See appendix B for method of occupational classification.
[33] PRO, BT31/20094/116486.

County had part of its overdraft guaranteed by different breweries, while a local newspaper and department store owned large stakes in Cardiff City. Yet one firm which gave Cardiff City the money to buy a player stayed anonymous, thus missing a seemingly good opportunity for some local publicity and gratitude.[34] Civic duty was not always about self-interest.

RUN AS A COMMUNITY BODY?

Directors may have argued that their clubs were communal and civic institutions, but did they actually run them as such? Clubs certainly tried to give something back to the community where they could. They often played benefit matches for popular causes such as mining disaster funds and local hospitals. In 1927, Cardiff City displayed the FA Cup at a local department store with everyone who came to see it encouraged to put a penny in a charity box. The club also ran a benevolent fund for the city's poor, to which both directors and players subscribed.[35] Charity collections were so common at matches that in 1922 the FAW decided that they were becoming a nuisance and detrimental to the game.[36] In 1921 Merthyr Town admitted the unemployed for free at half-time before the FA ordered it to cease the practice.[37] The FA did allow free entry during the last quarter of a game and it was not uncommon for Football League clubs to let the unemployed and children in for nothing towards the end of their matches. Mid Rhondda AFC even gave free admission to everyone in some of its unglamorous Western League matches which were not governed by price regulations.[38] Senior clubs also allowed their grounds to be used for junior cup finals and gave financial aid to schoolboy leagues. Such contact helped professional clubs to unearth local talent and encouraged local support, but it also, as Williams argues, suggested there was an 'organic relationship' between the town clubs and all those people who played for fun.[39] By helping junior sport and raising

[34] *SWE*, 10 January 1934.
[35] *SWE*, 5 May 1927; Crooks, *Cardiff City*, p. 151.
[36] FAW minutes, 27 December 1922.
[37] *SWE*, 11 October 1921.
[38] *FE*, 23 April 1921. A voluntary collection was held at the ground instead.
[39] Williams, 'One could have literally walked', p. 127.

money for local causes, clubs played an active role in the local community and ensured that they were seen as more than commercial organizations. Yet the 1921–2 season saw Cardiff City and Swansea Town refuse to play a benefit match for Glamorgan County Cricket Club because of the presence of a WFU official, who had publicly attacked professional soccer, on the cricket club's committee.[40] Community duty was not always above personal pettiness.

For all their appeals to civic duty, Football League directors were also happy to treat clubs as private businesses when it suited them. Chapter 4 argued that, although supporters' gripes about team selection were generally dismissed, complaints about entry prices were taken more seriously. The more practical suggestions of fans, such as Cardiff City's separate enclosure for boys where women were also allowed, were taken seriously. Directors felt obligated to supporters and the wider community to run the clubs in a competent manner.[41] The fund-raising and support of fans was appreciated and generally rewarded with places on the board, future promises or public statements of gratitude.[42] Yet, when all was going reasonably well on the pitch, directorates did feel they were fulfilling their primary community obligations. Crucially, since it was their money that sustained the clubs, they saw supporters as having no right or need to know or get involved in internal financial issues. Consequently, matters such as transfer fees and players' wages were largely kept confidential and the press did not try to pressurize directors into acting to the contrary.[43] This led to mistrust and misunderstandings. Attendances of tens of thousands made clubs sound wealthy without making the costs apparent. Some supporters even thought that directors received a share of the gates, while others thought them wealthy men who were doing little for the club. Other fans assumed that one big gate left a club with surplus cash which could be channelled into the purchase of new players.[44] Fans

---

[40] Andrew Hignell, *The History of Glamorgan County Cricket Club* (London, 1988), p. 73.

[41] Korr's work on West Ham United also concluded that the wishes and efforts of supporters were not ignored, with directors working with certain unspoken obligations to their club's followers. Korr, *West Ham*, chs. 2, 3.

[42] For example, see the statement by the club chairman in Newport County v. Derby County match programme, 1 May 1939.

[43] See, for example, the response to a reader's enquiry in *SWE*, 27 November 1937.

[44] See, for example, *SWE*, 19 January 1932; *FE*, 23 January 1932, 23 December 1933.

often accused directors of not spending enough on players, to which the retort was that the money was not there until gates rose. Cardiff City, Swansea Town and Newport County directors were all accused at different times of not wanting promotion, since a losing club in a higher division might make less money than a winning club in a lower division.[45] Such tensions did not change the reluctance to make internal financial details public. In 1933 the Newport County chairman said, 'If the supporters knew of all the difficulties the directors had to contend with they would not be so severe in their criticism.' He did not elaborate, and the financial situation remained confidential. Even with shareholdings and representatives on boards, the grievances of supporters of Football League clubs could fall on deaf ears. In 1922, another Newport County chairman told shareholders complaining about rises in the price of season tickets that they had no voice in the matter at all.[46]

Financial need, continuous problems on the pitch and pressure from the press could force a more open attitude. In 1928, with Cardiff City struggling near the foot of the first division, the *Echo* wrote: 'The directors have shouldered a responsibility and they must keep faith with the public whose loyal support all through has enabled them to maintain the club. It is not a private concern, neither should the running of the club be regarded as a hobby for the few.'[47] Yet it remained so, in effect, until the winter of 1931–2, when the club was in the third division and playing badly. Attendances had dropped to 4,000–5,000 and criticism of the directors for failing to buy new players began to intensify. In such a context, and given the club's civic importance, the board's previous secrecy was no longer acceptable. There were calls for more share capital to be made available and new blood to be introduced onto the board. The directors' pleas that the club was in serious danger of closing and that no one outside their circle understood the gravity of the situation did little to ease the pressure. As criticism mounted in the press, the board reluctantly abandoned its normally secretive attitude to finances. It held meetings with shareholders and revealed the full extent of the club's debts. Faced by the full

---

[45] Farmer, *Swansea City*, p. 53; *FE*, 22 January, 12 February 1938.
[46] *SWE*, 14 February 1933; *SWA*, 26 June 1922.
[47] *FE*, 7 April 1928.

financial facts, and with no one else willing to take on the debts, pressure on the directors and demands for their resignation subsided.[48] Such financial realities meant that, for all the claims that clubs were community institutions, they remained in the hands of a select few. With their club's best interests at heart, many individual directors were willing to resign should a more able benefactor appear. Following its relegation from the Football League in 1927, Aberdare Athletic invited nominations from shareholders for new directors to ensure that the club was more democratically run. None of the new nominations were willing to become involved.[49]

Financial pressures could also threaten the bond between a club and the local community. In 1926, the two Cynon valley clubs, Aberdare Athletic and Aberaman AFC, decided to merge. The idea was first put forward in 1922 by Welsh League Aberaman because of its financial difficulties, and finally went ahead four years later with Aberdare Athletic taking over the smaller club's debts. The Aberdare directors hoped to add 2,000 to home attendances, thus strengthening their own club's unstable finances. Three Aberdare directors resigned in protest, but both clubs' need for higher gates and financial stability was enough to transcend what had been a keen local rivalry before Aberdare's ascent to the Football League. Although the first team continued to use the title Aberdare Athletic, despite the new club bearing both towns' names, the merger was also a quick way for the smaller town to develop some kind of association with the prestigious Football League. The merger began to fail after the club lost its Football League place in 1927. Welsh League matches were switched to Aberdare, leaving Aberaman with infrequent reserve games in the Glamorgan League. To add to the insult, during the final season of the merger, the manager failed to visit the Aberaman ground once. No longer associated with first-class soccer, with the old debts cleared and just a few games being played on their ground, Aberaman supporters set up their own club again in 1928.[50]

[48] *FE*, 5 December 1931; *SWE*, 11–28 January, 4, 24 February 1932.
[49] *SWE*, 13 July 1927.
[50] Twydell, *Rejected FC*, vol. 1, pp. 23–5; *SWE*, 11 December 1922, 10 January 1924, 27 May 1926, 19 June 1928; *AL*, 30 June 1928. The clubs split in animosity, with Aberdare even attempting to block Aberaman's re-entry to the Welsh League first division.

Merthyr Town's financial difficulties led to the idea of moving the club to Pontypridd or somewhere in the Rhondda. In all probability, the club chairman had merely said that he was considering the idea to try to ensure greater support from the town itself, while the supportive letters in the press were from people outside Merthyr wanting to see first-class soccer nearer their home. Yet, in the same season, the club had unsuccessfully applied to the Football League to play its home matches at the opposition's ground, in the hope of bigger gates.[51] The quest for survival was enough to threaten the specific ties to the place where a club was based. Such changes of identity were naturally easier when the teams concerned were part of an identifiable wider geographical unit (as in the Aberdare and Aberaman case), but they nonetheless illustrate how clubs' perceptions of their relationships with communities were not rigid.

In search of success over the mountain

The financial realities of the professional game may have meant that the civic importance of clubs was often submerged beneath daily practicalities, but to what extent did concepts of civic pride in soccer mean anything to fans? Support for a team did not necessarily correlate directly with its geographical area. The large crowds that gathered at Ninian Park and the Vetch Field owed much to the number of workers who travelled down from the adjacent industrial valleys to watch soccer of a higher standard than was on offer at their home-town Southern and Welsh League clubs. Professional clubs from the Valleys and nearby towns consistently complained in the 1920s that the attraction of first-division football in Cardiff was reducing their gates. Rather than suggesting a lack of local pride, this illustrates how the coastal towns were the foci of large hinterlands. The primary industries of south Wales (in particular coal) were largely export-based and dependent on the ports of Cardiff, Swansea and Newport. The Valleys naturally looked on these urban areas

---

[51]   The idea of a new club, with the suggested name Valleys United, began with a letter to the *South Wales Echo* and was discussed by the Merthyr Town chairman in the press. There was also talk of the club switching to rugby league. *SWE*, 8, 11, 16 January 1930, 2 June 1930; *ME*, 18 January 1930.

as regional centres. Soccer boosted the towns' claims of being foci for their regions by adding a cultural dimension to the economic relationship. It gave the regional centres a relevance in people's lives that otherwise might remain inert and obscure. Newport County's original full title of Newport and Monmouthshire County AFC was an example of a club deliberately fostering such a regional image. What helped regional identities to supersede the civic identities of the Valleys towns was the fact that the Football League and FA Cup meant playing teams from beyond south Wales. There were no potential matches against travelling fans' own home-town clubs, and Cardiff City and others could assume the mantle of regional representatives.

Such representation did not necessarily infer a social unity between the two areas. The 'visitors from the hills' who descended on Cardiff for soccer matches and rugby internationals were the subject of some bemusement. In 1921 it was claimed that so many miners attended Cardiff City's big matches that such numbers from the Rhondda congregating in the city would have 'augured nothing short of revolution' had they not had soccer on their minds.[52] While they were not seen as socially threatening, the valleyites were subjected to patronizing comment and even – allegedly – deliberately poor café meals![53] In 1906, the Cardiff and District League, already containing teams from Barry, rejected applications from clubs in the Rhondda on the grounds that the travelling would cause unnecessary inconvenience and expense. The league chairman noted that people 'joined clubs with the object of playing the game on Saturday afternoons, and they did not feel inclined to go to the hills'.[54] Just as London cup finals exposed the differences between southerners and their northern visitors,[55] sport in the coastal towns of south Wales revealed the social divisions within the regional identities that they helped to develop.

Soccer was a commercial form of entertainment and a club that offered quality and success on the pitch could, contrary to the traditional picture of the immediate locality of fans, attract

---

[52] *SWE*, 27 August 1921.
[53] For example, see *SWE*, 27 August 1921, 3 February 1926. Also see Dai Smith, 'The Valleys: landscape and mindscape', in Morgan (ed.), *Glamorgan County History*, VI, p. 137.
[54] *SWDN*, 11 September 1906.
[55] Tony Mason, 'Football, sport of the north', in Hill and Williams (eds.), *Sport and Identity*, p. 47.

support from areas with which there was no interdependent economic relationship.[56] The crowds that travelled from Cardiff to Bristol to watch Football League matches at the start of the century demonstrate that people were willing to travel to watch high-class games if there was no senior club in their own town. Likewise, in 1912, young men were travelling from Bargoed to other Valleys towns such as Treharris so that they could watch Southern League soccer.[57] Even when a town had a Football League club, some locals would change their allegiance in search of success and entertainment. When Aberdare Athletic began to play well in 1921–2, nearby Merthyr Town's attendances fell as some supporters began to watch the more 'consistent team that was winning its matches over the mountain'.[58] By the 1927–8 season, the clubs' fortunes had been reversed, and there were even rumours that a prominent member of Aberdare Athletic's supporters' club was watching Merthyr Town instead of his own team.[59] The strong partisan loyalties that characterize modern British soccer had yet to emerge fully and, for some people, support was a relatively transient matter that could transcend local rivalries in search of a winning side. However, there were few fans who were prepared to watch regularly another town's club play badly. When Aberdare Athletic folded in 1928, its supporters did not transfer their allegiance to nearby suffering Merthyr Town in order to watch matches in the Football League again.[60] Watching one's home town languish at the foot of the third division was one thing; to watch your nearest neighbour do the same thing was quite another.

There was a body of supporters in south Wales that did not commit itself to any team but just liked to watch soccer of a high standard. One reporter thought that this group was large enough to warrant the arrangement of Cardiff City and Swansea Town home fixtures on alternate Saturdays.[61] Others would travel to a

---

[56] Mellor's study of north-west England has also shown how fans were drawn to higher-quality football outside their home towns. Gavin Mellor, 'The social and geographical make-up of football crowds in the north-west of England, 1946–1962: "super-clubs", local loyalty and regional identities', *Sports Historian*, 19, 2 (1999), 25–42.

[57] *ME*, 11 May 1912.

[58] *FE*, 1 April 1922. Aberdare's victory over Merthyr at the latter's ground was said to have begun the trend.

[59] Twydell, *Rejected FC*, vol. 1, p. 24.

[60] *FE*, 12 January 1929.

[61] *FE*, 16 November 1929.

different club to see a one-off important game or the visit of a
famous star player. However, many sports correspondents liked
to believe that at least some people were more interested in good
play and sportsmanship than in who won, and probably
exaggerated the number of neutral supporters. It was in the
industrial valleys, where towns' identities were weaker than in
the coastal towns, that support of clubs was most transient.
Because of their geography and rapidity of growth, such towns
often lacked central foci. Instead, they were collections of
dispersed but adjoining settlements whose populations identified
more with the concepts of the wider valley or the smaller villages
within them, than with the town or ward itself.[62] Hence a club
like Mid Rhondda AFC was not named after Tonypandy where
it was based, but rather a wider geographical unit. Yet ultimately, that supporters from a town like Merthyr, with its strong
civic pride, would go and watch Cardiff City's biggest games,
was more about soccer as entertainment than an as agent of civic
identity.

Despite this element of superficiality in clubs' support, the
popularity of derby matches illustrates the potency of local
rivalries and loyalties. Outside the Football League, 30,000 were
said to have watched Aberdare Athletic play Aberaman in 1920,
while 20,000 reputedly witnessed Mid Rhondda play Ton Pentre
in 1919. Jimmy Seed, who went on to be a successful club
manager, played in the latter match and said that there was
more excitement there than at any gathering he had ever
witnessed at Wembley, Hampden Park, Ninian Park or Windsor
Park.[63] In 1919, the *South Wales Echo* feared that the rivalry
between Aberdare Athletic and Aberaman was so strong that it
could lead to the downfall of both clubs, as it claimed had
happened before the war. It urged the directors to work together
to ensure that the clubs' fixtures did not clash, and thus present
an example of harmony to spectators.[64] The keenest rivalry in
south Wales was between Cardiff City and Swansea Town, the
region's two leading soccer clubs and urban areas. The 1919
Southern League match between the two at the Vetch Field took

    [62] Williams, *Democratic Rhondda*, pp. 18–19.
    [63] *FE*, 30 October 1920, 8 November 1919; Jimmy Seed, *The Jimmy Seed Story: Forty-
three Years in First-class Football as Player and Manager* (London, 1957), p. 71.
    [64] *SWE*, 3 May 1919.

place during a railway strike but, despite the loss of the primary form of transport, 5,000 people from Cardiff still managed to travel to the game. The interest in the return match, Cardiff City's record attendance at the time, was compared with that of a rugby international.[65] In 1929, Merthyr Town rearranged a Football League match because it clashed with a Cardiff–Swansea game. Special trains and buses were put on to that match from across the whole of south Wales.[66] The derby was so popular that calls for a special annual cup between the two clubs would arise from time to time. When Cardiff City was relegated from the first division in 1929, some people tried to take comfort in the fact that the prospective derby with Swansea Town might rekindle interest in Welsh soccer.[67]

During Cardiff City's first-division heyday, the derbies were more important to Swansea Town and its supporters, who were keen to prove that they could hold their own against their bigger neighbour. This was illustrated by a 1925 fifth-round Welsh Cup match between the two. Cardiff City, feeling that the league and its imminent FA Cup match were more important, played badly and indulged, according to one Swansea newspaper, in 'childish methods' and 'pompous swank'. Despite winning 4–0, Swansea Town had missed out on an opportunity to secure a meaningful victory over its rival, and thus its supporters felt insulted.[68] As the fleeting attention generally given to meetings between the two clubs in the unvalued Welsh League shows, the derbies were about footballing prestige rather than an all-out clash of two rival towns. In 1925, Cardiff City felt no need to prove its superiority and thus placed little importance on the Welsh Cup match. Nevertheless, the rivalry between the two clubs did of course reflect a wider tension between the towns. Although Cardiff was not officially the capital of Wales, Swansea felt somewhat over-shadowed by its larger neighbour and was anxious to demon-strate its equality. Sport offered one route by which this might be

---

[65] Most went by sea on specially chartered passenger steamers. *FE*, 4 October 1919, 6 April 1929; *SWE*, 2 October 1929, 7 February 1920.

[66] *SWE*, 2, 5 October 1929.

[67] See *FE*, 6 April 1929.

[68] The Swansea press naturally felt that their team still would have won even had Cardiff City played properly. Meanwhile the Cardiff press felt that City's performance was justifiable, considering the club's impending engagements, and claimed that the Swansea team had itself not put in much effort once it had established a lead. *Sporting News*, 7 March 1925; *WM*, 3 March 1925.

achieved. After the club's promotion to the second division, the Swansea Town chairman suggested that a match between the two clubs might help decide the 'vexed question' of the capital of Wales.[69] Hosting Wales's international matches was a vital symbolic point in defining the status of the two towns. Rugby internationals were shared fairly equally between the two but in soccer just three inter-war internationals were held at the Vetch, in contrast to Ninian Park's fourteen.[70] Swansea was anxious to have its share, and ground improvements were undertaken with this in mind. Further resentment arose in the town when Benjamin Watts Jones, a Swansea Town director, was appointed secretary-manager of Cardiff City in 1934. Despite being in a higher division, Swansea Town had again failed to move out of Cardiff City's shadow.[71] While Swansea was eager to use soccer to state its equality, Cardiff was keen to use it to declare its superiority. In the 1930s, when Cardiff City was no longer the leading Welsh club in the Football League, there were calls to make Ninian Park the national ground.[72] This would confirm the city's status as the premier Welsh urban centre. Soccer not only illustrated civic rivalries but also helped to shape them. For the inhabitants of Cardiff and Swansea, competitions between the towns' two clubs brought alive a latent rivalry, giving it a symbolic but popular relevance which otherwise was not often visible.

THE CIVIC IMPORTANCE OF PROFESSIONAL SOCCER

Despite the efforts of directors and the press to portray clubs as community institutions, soccer normally only reached a fraction of the population. Yet when a town's club won something it was difficult for the rest of the population to escape the subsequent impact. Cardiff City's 1927 FA Cup victory was the ultimate sporting success in inter-war south Wales. It was an event that

---

[69] *SWE*, 5 May 1925.

[70] Between 1920 and 1939 eighteen rugby internationals were held in Cardiff and seventeen in Swansea. However, there were concerns in Swansea that a movement was afoot to hold all internationals at the Arms Park. See Peter Stead, 'The entertainment of the people', in Glanmor Williams (ed.), *Swansea: An Illustrated History* (Swansea, 1990), pp. 274–5.

[71] *SWEP*, 5, 6, 10 March 1934.

[72] See *FE*, 24 October, 14 November 1936.

gripped the city: thousands gathered in the civic centre to listen to the match on specially erected loudspeakers, while hundreds more assembled outside wireless shops to hear the events at Wembley.[73] After the final whistle, an excited crowd spread news of the triumph around the city centre. One old woman was charged for being drunk and disorderly that night after shouting 'Good old Cardiff' at people on the street.[74] The return of the victorious team to Cardiff was a true civic celebration, with the players proceeding through streets decorated in blue and white and swarming with admirers:

> the enthusiasm knew no bounds. It was a democratic demonstration, an unrestrained idolatry of popular heroes. The victors' chariot was a storm-centre: it progressed through a hurricane of joyous clamour and a carnival of colour . . .
>
>   The police were helpless to dam the human stream as it flowed in ever-increasing volume as uninvited parts of the procession. That loss of discipline, good motivated though it may have been, inevitably spelled danger. Screaming women and the cries of half stifled children brought some of the over-exuberant to their senses when, less than half-way down St. Mary-street, a jam called for the intervention of police and Red Cross nurses. And ahead was the dense solid mass of gesticulating citizens seething over the quadrangle of Cathays Park, packing every inch of space from North-road on the one side to Park-place on the other. There were, it is easy to believe, quite 150,000 in that vast throng.[75]

To those who witnessed the scene, 'it was one of them things that you will never forget'.[76] Given the size of the crowds, many of the people there had probably never shown any real interest in soccer before. Soccer had brought Cardiff together in celebration, awoken people's pride in their city and placed the game firmly in the public consciousness. The crowds encompassed men and women of all classes, ensuring that the community loyalties that such events helped to shape were socially inclusive. The press attempted to develop this view. Before the 1927 final,

---

[73] Similarly, the *Western Mail* claimed that 2,000 people had waited outside its offices for early news of the 1925 cup final. *WM*, 27 April 1925. Estimates of the size of the crowd in the civic centre listening to the 1927 final varied from 2,000 to 10,000.

[74] *SWE*, 25 April 1927.

[75] *WM*, 26 April 1927. The police estimated that the crowd was at least 100,000 strong, while sensational headlines in the *Western Mail* put the figure at 250,000.

[76] Ivor Harris, interview.

the *Echo* featured a short interview with 'Ali', an Arab said to be one of Cardiff City's most consistent supporters.[77] A cartoon printed in the *Western Mail* (see Figure 3) depicted everyone enjoying the cup win, from smart businessmen and migrant Scots to fashionable young women and even dogs. Such social unity may not have been permanent, but at the very least the match put a smile on the city's face.

With rugby having no equivalent club competition to the FA Cup, it was only soccer that could bring a town together in such a way. With the exception of war, there was no other event outside sport, political or cultural, that could have quite the same impact. The crowd that had turned out to watch the king and queen open the National Museum of Wales in Cardiff two days before the final was as patriotic as but smaller than the victorious team's welcome. The press played an important role in developing celebrations of sporting successes into expressions of civic pride. By emphasizing the importance of the occasion to the community at large, newspaper coverage ensured that the event was a true civic celebration.[78] The press was also keen to show how the crowds of Welshmen that visited London for cup finals were well behaved and orderly.[79] The occasions provided opportunities to try to dispel south Wales's reputation as a centre of unruly extremists.

When Cardiff City's 1925 defeated cup final team returned to the city, the *South Wales Echo* declared that

> Those who imagined that the spirit of Celtic exuberance would be less in evidence today on the return of the non-successful team calculated without knowledge of their sense of good sportsmanship which characterises Welsh football crowds.[80]

The paper was trying to stress the sporting characteristics of the town or, in Cardiff's case, the nation. Newspapers estimated that 50,000 people turned out to welcome the Cardiff City team home in 1925. Despite the claims that they 'could not have

[77]   *SWE*, 19 April 1927.
[78]   See Jeff Hill, 'Rite of spring', for a further examination of the role of the local press in reporting cup finals.
[79]   For example, see *SWE*, 27 April 1925.
[80]   *SWE*, 27 April 1925.

expected a more tumultuous welcome had they won', the size of the crowd was dwarfed by that of two years later.[81] The reception may not have been any warmer, but the fact that it was so significantly larger does indicate that actually winning had raised the importance of the event. The victory and its British context made Cardiff the focus of celebration across the whole of Wales, lending weight, inside and outside the Principality, to the city's claim to be the Welsh metropolis, the premier civic and urban centre of the nation. It was a more accessible and popular achievement than placing national institutions in the city or the other symbolic ways with which Cardiff had tried to demonstrate its status.[82] Thus, success could make soccer one of the most potent elements in civic pride. It was something to be savoured by everyone connected with the town and the bigger the prize, the greater the proportion of the population that celebrated.

With soccer acting as a source of civic pride, local dignitaries were eager to be involved in its triumphs. Mayors and local MPs were VIP guests at cup finals and local authorities gave civic receptions in honour of their local clubs' triumphs. David Lloyd George, in the autumn of his career and perhaps desperate for votes, made one of his symbolic gestures to Wales by attending the 1927 cup final and then publicly congratulating the team on its victory.[83] The receptions given to the 1925 and 1927 Cardiff City cup final sides involved dining with the lord mayor and speeches outside the city hall after a procession through the city streets. The city hall was even decked out in blue and white after the 1925 final.[84] The grand architecture of the period's municipal buildings has been seen as towns projecting their greatness to themselves.[85] Thus, the use of the city hall, a symbol of Cardiff's Edwardian achievements, reinforced the idea that the cup finals were civic achievements for the whole community. Furthermore, as Hill points out, the involvement of the local council helped to turn such receptions into semi-official

---

[81] *SWE* and *WM*, 28 April 1925; *Cardiff Times*, 2 May 1925. The *Western Mail* did mention the figure of 100,000 but referred to 50,000 more often.

[82] See Neil Evans, 'The Welsh Victorian city: the middle class and civic and national consciousness in Cardiff, 1850–1914', *Welsh History Review*, 12, 3 (1985), 350–87.

[83] *Athletic News*, 25 April 1927. Similarly, Lloyd George had become a patron of London-Welsh AFC in 1921. *SWE*, 7 September 1921.

[84] *SWE*, 28 April 1925.

[85] James Vernon, *Politics and the People: A Study in English Popular Culture, c.1815–1867* (Cambridge, 1993), p. 49.

celebrations of a town itself.[86] Club directors consistently argued that the civic importance of soccer extended beyond winning trophies, and the involvement of local dignitaries was certainly not limited to cup finals or promotions. They opened new stands and made a point of being seen at prominent matches. Such activities appear to have been often treated as standard civic duties rather than a concerted effort to be involved in soccer. However, other local politicians must have hoped that being associated with a club, no matter how briefly, would boost their popularity. The Conservative and Labour candidates in Aberdare sat together at a match during the election campaign in 1924. This, no doubt deliberately, gave the impression that they could forget their rivalries in the higher interest of the town's soccer club.[87] Clement Kinloch-Cooke, a Conservative Cardiff MP, unsuccessfully took up the case of his constituents who could not get tickets for the 1927 final with the FA, in what could be interpreted as opportunism.[88] Whatever their motives for associating with soccer, municipal and local dignitaries could also be fans. The *Western Mail* excused Cardiff's lord mayor for his lack of decorum in the Royal Box at the 1927 cup final as he joined the 'throng in a demonstration of enthusiasm'.[89] There was no reason why one should not enjoy one's responsibilities.

FA Cup final appearances were rare and, as the depression deepened, the experience of most clubs was a battle for survival. The reaction to these struggles illustrates the potency of the idea of clubs as something more than providers of entertainment. When Merthyr Town folded in 1934, the editorial of the local newspaper stated that

> The demise of the club is a real loss to the Town in more senses than one. We can ill-afford to part with any sport or attraction which provides healthy entertainment for our young people, and interest for adults, too many of whom find their enforced leisure a burden.[90]

[86]   Hill, 'Rite of spring', p. 100.
[87]   Undated clipping from the *South Wales Football Express* held at Aberdare public library.
[88]   *WM*, 21 April 1927.
[89]   The king had told the lord mayor to cheer as much as he wanted. *WM* and *South Wales News*, 25 April 1927.
[90]   *ME*, 30 June 1934.

It went on to attack the FAW for its lack of support and its refusal to allow the cheaper admission prices that could have saved the club. The editor feared that it would be a long time before there was first-class soccer in the borough again. The closure of the club seemed to sum up the fortunes of the town. It was suffering through no fault of its own, felt let down by those in authority and saw little immediate hope for the future. In 1936, a *South Wales Echo* editorial welcomed Newport County's re-election to the Football League, acknowledging that during such times of economic hardship sport played an important role in the well-being of towns.[91] Soccer's contribution to the life and identity of a town was not just limited to times of success; simply having a senior club was regarded as helping the mental and physical health of a town. Because of such beliefs, local author-ities sometimes helped clubs in times of hardship. Mayors and other councillors often attended and chaired fund-raising meetings. The Cardiff City Corporation owned Ninian Park and was flexible about the rent as the depression deepened. The club tried to foster good relations with the corporation by offering free entry to Ninian Park to any interested local councillors.[92] In 1912, the mayor of Merthyr played an active role in raising money for a successful but financially weak Merthyr Town. He chaired meetings, made public appeals and generally did his best to raise the profile of the club. He drew analogies between the town's other achievements (such as setting up its own police force and being a county borough) and the club's success. He said he wanted to help the welfare and good of the town and would help the club where he could. To him, the thousands of people whom soccer brought into the town were a small means of making up for the failure to attract new industry.[93]

In 1935, Swansea Town found itself with serious financial problems and there were genuine fears that the club would go bankrupt. With the help of the press, the club began a campaign based on an appeal to community spirit and the conscience of supporters. Its launch was presided over by the mayor with 'moral support' from representatives of Swansea RFC and the

---

[91] *SWE*, 9 June 1936.
[92] *FE*, 12 September 1936.
[93] Not all the town appreciated his efforts and some felt that he should be doing rather more to help Merthyr's industry. *ME*, 4, 11 May 1912.

best wishes of a local MP. A doctor was even there to encourage attendances through the benefits of being out in the air: 'Speaking scientifically, every time you go to a match you do yourself as much good as if you took a 3s. 6d. bottle of medicine'! An editorial in the *South Wales Evening Post*, under the heading of 'Swans must be saved', asked supporters if they were 'going to leave in the lurch the people who have provided them with the opportunity of seeing most of the best sides in the game'. A shilling fund, a boxing match, a dance at the Vetch and smaller events all around the town were organized by locals to raise funds for the club. Here was a community fighting to help *its* soccer team.[94] But when the public failed to respond to such fund-raising initiatives there was anger amongst club directors and in the press. In 1930, the chairman of financially crippled Merthyr Town argued that the club had brought considerable numbers of visitors and publicity to the town and that this service should be repaid.[95] The Newport County reporter who felt that the club should be 'part and parcel of the town' argued that it was unfair that such a small number of directors should carry the club for the whole community. After Aberdare Athletic lost its Football League status in 1927, a member of the board said that he was disgusted at the lack of public spirit that had been shown in the club's efforts to stay financially viable. Like his peers at other clubs, he felt that the community should have done more to help its soccer club in its hour of need.[96]

Directors may have felt that their clubs deserved more support, but for local authorities struggling to serve the community amidst competing social needs, soccer was not a priority. Their involvement was limited, sporadic and often down to the enthusiasm of individual councillors. Despite some well-publicized speeches from local politicians on the responsibility of their authorities to assist clubs in financial need, help was never forthcoming on any significant scale.[97] The mayor of Newport thought that the Cardiff Corporation had poured thousands of pounds into Cardiff City. He called on his council to help

[94] *SWEP*, 15 June 1935; Farmer, *Swansea City*, p. 95.
[95] *SWE*, 8 January 1930.
[96] *FE*, 12 January 1935; *SWE*, 13 July 1927.
[97] Such a speech was reported in 1928. The paper did not name the mayor who made it or the borough he represented, perhaps because his idea was potentially unpopular with ratepayers and voters. *FE*, 20 October 1928.

Newport County (and rugby club) in a similar fashion. However, the Cardiff Corporation had never been either prepared or financially able to offer soccer such direct help, and similarly nothing came of the mayor of Newport's request.[98] In 1912, the local corporation had even begun legal proceedings against Cardiff City over the unpaid rent on Ninian Park.[99] The Swansea Corporation refused permission in 1920 for a new stand at the Vetch Field owing to a shortage of building materials. It understandably felt that the housing projects being carried out at the time should take priority.[100] Six years later, the Cardiff Corporation refused to lease to Cardiff City some empty ground adjoining Ninian Park, which the club wanted to use as a training ground, because there was a firm interested in building houses on the land. Another application to extend Ninian Park was rejected since it would have meant turning over council-owned allotments to the club, an acknowledgement that leisure facilities outside sport were important too.[101] Not all the help that local authorities did provide was popular. The Cardiff Corporation's decision to forgo a year's rent on Ninian Park in 1934 brought complaints and criticism. Some ratepayers felt that they were being asked to subsidize the enjoyment of a minority, whilst others thought it wrong when there were people losing their homes because they were not able to pay their rent.[102] Similar anger followed the decision of the Newport local authority to hold a private banquet, at the ratepayers' expense, for Newport County, after it had won the 1939 third-division south championship.[103] Few may have shared the views of one Welsh Labour MP, who thought professional sport a luxury and argued for a tax on transfer fees in these times of adversity,[104] but, for all its civic importance, soccer was hardly the most pressing need of the communities of south Wales.

[98] *SWE*, 25 August 1936.

[99] Cardiff Corporation, Parks etc. Committee minutes, 18 October 1912.

[100] The application was not helped by the fact that the surveyors were not convinced that the proposed stand was safe. In refusing permission, the corporation classed the project as a 'luxury building'. *SWE*, 24 July 1920.

[101] The decision was much to the indignation of the club which claimed that it was not fully realized what an asset it was to the town. *SWE*, 15 February 1926, 22 August 1923; Cardiff Corporation, minutes of Waterworks Committee (19 March 1923), and Small Holdings and Allotments Committee (29 March, 25 June 1923).

[102] See *SWE*, 2 October 1934.

[103] See the letters of protest in the *SWA*, 18 April 1939.

[104] D. Watts Morgan, MP, *SWE*, 21 January 1929.

CONCLUSION

Two publications of the 1930s illustrate the civic nuances of professional soccer. The cover of Cardiff City match pro-grammes regularly featured a picture of the city hall, a reminder to all that the team was representing more than just a soccer club. In 1932, Newport County produced a brochure for its campaign to be re-elected to the Football League. Featuring photographs and descriptions of local industry and business, it was as much an advertisement for the town of Newport as it was for the club.[105] There were strong practical reasons for this: an economically strong district promised the potential for the high gates that the Football League electorate sought. The pro-fessional game revolved around this paradox of civic and com-mercial roles. Professional clubs may not have been profit seeking but they were private businesses that had to operate within financial constraints. As such, the small business and professional men who dominated the boards of directors liked to keep the financial affairs of clubs secret from supporters. When clubs ran into monetary difficulties, such a secretive approach was neither practical nor acceptable to the public and press. Clubs then tried to raise funds by appealing to the idea that they were institutions with communal and civic functions. There was often a community response to such appeals, embracing the club, supporters, local press, local dignitaries and other sporting institutions. At the heart of such a response was a complex moral relationship that bound professional clubs, fans and the community.[106] That relationship was dependent on the civic importance of professional soccer, and on a belief that, for all the financial realities of the game, clubs were ultimately communal rather than commercial institutions.

Professional soccer's civic importance lay not in its alleged ability to divert the masses from politically or morally unaccept-able thoughts and behaviour, but in its role as one of the few spheres where people and institutions could express a common membership of a town. Indeed, such feelings of membership were often inert, but soccer helped to give them life; as such it

[105] *SWA*, 3 June 1932.
[106] Hill, 'Cocks, cats, caps and cups: a semiotic approach to sport and national identity', *Culture, Sport, Society*, 2, 2 (1999), p. 6.

became an acknowledged part of civic life. Amidst social inequalities, a 'common mood' in urban life was often not evident
but, as Williams argues, professional soccer, particularly at times
of achievement by a local club, is evidence that it could exist.
Supporting a club offered people an opportunity to 'define themselves and articulate a shared geographical identity'. More
people may have gone to religious services and the pictures, but
'no single cinema or church had so many patrons for one
performance or service as did a football match'.[107] 'Nothing
mattered but the game on Saturday', wrote one reporter in 1922
after Cardiff City had entertained Spurs.

> From early morning till nightfall the [only] topic was of football and the
> crowds . . . No Mabon's Day, Bank Holiday, Eisteddfod gathering, Royal
> visit, or any other function or holiday presented such a scene in the City. It
> was impossible for anyone to avoid it. One simply moved in the crowd;
> was absorbed and moved along.[108]

What such common moods actually meant to people is more
elusive. There were no homogeneous attitudes within classes, let
alone in whole communities. To some supporters at least, professional soccer was about entertainment, and they went where it
was at its best. To other people it was an annoyance that could
mean that 'every place of entertainment, restaurant, street, and
thoroughfare was engulfed'.[109] Yet there must have been few
who witnessed the ecstatic scenes in Cardiff after the FA Cup
final who could have denied that professional soccer had some
role to play in generating and articulating people's pride in their
town.

---

[107] Williams, 'One could have literally walked', p. 138.
[108] *SWE*, 6 March 1922.
[109] Ibid.

VI

'AN ALL WALES OCCASION': SOCCER AND NATIONAL IDENTITIES

[T]he English Cup Final is much more than a great football contest . . . it is a tremendous festival, and this year . . . was added the flavour of an international: something of the flavour of an England v. Wales Rugby contest at Cardiff or at Twickenham.

From Wales the men and women went up to London in legions. All through the Friday night and the early hours of Saturday morning the streets of London were musical with Welsh hymns and songs. The leek and the daffodil were almost as abundant, worn as favours, as the City's colours. It was not merely a Cardiff City occasion. It was an all Wales occasion. The mayors of Swansea and Brecon and many other Welsh towns were there, civic rivalries forgotten in the national pride.

Western Mail, 25 April 1927

'Wales is an artefact which the Welsh produce', wrote historian Gwyn A. Williams.[1] Exactly what that artefact was, and how it was produced, are contentious questions obscured by current political ideas about Wales's future, the absence of a nation state and internal geographic, linguistic and ethnic divisions. Wales and Welshness have a plethora of different meanings for the people who possess and make it.

Whatever definition one believes in, it would be difficult to deny sport's place in the articulation of Welsh national identity. Indeed, few other cultural forms are so well equipped to express national identity. Sport's emotions, national colours, emblems, songs and contests all make it a perfect vehicle through which collective ideas of nationhood can be expressed. It has been a central agent in inventing, maintaining and projecting the idea of a single Welsh national identity in and outside its blurred borders. Rugby internationals at Cardiff Arms Park mobilized Wales's collective identities and passions. They helped gloss over the different meanings that the people of Wales attached to their nationality, enabling them to assert their Welshness in the face of

---

[1] Gwyn A. Williams, *When was Wales?* (London, 1985), p. 304.

internal division and in the political, social and cultural shadow of England. Association football too has played its part in producing and projecting Wales. This chapter looks at how the game in south Wales interacted with Welsh national identity; it explores national passions in the club and international game and argues that soccer sheds vital light on an understanding of what Wales meant to the people who lived there.

NATIONAL IDENTITY AND CLUB SOCCER

Linda Colley has argued that 'Identities are not like hats. Human beings can and do put on several at a time.'[2] Some supporters may have articulated civic partisanships through following pro-fessional teams, but such rivalries were subsumed at important matches when a sense of national identity united south Wales behind a specific club. The south Wales press was prone to speak of 'national' contests and did its utmost to present a united front of support for Welsh clubs in the FA Cup and other important ties. As Michael Billig argues, such 'flaggings' of nationhood in the media were not mere rhetoric. They communicated a sense of nation and unobtrusively drew readers into that community.[3] The special trains that travelled to and from Swansea and Cardiff for important cup-ties indicate that significant numbers of supporters of the rival clubs actively joined together when their interests did not clash. Of the 20,000 Welsh supporters at the 1925 cup final, only half were estimated to have come from Cardiff, while, for the 1927 final, around 1,700 travelled by train from Swansea alone.[4] Of course, the levels of interest in the cup-runs of Welsh clubs cannot be put down to national sentiment alone. As the press conceded, Welsh interest also owed something to an appreciation of good soccer.[5] Important cup matches were exciting fixtures no matter who was involved, and the FA Cup final was the season's climax. English clubs generally enjoyed bigger gates for cup-ties irrespective of the opposition, and

---

[2] Linda Colley, *Britons: Forging the Nation, 1707–1837* (London, 1994 edn), p. 6.
[3] Michael Billig, *Banal Nationalism* (London, 1995).
[4] *SWE*, 25 April 1925; *Sporting Post*, 23 April 1927. The FA's methods of ticket allocation both diminished the number of supporters from Cardiff and increased the number from elsewhere in Wales.
[5] *SWE*, 11 March 1924.

spectators from the West Country were attracted to such games in south Wales. For the 1924 FA Cup quarter-final replay between Cardiff City and Liverpool, special trains were put on to Ninian Park from Bristol, Gloucestershire and the Wye valley, as well as from all over south Wales.[6] Yet even at run-of-the-mill league games not flagged as national contests by the press, supporters could inject them with such qualities. When first-division Cardiff City played league games in Liverpool or Manchester, special trains were put on from north Wales for people to support their compatriots from the south. Welsh exiles also turned up to the games in large numbers.[7] In 1923, a letter in the *South Wales Echo* by a 'Merthyr supporter', said that he, like 'every true Welshman', hoped that Cardiff City would soon be on top.[8] The writer apparently saw no conflict between his support for Merthyr Town and his hopes for his compatriots in a higher division.

For supporters of all clubs, important away matches offered a festive day out, but for the Welsh fans they also offered opportunities to celebrate their nationality. Large groups of Welsh supporters swarmed by train into English towns and cities, making their presence seen and heard. They formed processions behind Welsh flags, sang Welsh songs and hymns and wore countless leeks and daffodils. The occasional woman even dressed up in 'traditional' costume with 'Wales Forever' emblazoned across her tall hat.[9] Leeks were worn by so many at Cardiff City's two FA Cup finals ('Wembley was a maze of leeks') that traders at Covent Garden tripled the normal price of the vegetable.[10] Such symbolic manifestations of nationhood were not lost on the English press, which saw the Welsh supporters as 'invaders from the land of leek' come to take the *English* cup away.[11] An 'intolerable thought' reported *The Times* before the 1925 cup final. It went on:

> an invasion such as this has not been witnessed in the south since the days of primitive warfare a thousand years ago . . . thousands of enthusiasts carried

---

[6] *SWE*, 10 March 1924.
[7] See, for example, *FE*, 22 November 1924; *WM*, 19 March 1921.
[8] *SWE*, 6 January 1923.
[9] See, for example, *FE*, 31 January 1920; *SWE*, 23 April 1927.
[10] *SWE*, 25 April 1927, 27 April 1925.
[11] *The Morning Advertiser*, quoted in *WM*, 27 April 1925.

leeks with them throughout the day . . . [which] looked very formidable indeed.[12]

A melodramatic, perhaps tongue-in-cheek, reaction but no one could doubt that the Welsh had come to town. Scottish supporters made similar highly visual and audible proclamations of their nationhood when they followed their national team to matches in England.[13] Such occasions presented supporters from the so-called Celtic fringes with rare opportunities to remind the English of the cultural traditions of a divided Britain, while a patriotic Welsh press was keen to emphazise any behaviour that demonstrated Wales's distinctiveness.[14] By doing so, it was not inventing or contriving the matches as national affairs but rather reinforcing and emphasizing an idea and behaviour that were already there. Yet newspapers do more than just report the events. They frame the terms in which we think about what we read. Thus the treatment that the English and Welsh press accorded the games ensured that the wider reading public also saw such matches as celebrations of Wales and Welshness. The reports told people that Wales was a nation and that soccer was more than just a game.

Encouraged by the press, the whole of Wales rejoiced in Cardiff City's 1927 cup victory, treating it as a national achievement. 'The Cup comes to Wales', declared the headlines of the Swansea-based *Sporting News*. It went on to say that City had represented the whole principality in a struggle against England. The winning team was given official civic receptions in Merthyr and northerly Wrexham. The game was broadcast at Mid Rhondda's ground on loudspeakers, and the scheduled match delayed until after the final whistle had gone at Wembley. The national importance of the 1927 final to Welsh soccer was

[12] *The Times*, 27 April 1925. Hill argues that the FA Cup final became a representation of a certain kind of Englishness. Hill, 'Rite of spring', p. 88. Thus the possible loss of the trophy to a Welsh team helps to explain such rhetoric. After the 1927 final, the English press made much of the fact that Cardiff City had been lucky and scored through a Welshman's mistake. Again, this was to help compensate for the loss of the English cup to a 'foreign' team. Meanwhile, the Welsh press just saw this as bad sportsmanship.

[13] H. F. Moorhouse, 'Scotland against England: football and popular culture', *International Journal of the History of Sport*, 4, 2 (1987), 189–202.

[14] Similarly, supporters of clubs from the north of England (and the watching southern press) at FA Cup finals saw the occasion as an opportunity to assert the 'otherness' of northern England. Hill, 'Rite of spring', pp. 102–3.

so strong that the *Sporting News* conceded that it was perhaps 'fitting' that it was Cardiff City, the 'senior' Welsh club, that had the honour of playing.[15] Likewise, the Cardiff press celebrated Swansea Town's 1925 promotion to the second division with front-page headlines and proclamations of a national achievement.[16]

Such national rejoicing was not just found at away games. In the sixth round of the 1926 FA Cup, Swansea Town were led onto the field by a girl in national costume to the accompaniment of 'Land of my fathers'.[17] Traditional Welsh hymns and anthems were played regularly by pre-match bands and sung fervently by the crowds; soccer played its part alongside rugby in the inter-war invention of a Welsh tradition of community singing. By the late 1930s, the singing of 'Cwm Rhondda' and 'Sospan Fach' at a cup match was seen as inevitable.[18] The icons of a later popular national identity were gradually being incorporated into any significant match between Welsh and English clubs. Such celebratory nationalism did not indicate a wider political national consciousness. It was fun, depoliticized, laced with sentimental clichés and, in the midst of a depressed economy, acted as a harmless piece of escapism, a distraction from the harsh realities of life. The behaviour of supporters had more in common with the traditional rituals of the local community which Fishwick noted at Swindon Town matches than the defiant exertion of nationalism seen in Ireland through the promotion of Gaelic football.[19] It was all part of the atmosphere of festivity that helped to establish soccer everywhere as a popular pastime. As in rugby, mixed in with the crowd's singing of Welsh hymns were popular music-hall and wartime songs.[20] Drinking, swearing, and sometimes fighting, were as much a feature of prominent rugby and soccer games as the celebrations of Welshness. The behaviour displayed in both sports is indicative that a pride in Wales coexisted with membership of a wider British popular culture based upon agencies such as the shared experiences of war, class and commercialized mass leisure.

---

[15] *Sporting News*, 23 April 1927; *SWE*, 29–30 April 1927; *RG*, 30 April 1927.
[16] *SWE*, 2 May 1925.
[17] *FE*, 6 March 1926.
[18] *FE*, 8 January 1938.
[19] Fishwick, *English Football*, p. 59.
[20] See, for example, *Sporting News*, 31 January 1925.

Hill has demonstrated how the FA Cup final was a narrative and icon of England, but one that was also interwoven with British meanings in the typical English fashion of conflating the two nations.[21] The 1925 and 1927 finals represented Wales proudly and publicly taking her place in a British national institution and reminding people on the other side of the border that Britain did not just mean England. The national and imperial prestige of Wembley (or the Empire Stadium as it was officially known), the fact that the final was the first to be broadcast live on the wireless, and the presence of the king and his appreciation of the Welsh singing, all added to Welsh pride in their role in this most English of occasions.[22] While the press emphasized the distinctiveness of the Welsh fans, it also stressed a wider British unity. To a *Western Mail* reporter, the joining together of English and Welsh supporters at the 1927 cup final to sing 'Abide with me' was an emotional moment that brought back memories of the Great War.[23] The Welsh trips to London for the final helped to reinforce the idea that the city was the British capital, just as cup finals helped to develop northerners' view of it as the English capital. Furthermore, the visits to the cenotaph made by supporters and club officials at inter-war finals indicated not only the continuing sense of personal and collective grief left by the First World War, but also the sense of a British nation felt by both northerners and Welsh people. Thus, Cardiff City's cup finals are evidence not only of a celebratory pride in a Welsh national identity, but a feeling of Britishness too. To the leek-wearing supporters eagerly visiting the metropolis, the two were not contradictory.

PROFESSIONAL PLAYERS AND NATIONAL IDENTITY

As was roughly typical of Welsh professional clubs of the time (see table 6.1), only three of the Cardiff City's 1927 cup final team were actually Welsh. In contrast, rugby was a game of

---

[21] Hill, 'Rite of spring' and 'Cocks, cats, caps'; Colley, *Britons*.
[22] George V was so impressed that he asked for the Welsh national anthem to be sung again. *FE*, 23 April 1927. *The Times* (25 April 1927) felt that it 'was the unmistakable quality of Welsh voices that enabled the national song "Land of My Fathers", and the hymn "Abide with me" to sound so impressive'.
[23] *WM*, 25 April 1927.

Table 6.1

Birthplaces of first-team players at leading clubs in south Wales, 1925–1926 season[1]

	Cardiff City	Merthyr Town	Newport County	Swansea Town
South Wales	5(3)[2]	7(4)	7(1)	7(4)
North and mid-Wales	2	0	0	2
North-east England	7	3	5	5
North-west England	2	0	0	0
The Midlands	1	7	4	1
South-east England	1	0	1	4
South-west England	0	0	1	0
Scotland	6	4	5	3
Ireland	3	0	0	0
Uncertain	0	0	0	1
Total	27	21	23	23

[1] Merthyr Town and Swansea Town players are those registered at the beginning of the season while the Cardiff City and Newport County players are those who made first-team appearances in the Football League during the season. *Sources: FE*, 29 August 1925; John Crooks, *The Bluebirds: A Who's Who of Cardiff City Football League Players* (Pontypool, 1987); Tony Ambrosen, *The Ironsides – A Lifetime in the League: A Who's Who of Newport County* (Harefield, 1991); *Athletic News*. I am grateful to Ian Garland for his help in completing this table.

[2] Numbers in brackets indicate number of players born in the town that the club represents.

predominantly local, or at least Welsh, players, as critics pointed out in the aftermath of Cardiff's triumph:

> It is, of course, a matter of money. [In soccer] if you have a rich city and a big gate, you can hire a fine team. But where is it going to end? . . . [a] huge long-limbed Zulu whose arms span half-way between the posts for goal. From China may come a couple of imperturbable, hardworking backs. From India quick and cunning Gurkhas could be brought in as half-backs. And the forwards might be big, swift and versatile Maoris . . . Long may Rugby football flourish, where we can take a personal interest in, and enjoy a reflected glory of the prowess of our own townsmen and fellow nationals, and tell the world with some show of truth that 'that's the stuff that *we* are made of!'[24]

[24] *WM*, 26 April 1927.

Such letters were not new; professional foreign players always provided the rugby fraternity with a stick to beat soccer with.[25]

> May I call attention to the absurd and preposterous sum paid for the services of men in order to kick a bit of leather about? Ye God! the salary of a prime minister! Is it seriously suggested that there are not local men who make as good show as these 'stars'?
>
> Although I am an old Rugby player I have attended matches at Ninian Park in order to get interested, but there, I simply can not. It is a fluky game anyway. Again is it any credit to Cardiff or any other city to get to the top of the tables with the assistance of imported players? . . . I don't blame the players but I do resent the introduction of strangers.[26]

The fact that such letters tended to appear in the press when soccer was enjoying success and a high profile suggests that the sentiments expressed were more indicative of fears that rugby was being marginalized by this 'alien' game, rather than of any widely held prejudice. Some peripheral purists within soccer also resented the foreign composition of the Cardiff City side, but this represented anger at the professional status of the game rather than the fact that it brought in non-locals. The language of many complainants was of nationality rather than locality.[27] In the mobile societies of Edwardian and inter-war south Wales, civic membership was too fluid to be too rigidly defined or adhered to. Even in rugby, players were not confined to their home towns. Towns like Cardiff and Swansea were regional centres. It mattered not that players were from other parts of south Wales but, when English or Scots were brought in to play for a wage, that did offend the purists. The players themselves were certainly aware of the nationality issue and did their best to make it clear that they were representing Wales. Jimmy Blair, Cardiff City's Scottish captain in the 1925 cup final, boarded the train for

---

[25] Similarly, there was controversy in the late nineteenth century over whether success gained by English clubs with Scottish professionals was really bringing honour to the areas concerned. As in inter-war south Wales, such voices were in a minority, with most preferring to enjoy the better standards of play that such professionals brought. Steven Tischler, *Footballers and Businessmen: The Origins of Professional Football in England* (London, 1981), p. 46.

[26] *SWE*, 7 November 1925. Other members of the local community resented the imported players because of the attention they received from girls! Charles Jones, interview.

[27] For example, *SWE*, 17 March 1924. Other letters used the concepts interchangeably.

Wembley carrying a Welsh flag. Hughie Ferguson, another Scot, acknowledged that not all the team was Welsh but assured City's supporters in 1927 that the players had only one thought, 'to win and so bring the coveted trophy to Wales'.[28]

To the majority of supporters such issues were not important. As one fan wrote, supporters paid 'to see a good game of football irrespective of nationality . . . all football enthusiasts in the British Isles care not about nationality as long as their pet team is a successful one.'[29] The thousands who turned out to welcome home Cardiff City's FA Cup winners saw no irony in celebrating, complete with every form of Welsh paraphernalia, a side that contained only three Welshmen but four Irishmen, three Scots and one Englishman. The players had brought honour to the city and to Wales; their nationalities as individuals mattered not. As the mayor of Merthyr said, anyone who came to play for a Welsh club became a Welshman whether he liked it or not.[30] The in-migration of the Edwardian period had made south Wales, and in particular Cardiff, a cosmopolitan society. Throughout modern history, Welsh identity has been malleable and constantly reshaped by the people of Wales. By the Edwardian and inter-war years, it incorporated a multiplicity of different peoples under one broad label. Clubs thus had Irish-, English- and Scottish-born supporters as well as players and the professional soccer clubs of south Wales reflected this. The occasional sceptic might joke about players wearing kilts, and fans with Welsh accents being ejected, but far more common was the objection that a team of Welshmen would probably bring relegation.[31]

Supporters acclaimed talent and success, not nationality. Welsh players were not more popular on account of their birth-place alone. Fred Keenor owed some of his popularity to being a 'Cardiff boy' but more to his strong tackles, courage and resilience on the pitch. These were exactly the qualities that appealed to an audience of skilled working-class men, and he became a favourite with fans at his next club, Crewe Alexandra.[32] Welsh

---

[28]   *SWE*, 24 April 1925, 22 April 1927.
[29]   *SWE*, 11 November 1925; Charles Jones, interview. Fishwick has shown that in England success, and thus value for money, was viewed as more important than having a team of locals. Fishwick, *English Football*, p. 65.
[30]   *SWE*, 30 April 1927.
[31]   Supporters' letters in *SWE*, 11 November 1925.
[32]   Johnes, 'Fred Keenor'.

international Len Davies's Cardiff birthplace did not protect him from strong criticism after he missed the penalty that cost Cardiff City the league championship in 1924.[33] When the abilities of a club's foreign contingent were recognized through selection for their national side, it was a source of pride in the town for which they played. There was lingering resentment that Billy Hardy, widely acknowledged as one of the finest halfbacks in Britain, was never picked for England, allegedly because he played for a Welsh club. Hardy was the 'unquestionable idol of the crowd'; the fact that he was English was not an issue to his fans.[34] Richard Holt has argued that Billy Meredith, the greatest foot-baller in Edwardian Britain, was not a heroic national figure in Wales because he was a soccer rather than a rugby player.[35] Yet Meredith was treated with reverence when he played for Wales in the south of the principality. His failure to achieve the same heroic status in south Wales as the greatest rugby players was because he was from north Wales and lived and played in Manchester. Many Welsh rugby players accorded heroic status were not actually born in Wales. But, as in soccer, living and playing in Wales was enough to make them representatives of the Welsh people. In contrast to the situation in Wales, English soccer players in Scotland were generally treated with distrust and contempt. Scottish soccer saw itself as superior in skill and style to the English game, and thus imports from the latter were viewed as a threat that could dilute the quality of indigenous play.[36] In Welsh soccer there was no such sense of superiority, and supporters were happy to embrace good players of any nationality that came their way.

When local and Welsh players were successful, it was some-thing to be celebrated. The Cardiff press took some added pride

[33] See *SWE*, 6–7 May 1924.

[34] See, for example, *SWE*, 17 October 1922, 17 March 1921. Lovell's, the Newport confectionery manufacturers, even ran a newspaper advertisement based on the grievance. See *FE*, 19 December 1925.

[35] Holt, *Sport and the British*, p. 247. In 1912, the FAW organized a benefit match for Meredith at Ninian Park between a south Wales XI and a team selected by Meredith himself. The £62 gate was meagre compared with the £1,400 he received from a benefit in Manchester that year. The figure was described as very disappointing by the local press, which claimed nonetheless that Meredith was a popular figure in south Wales. A benefit match in Wrexham also failed to raise a large sum. *SWDN*, 9 December 1912; John Harding, *Football Wizard: The Story of Billy Meredith* (Derby, 1985), pp. 168–73.

[36] H. F. Moorhouse, 'Shooting stars: footballers and working-class culture in twentieth-century Scotland', in Holt (ed.), *Sport and the Working Class*, pp. 182–4.

in that the three Welshmen in the FA Cup-winning side came from the city itself. In 1921, the press could be found wistfully dreaming of an all-Welsh Cardiff City, but they were content with the fact that no longer did all the Welsh talent end up in England.[37] However, when teams were not playing well, there were calls for more Welsh players and criticisms of existing foreigners. Letters to the press demanding that the Cardiff City directors buy the entire Welsh national side were printed together with the claim that this would bring higher attendances and better results.[38] Notably, the calls were for Welsh players, not men from the city itself; again soccer seems to suggest that Welsh identity was interwoven with civic feeling. These nationalist calls-to-arms were not universally popular, one being attacked with the retorts that it was the football that mattered and that a Scottish player could not help where he was born.[39] As in England, crowds also tended to barrack local players more than others.[40] One local reporter was even accused of excessive Welsh sentiment for defending Cardiff City's Len Davies.[41] Thus, the popular perceptions of professional players in south Wales drew upon the ambiguities of Welsh national identity. Individuals' origins could be forgotten in times of success, but in times of hardship foreign players could also be made scapegoats for poor results. There was never any universal agreement on this, especially in the cosmopolitan city of Cardiff, but nationality was never a clear concept and it meant different things to different individuals. It was rejoiced in during the good times, but in bad times it could either become an irrelevance or a perceived solution.

During the early to mid-1920s, with successful local clubs spending thousands on good players from Scotland and elsewhere, neither the press nor supporters had expressed anxiety about Welsh talent being bought by English teams. Yet, by the 1930s, the decline in the fortunes of south Wales's senior clubs led to concern at the number of Welshmen who ended up

[37] *FE*, 26 November 1921.
[38] For example, *SWE*, 2 February 1926, 8 December 1933.
[39] *SWE*, 4 February 1926.
[40] The press claimed that this was causing many young local players to move out of Wales altogether. *FE*, 16 November 1929, 15 February 1930, 21 December 1935. See Fishwick, *English Football*, p. 62, for a discussion of a similar situation in England.
[41] *FE*, 30 December 1922.

playing in England. The local scouts who unearthed talent for English clubs were attacked for lacking 'local sentiment' and 'national pride'.[42] It was difficult to reconcile the success of the international side (comprised almost entirely of men from south Wales playing for English clubs) with the dire situation in the domestic game. Local soccer reporters never shared the view that Welsh clubs should confine themselves to employing Welsh players, but they felt that the decline of the 1930s could have been avoided had many of the leading players from the region been signed by local rather than by English teams. In what sounded like an effort to deflect the blame, one Cardiff City director said that it was up to the players to want to play for the town in which they were born. Another felt that local employers should help by giving jobs to promising players so that they did not move away in search of work.[43] The press was convinced that Welsh soccer's salvation lay at home and did its utmost to encourage the senior clubs to develop their links with junior clubs and leagues in order to unearth players of potential. This was not nationalistic sentiment but rather a realistic appraisal of the situation. Rising transfer fees and falling attendances meant that Welsh clubs could not afford to continue buying in talent from elsewhere.

The patriotism of Scots playing for English clubs was often doubted.[44] Domestic Scottish association football, with its history, traditions and independent competitions, was a stronger component in Scottish national identity than soccer was in Wales. Like Welsh rugby, Scottish soccer did not see itself as secondary in quality to its English peers. Thus, Scottish soccer and its supporters were protective of its status and apprehensive of anything that might challenge it or expose any weaknesses. Scottish supporters did not like to think of a transfer south as a move upwards, and the number of good players who made the transition threatened that confidence. In contrast, in south Wales soccer was built on competing in an English context, not in an independent sphere. There was a sense of regret about the talent that left, but players were not blamed personally.[45] In the

[42] For example, *FE*, 16 November 1929.
[43] *SWE*, 30 May 1936; *FE*, 14 September 1935.
[44] Moorhouse, 'Shooting stars', p. 186.
[45] For example, Charles Jones, interview.

Edwardian era, south Wales did not have any clubs that could compete with the attraction of the Football League for the best players. In the early 1920s, there were not enough local successful clubs to cater for all the region's talent. After that, the depression meant that the economic pull of England was accepted and, given the mass migration from the Valleys, it was hardly just professional soccer players who were leaving. They were part of a general migration of young men and their families desperate to escape the constraints and poverty of the depression. South Wales may have been unhappy about its weak economic position, but it was not bitter towards the individuals who escaped.[46] Those players who left were simply taking a step up a career ladder that Welsh clubs could not provide.

INTERNATIONAL SOCCER AND SOUTH WALES

The 20,000 who watched Wales play England at the Arms Park in 1906 constituted a new record gate for soccer in south Wales. The game may have offered an opportunity to see a better standard of play than was available locally but it was not a celebration of Welshness in the way that Edwardian rugby internationals were. The press expressed regret that Wales could not produce 'an eleven from regular players in the principality to uphold the honour of the country'.[47] Even in the inter-war years, international soccer in south Wales was not associated with the nationalistic paraphernalia, celebration or Welsh *hwyl* that could be found at important cup games or international rugby.[48] In contrast to the way it treated important FA Cup matches, the press did little to give international soccer a sense of occasion or national importance. Poor results did not help (see table 6.2).

---

[46] This is further illustrated by the fact that rugby players who turned professional were not resented personally, even during the game's Edwardian 'high noon'. In a working-class and amateur game, no one begrudged those who left when tempted by northern riches. See Smith and Williams, *Fields of Praise*, p. 178, and Gareth Williams's review of Phil Melling, 'Man of Amman: The Life of Dai Davies' in *Sports Historian*, 16 (1996), 238. When successful Mid Rhondda sold Jimmy Seed in 1920, there was considerable disquiet amongst supporters, who felt that it was being done for financial reasons. However, when Seed himself explained that he was going of his own accord the situation was pacified; his ambition was understood. Seed, *The Jimmy Seed Story*, p. 73.
[47] *SWDN*, 12 March 1906.
[48] See, for example, *SWE*, 17 March 1924; *FE*, 30 January 1926.

Table 6.2
Results of Wales's international matches, 1900–1939[1]

	1900–14	1919–29	1930–9	Total
Won	11	10	12	33
Drawn	11	10	3	24
Lost	23	14	13	50

[1] Includes unofficial 1919 victory matches but not 1939 wartime internationals.

Although Wales won the home championship for the first time in 1907, it did not beat England once between 1900 and 1914. Results were hindered by the FAW being dependent on the goodwill of English clubs to release their Welsh players for international matches. In 1908 only four of the players initially selected for Wales against Ireland were released from their club duties in order to play.[49]

At the heart of international soccer's marginalization in south Wales were the players who were picked. Before 1914, the Welsh team was dominated by players born in north Wales and employed there or in England (see tables 6.3 and 6.4). Rural north Wales was economically and geographically marginalized from the industrial south, and it was also becoming increasingly so in linguistic and political terms. A team of unsuccessful northerners wearing a Welsh shirt might attract supporters wanting to see a higher class of football than was available at local clubs, but it would not generate a celebration of shared Welshness. Eric Hobsbawm has famously argued that 'the imagined community of millions seems more real as a team of eleven named people'.[50] Yet those players still had to represent the imagined community of which spectators felt part. Not only were Welsh international soccer's eleven named men not very successful but, more crucially, they were from environments remote from supporters in the south. In stark contrast, Edwardian Welsh international rugby could offer both repeated successes and a team of players from the south.

---

[49] *SWDN*, 13 April 1908. A football association could only demand the release of a player from his club commitments if the club came under the association's jurisdiction.
[50] Hobsbawm, *Nations and Nationalism since 1780* (Cambridge, 1990), p. 143.

1900–1914

	No. of players	%	No. of caps	%
Clwyd	41	48.8	275	55.4
Dyfed	6	7.1	25	5.0
Glamorgan	10	11.9	40	8.1
Gwynedd	7	8.3	19	3.8
Monmouthshire	0	0.0	0	0.0
Powys	13	15.5	65	13.1
Elsewhere	7	8.3	72	14.5
	84		496	

1920–1929

	No. of players	%	No. of caps	%
Clwyd	20	30.8	92	26.1
Dyfed	0	0.0	0	0.0
Glamorgan	35	53.8	210	59.7
Gwynedd	2	3.1	6	1.7
Monmouthshire	6	9.2	40	11.4
Powys	2	3.1	4	1.1
Elsewhere	0	0.0	0	0.0
	65		352	

1930–1939

	No. of players	%	No. of caps	%
Clwyd	13	17.8	36	10.9
Dyfed	1	1.4	7	2.1
Glamorgan	45	61.6	237	71.8
Gwynedd	2	2.7	3	0.9
Monmouthshire	11	15.1	46	13.9
Powys	1	1.4	1	0.3
Elsewhere	0	0.0	0	0.0
	73		330	

[1] Table drawn up from information in Davies and Garland, *Who's Who of Welsh International Soccer Players*, and Gareth M. Davies, *Soccer: The International Line-ups and Statistics Series – Wales, 1876–1960* (Cleethorpes, 1995). Includes D. Davies's appearance as a substitute in 1908 against England. Does not include the unofficial 1919 victory internationals, for which caps were not awarded, or the 1939 wartime internationals. International matches were not played during the First World War. In line with the contemporary regulations, players born outside Wales should not technically have been selected. The players concerned were all either born near the border or selected in ignorance of their place of birth or for unknown reasons. One Robert Evans actually played for both Wales and England before the First World War. He had been born in Chester but allegedly claimed, when signing for Wrexham, that he was born in Wales for which he went on to win ten caps. He appears to have later decided to play for England, and the truth about his place of birth came out. The disgruntled FAW claimed that he was Welsh in all but birth and selected him for a match against Ireland in 1911, despite the fact that he had already been picked for the England team. See *SWDN*, 19 and 23 January 1911.

Table 6.4

Distribution of players appearing for Wales by club[1]

1900–14	No. of appearances	1919–29	No. of appearances	1930–9	No. of appearances
South Wales					
Aberaman	1	Aberdare Athletic	2	Cardiff City	12
Aberdare	3	Cardiff City	79	Newport County	4
Cardiff City	4	Merthyr Town	2	Swansea City	16
Cardiff Corinthians	1	Newport County	4		
Llanelly	3	Swansea Town	36		
Merthyr Town	3				
Treharris	1	Cardiff Corinthians	1	Cardiff Corinthians	2
		Llanelly	1	Llanelly	1
		Lovell's Athletic	1		
	16 3.23%		126 33.69%		35 10.61%
North and mid-Wales					
Miscellaneous	45	Non-League	1	Non-League	4
Wrexham	67	Wrexham	18	Wrexham	16
	112 22.58%		19 5.08%		20 6.06%
England					
Professional Clubs	352	Football League	220	Football League	265
Amateur Clubs	13	Non-League	9	Non-League	1
	365 73.59%		229 61.23%		266 80.61%
Other					
Hibernian	3	None		Hearts of Midlothian	2
				Linfield (Ireland)	1
				Motherwell	6
	3 0.60%		0 0.00%		9 2.73%
Total appearances	496 100%		374 100%		330 100%

[1] Includes unofficial 1919 victory internationals.

As the Edwardian development of soccer in south Wales began to bear fruit, the region contributed an increasing proportion of players to the national side. This, together with the presence of Cardiff City players in the Scottish and Irish teams, developed the popularity of international matches in the south. There was particular pride at Ninian Park in 1924 when the opposing captains of Wales (Fred Keenor) and Scotland (Jimmy Blair) were both Cardiff City men. Yet attendances remained smaller than at prominent clubs. Thirty thousand watched the above game, but the following week 45,000–50,000 saw Cardiff City play Bristol City on the same ground.[51] There were as many as nine players with south Wales clubs in the Wales team that faced England at the Vetch in 1925, but the crowd was just 8,000. Before that match one fan complained that it 'would be a national (Welsh) calamity if Cardiff City failed to steer clear of relegation because their star players' services are claimed for the Welsh international side'. The concerned Cardiff press appealed that the struggling club's cause was a national one and that no Welsh victory would make up for relegation.[52] The FAW refused to change the selection despite the appeals of the City directors. But, by 1929, with confidence in Welsh club soccer at a much lower ebb, it was suggested that some Cardiff City and Swansea Town players were overlooked for selection for Wales because their clubs were in danger of relegation.[53] International soccer was playing second fiddle to the club game.

The reception given to success in the home championship never remotely approached the patriotic celebrations of the 1927 triumph.[54] As the press often pointed out, international soccer in south Wales was still being hindered by the number of players representing Wales who did not play for local clubs.[55] In the 1920s, nearly two-thirds of Welsh international players were with English or north Wales clubs. The majority may now have been born in the south, but they were more representative of their English teams than of their nation; there was not the same

[51] *FE*, 16, 23 February 1924. As well as Blair in the Scottish team, there were three Cardiff City players and one Swansea Town man in the Welsh team.
[52] *SWE*, 3, 6, 11 February 1925. The attendance was affected by heavy rain.
[53] *FE*, 26 January 1929.
[54] For example, see the muted reporting of Wales's winning of the home championship in *FE*, 15 March 1924.
[55] See, for example, *FE*, 23 January 1926, 26 January 1929.

relationship with players that existed at club matches, rugby internationals or even cricket.[56] Too many international players were famous names rather than actual personalities whom supporters knew and closely related to. Indeed, there was only a handful of players, such as Alex James, 'Dixie' Dean, Nat Lofthouse and Tommy Lawton, who were national figures.[57] Other Welshmen who achieved notable success beyond their native borders did become national heroes. Politicians like Lloyd George and boxers like Tommy Farr or Freddie Welsh established themselves outside Wales but did not lose their connection with their nation. The spheres they operated in did not allow them to reach the top at home; they had to go away to achieve success.[58] But in soccer during the 1920s, the Welsh clubs offered a route to the top, and thus those who made it with English teams were never going to be national heroes in the same way as those who stayed at home. Holt argues that league soccer was too self-absorbing, with an exhausting programme and strong club loyalties, for the English national side to be supported wholeheartedly.[59] It was no different in south Wales.

Thus, when a player left a club, his status as a representative of that area diminished. There was great pride in his achievements in his home town, but interest in him in the rest of south Wales was of a more anecdotal nature. When someone talented like Leslie Jones turned out for Arsenal, he was representing the London team more than Wales or even his home town of Aberdare. Thus, the pride in Welshmen who had made it with English clubs was never quite on the same level as a rugby hero, a boxing champion or even a good English player at the local soccer club. From time to time the press would mention how

---

[56] During the late nineteenth century, struggling Glamorgan County Cricket Club always retained some local players to ensure that it kept up local support. Hignell, *A Favourit' Game*, p. 179. In 1931, the need to be seen as representing south Wales in order to attract bigger gates was partially behind a decision by Glamorgan CCC to release three prominent English players. Hignell, *History of Glamorgan CCC*, p. 98. As in club soccer, this would not have been so important had the team been doing well.

[57] McKibbin, *Classes and Cultures*, p. 344.

[58] For example, see Dai Smith's discussion of Tommy Farr in his 'Focal heroes'.

[59] Holt, *Sport and the British*, p. 273. Instead, in England the north–south rivalry was more important in soccer. During a match against England at Wolverhampton, both leading soccer correspondents of the *Echo* noted that much of the English crowd had been cheering Wales. They put this down to the 'Arsenal complex': a provincial reaction against the selection of so many London-based players in the England team. *SWE*, 6 February 1936.

former players of the local club were doing, but such treatment
did not just apply to Welshmen but any former player of note.
When players at top English clubs came home to Merthyr for the
summer, while some soccer fans in the town 'adored' them, to
others they were not so much returning heroes but lucky men
who had a job, a regular income and the attention of the local
girls. And then when they took up the 'bank manager's game' of
golf they were deemed 'snooty'.[60] Of all the great south Wales
players in England in the 1930s, only Bryn Jones, after his
sensational world record transfer to Arsenal, stimulated any
widespread interest in the region itself. Success was sweetest
when it was tasted at home.

In 1930 the Welsh team was severely hit by a ruling by the
Football League that forbade English clubs from releasing any
non-English players on a Saturday.[61] Before the ruling was
relaxed somewhat in 1931, Wales was forced to play Scotland
with a team of 'unknowns', including nine new caps (three of
whom amateurs) and just one established international.[62] That
year, one first-division club refused even to release a selected
international who played in its reserves.[63] When internationals
were played in mid-week, obtaining the release of players was
not a problem, but the FAW preferred to play on Saturdays
when gate receipts were invariably bigger. The position improved in 1934 when, after the FAW withdrew from the 1931
compromise, a new agreement was secured whereby the English
Football League clubs consented to release the growing crop of
talented players for one Saturday international match in Wales a
year.[64] This led to consistently improved performances, and
Wales won the home international championship outright in
1933, 1934 and 1937 and shared it in 1939.

[60] W. R. King and Charles Jones, interviews.
[61] This was a rule voted for by Swansea Town (but not Cardiff City or Newport
County) despite the fact that it had no non-Welsh internationals. The Cardiff press self-
righteously insinuated a lack of loyalty to Wales when it reported the news. *FE*, 30
November 1929.
[62] Only four of the side regularly played in the Football League. The result, a 1–1
draw, led to the side receiving widespread acclaim outside Wales. For example, see match
report headed 'The glorious unknowns' in *Daily Record and Mail*, 27 October 1930. In line
with its general attitude towards international football, the south Wales press gave the
result a much more low-key reception.
[63] *FE*, 14 November 1931.
[64] The ongoing saga over the release of players is described in Geoffrey Green, *The
History of the Football Association* (London, 1953), pp. 313–18.

From the mid-1930s, success, allied with a slowly recovering economy and the belated FAW decision to play more often in Cardiff, brought attendances of over 40,000 and the biggest crowds that Welsh international soccer had ever enjoyed. A contest against England in 1938 set a new record for south Wales soccer with a gate of 55,000 at Ninian Park. Wales's talented forward line of the late 1930s was largely made up of former south Wales miners, and this no doubt drew men from the Valleys to the games. The performances were exciting and the achievements joyfully celebrated:

> Goal number four sent the crowd crazy. Bryn Jones started it with a wide sweeping pass to Cumner. Cumner beat Sprosten before turning the ball inwards to Astley. This brilliant centre-forward still had to beat Young, but he swept past him as if he did not exist. Woodley, scenting danger, came out, but Astley, cool and calculating, placed the ball past the advancing goalkeeper like a master.[65]

Yet, after the excitement had died down, the fact that the southern players played over the border brought out a sense of sadness. The decline of the local clubs meant that it was understandable that the region's best players went to England, and there was some pride that Welshmen were playing in Britain's top teams. But the performances of the Welsh side presented a stark contrast to the poor state of the domestic game and were a reminder of what could have been had the players whose 'mastery was nurtured on the slag-heaps of Merthyr, Bargoed or Pentre' stayed in Wales.[66] Victories were celebrated with pride but also with a touch of sadness. People flocked to see the successful Welsh side, heartily cheered their wins and sang the inevitable Welsh hymns but, with very few home-based players, neither they nor the press treated it as an unrestrained national celebration. Thus international soccer in Wales never quite had the same symbolic significance enjoyed by Welsh rugby or the game in Scotland where, thanks to home-based players and a

---

[65] *WM*, 24 October 1938.
[66] Ibid. Also see *WM*, 19 October 1936; *SWE*, 29 October 1937; *FE*, 30 October 1937, 22 October 1938.

history of successful results, any match against the 'auld enemy' was seen as an outright national competition.[67]

While the commitment of supporters in south Wales to the national side may not have been as nationalistically fervent as in Scotland, the attitude of the players reveals a different picture. Ron Burgess, a Welsh international in the 1940s and 1950s, said of his childhood in Cwm: 'one of the birthrights of every boy born in that humble mining community is to play football for his beloved Wales.'[68] Such patriotism owed as much to the inspiration of the FAW's extrovert secretary Ted Robbins as it did to national sentiment. The son of a Wrexham music-hall owner, Robbins was a showman and a patriot who dominated the association and was a 'father, friend and philosopher to the Welsh team'.[69] Walley Barnes, a Welsh captain in the 1940s and 1950s, wrote that Robbins 'appealed to the players through their mam and their dad, inspiring them to fight against the odds, and beyond normal ability; not as individuals, but as a team for the honour and glory of our little country'.[70] Some clubs tried to attract players by offering them contracts that guaranteed they would be released for international matches,[71] but money often took precedence. Birmingham City told Ernie Curtis that he could play for Wales, but should he do so his wages for the next season would be reviewed. He was forced to withdraw from Welsh teams and say that he would rather play for his club.[72] Ralph Williams was promised a Welsh cap by Ben Watts Jones, then a Swansea Town director and a member of the FAW council, if he signed for the club. However, Crewe Alexandra's offer of better wages meant that Williams ended up there instead.[73] A comment by Fred Keenor reveals a different aspect

[67]   See Moorhouse, 'Scotland against England'.
[68]   Burgess, *Football: My Life*, p. 8.
[69]   *SWE*, 6 October 1935.
[70]   Walley Barnes, *Captain of Wales* (London, 1953), p. 18. The informal and rousing approach used by the FAW was in complete contrast to the curt way in which the FA operated; it had the aloofness of an employer–employee relationship. See Rogan Taylor and Andrew Ward, *Kicking and Screaming: An Oral History of Football in England* (London, 1995), ch. 7.
[71]   In 1930, the Football League refused to endorse any such contract, thus further putting the selection of the Welsh national team at the mercy of clubs. *FE*, 15 March 1930; C. E. Sutcliffe, J. A. Brierley and F. Howarth, *The Story of the Football League* (Preston, 1938), p. 137.
[72]   Ceri Stennett, *The Soccer Dragons* (Cardiff, 1987), p. 7. Despite being at the height of his career, Curtis won only two further caps.
[73]   Letter from Alan Ralph Williams to Derrick Jenkins, 20 August 1987.

of Welsh patriotism amongst players: 'We Welshmen do not mind much if we have to bow the knee to Scotland or Ireland but we do take a special delight in whacking England.'[74] Amidst the competitive banter of nationally mixed dressing-rooms, such victories must have boosted the pride of Welsh players. In the eyes of fans, players may have lost something of their connection with Wales by moving to England, but as individuals they retained their own personal patriotism within a pragmatic realization of the need to make the most financially out of a short career.

THE WELSH CUP AND LEAGUE

Despite its national consciousness and patriotic celebrations, inter-war soccer in south Wales was essentially bound to the wider English club scene and it paid little regard to all-Wales competitions such as the Welsh Cup and League. Before 1914, the emerging soccer fraternity in the south had seen the Welsh Cup as an important route to establishing its credentials but, after the war, with local teams now playing in the higher standard and more prestigious Football League, the competition lost its appeal. Cardiff City et al. rarely fielded their first teams in the cup, and even the date of the final was often fitted around southern clubs' league fixtures.[75] Matches were generally not well attended and the local press rarely made any effort to hype the games. The venue of the 1920 Welsh Cup final was moved from Cardiff to Wrexham because it was felt that the latter town's team would not attract a large crowd in the south where crowds were used to watching the higher standard Southern League soccer.[76] For the clubs from the south, becoming champions of Wales held no appeal compared with the possibility of success on the English stage that the Football League and FA Cup offered; prestige was about recognition from outside the principality, not from the politically, culturally and economically distant north.

In contrast, clubs from the north were eager to use the Welsh Cup to proclaim their equality, and there was a sense of regret

[74] *FE*, 22 September 1934.
[75] Garland, *Welsh Cup*, p. 100.
[76] *SWE*, 15 April 1920.

about the south's apathetic attitude.[77] This attitude might have been different had north Wales possessed enough clubs of a sufficient standard to challenge consistently for the trophy. However, between 1920 and 1939, the trophy was only won five times by teams from the north. In the hope of raising the competition's status, the FAW invited English clubs to enter in the 1930s. Yet that failed to raise interest in the south.[78] The English teams that entered were mostly small clubs from the counties that bordered north and mid-Wales and meant little to the inhabitants of south Wales. The only result was embarrassment for the FAW, as the trophy left Wales on seven occasions during the 1930s. The FAW appealed for stronger efforts to bring the cup back to Wales, but the calls fell on deaf ears amongst south Wales clubs, whose eyes were focused on the more prestigious English competitions.[79]

The Welsh League, born out of a change of name by the Glamorgan League in 1912, initially set out to be as 'strong and important' as the Football League.[80] Like the creation of other Welsh national institutions in the Edwardian period, this drew upon a desire to declare Wales's nationhood and equality with England. However, it faced difficulties from the outset, with Cardiff City deciding to join the English-orientated Southern Alliance instead.[81] Newport County, Merthyr Town and Ton Pentre also temporarily resigned from the Welsh League in 1913 to concentrate on other competitions.[82] Although Cardiff City joined that year, the Welsh League was never a priority for clubs who also played in the higher-standard English leagues. In 1920, the Welsh League itself requested that its top two sides each season be promoted to the Football League.[83] The rejection of this request ensured that the League was consigned to a back seat. The Welsh League could not even guarantee its smaller members Saturday fixtures, as clubs with other commitments

[77] Garland, *Welsh Cup*, pp. 113, 115.
[78] Nor did it raise attendances as much as had been hoped in the north. Garland, *Welsh Cup*, p. 142.
[79] For example, the 1938–9 FAW *Annual Report* declared that it was the duty of every Welsh club to field its strongest sides and bring the trophy back to the principality.
[80] *SWDN*, 30 May, 1 July 1912.
[81] *SWDN*, 25 July 1912. The Welsh League unsuccessfully tried to get the FA and the FAW to block Cardiff City's action.
[82] *SWDN*, 11 June, 25 July, 9 October 1913.
[83] Inglis, *League Football and the Men who Made it*, p. 122.

struggled with a congested programme. Putting footballing practicalities before national sentiment, the leading south Wales clubs often only fielded reserve teams despite the League's rules insisting that they field their strongest sides. Yet such clubs felt the Welsh League's standard was not high enough to develop even their reserves sufficiently.[84] Cardiff City and Swansea Town both looked elsewhere for alternative competitions and, on various occasions, were members of the London Combination and the Birmingham and District League. With clubs treating the League so dismissively, its chances of ever becoming any kind of serious alternative to the Football League were minimal.

As the depression forced the closure of many senior south Wales clubs, the Welsh League plunged towards crisis. By 1929 there were only eleven clubs in its southern section, and seven of those played in other leagues as well.[85] With fewer teams and professional players, gates and the standard of play declined, further reducing the competition's status. Thus there was little incentive for Cardiff City and Swansea Town to use the competition as anything but a reserve league. The two clubs used Saturdays for matches in the Southern, London or Birmingham Leagues, whilst their Welsh League games were relegated to mid-week. For any Welsh League matches that had to be played on a Saturday, the clubs resorted to fielding third-choice teams. This led to anger and frustration amongst the League's other teams who accused the big two of lacking national pride.[86] As the depression began to bite deeper, and the senior clubs slipped down a Football League perceived to be hostile to Wales, the demands from the press and smaller clubs for a stronger Welsh League grew, using national prestige as an emotional motive. There were even isolated calls to make the League Welsh in ideals and inspirations through clubs supporting each other and only fielding Welshmen.[87] In reality such complaints were based on financial rather than patriotic concerns. Matches against the likes of Cardiff and Swansea brought the biggest attendances, so constantly having to play half-hearted reserve sides represented important missed financial opportunities for the smaller teams,

---

[84] For example, see *SWE*, 26 February 1925.
[85] *FE*, 4 May 1929.
[86] For example, see the complaints of Merthyr Town in *FE*, 19 December 1931.
[87] For example, *SWE*, 16 November 1931; *FE*, 4 May 1929.

particularly now there were no longer clubs in populous areas like Merthyr and Mid Rhondda to play against.[88] Yet, for the biggest clubs, footballing and financial concerns meant that the Welsh League was simply not a priority. Had the Welsh League been able to offer soccer of a similar standard to the Football League, then it might have stood a better chance. However, there were simply not enough populous towns to sustain a competitive league with high-quality players.

Despite its title, the Welsh League was not a national organization, and a competition of the same name also existed in the north. In the early 1920s, the competitions carried the titles of southern and northern sections, although both operated autonomously. Southern clubs rejected a proposal to merge the two sections in 1923, while the FAW gave the idea brief consideration on a number of occasions but never followed the idea through.[89] Support for such a truly national league was always stronger in the north. Playing the southern giants, even if it was only their reserves, promised better gates than a northern league and offered the challenge of proving equality with the other half of the nation. The 1938–9 *North Wales Football Annual* carried an appeal for a national league but also contained a note from Ted Robbins, the FAW secretary, claiming that the geography and multiplicity of thinly populated areas in Wales made such a proposal impractical.[90] This was recognition that Wales was as much a collection of regions as it was a unified nation. Thus north and south retained their own separate leagues, with travelling expenses and the lack of large urban areas in the north making any other arrangement impractical. The poor support inward-looking Welsh club rugby received compared with its international matches illustrates that the public was more interested in competing with the English. Thus the failure of the Welsh League to rival the Football League owed much to the nature of Welsh identity in the south. As in political spheres,

---

[88] See *FE*, 8 October 1938, 19 November 1938.

[89] The southern section dropped the title in 1923 and the northern section folded in 1930, to be replaced by a competition that had formerly been a Cheshire league. Alun Evans, 'Football on the edge: the relationship between Welsh football policy-making and the British international championship' (De Montfort University, unpublished MA thesis, 1996), pp. 33–4; Garland, *Welsh Cup*, pp. 129, 109; *SWE*, 27 March 1930.

[90] *North Wales Football Annual 1938–9*, quoted in Gareth M. Davies, *A Coast of Soccer Memories, 1894–1994* (Colwyn Bay, 1994), pp. 64–5.

Welsh aspirations overwhelmingly lay in competing with England and not in chasing independence or separation. Achieving equality with England meant clubs playing in English competitions.

'SEVERELY ANTI-WELSH'

Welsh clubs saw themselves as a community of sorts in a way that does not appear to have any parallel in England. In 1930, Swansea Town lobbied other clubs to try to help Merthyr Town get re-elected to the Football League. A year later, Llanelly AFC withdrew its Football League application in order to strengthen Newport County's bid for re-election.[91] Cardiff City played financially struggling Caerphilly Town in an effort to raise both money and interest in its smaller neighbour.[92] The co-operation between Welsh clubs may never have gone as far as the press would have liked, but it nonetheless illustrates that directors did feel a sense of regional and Welsh identity.[93]

The often marginal position of Welsh clubs within the English soccer establishment was key to this sense of identity. In 1910, the south Wales clubs that resigned from the Western League complained that some of the league's administrators and members were 'anti-Welsh'.[94] The presence of Welsh teams in English competitions was a source of tension throughout the period. The result was a sense of persecution and a heightened feeling of Welsh identity in south Wales soccer circles as its sense of 'otherness' was exacerbated. In 1921, amidst much dismay in south Wales, the FA put forward a proposal to prevent non-English clubs taking part in the FA Cup.[95] In opposition, the

[91]   *ME*, 28 June 1930; *SWA*, 1 June 1931.
[92]   *SWE*, 25 October 1921.
[93]   The press frequently urged co-operation between Welsh clubs over everything from the loaning of players to the dates of fixtures. See, for example, *FE*, 9 February 1929.
[94]   Had there not also been financial issues at stake, the clubs would not have acted so drastically. *SWDN*, 20 June, 1 July 1910.
[95]   The FA was said to be angry over various incidents in Wales, such as a junior club disbanding rather than paying the cost of an FA commission it had requested. The loyally British *Athletic News* was a defendant of the Welsh clubs' right to play in the competition, even arguing that it was only fair, since Wales had fought for England in the Great War. It also argued that, in light of the FA's efforts to promote the game on the Continent, it was wrong to impoverish neighbouring clubs at home. *SWE*, 20 December 1921; *Athletic News* quoted in *ME*, 28 January 1922; *SWE*, 16 January 1922.

South Wales Echo even brought up the hardened rugby follower's adage that south Wales clubs were, for practical purposes, English, playing in English competitions under English rules.[96] The end result was a compromise whereby only fourteen Welsh clubs were allowed to enter each year, although fears for the deal continued to arise periodically. The Football League's attempts to prevent Welsh players from being released for Saturday internationals was another source of lingering tension. The English authorities' obstinate attitude to Wales was typified for many people by the FA's refusal to pick Billy Hardy for England, widely believed to be because he played for a Welsh club.

In 1931, with the Football League's intransigence over the release of players under debate, the sense of persecution in Wales intensified. That year, it looked as if Cardiff City was going to be forced to play in an FA Cup qualifying round. The club directors felt insulted, especially since the Corinthians, an English amateur side, were given a bye until the third round. Also that year, Newport County was expelled without a hearing from the competition for involvement in an illegal sweepstake. All this, together with the failures of Aberdare Athletic, Merthyr Town and Newport County to secure re-election to the Football League, encouraged the belief that the English soccer authorities wanted Welsh clubs out of their competitions. Among the advocates of this theory were the Merthyr Town chairman, the mayor of Newport and, after initial scepticism, the *South Wales Echo*'s chief soccer reporter.[97] The *Echo* claimed that the FA and Football League had become

> severely anti-Welsh . . . [and] they are missing no opportunity of demonstrating it and they will continue to do so at the slightest provocation . . . readers need no reminder of the extremely harsh treatment Wales and Welsh clubs have received from their so called friends across the border.[98]

Welsh clubs, it was felt, should be helped through their financial difficulties, not further attacked. A Swansea Town correspondent claimed that Welsh clubs were unpopular with their English peers

[96] *SWE*, 2 January 1922.
[97] *SWE*, 2 May, 2 November, 1 June 1931; *FE* 28 November 1931. The Newport mayor was a club director.
[98] *FE*, 12 December 1931.

because of the higher travelling expenses incurred in playing there, and 'the strange idea that they are in some foreign land'.[99] There was certainly some resentment amongst English clubs that their share of the receipts at Aberdare or Merthyr often did not cover travelling expenses. Whether or not there was a genuine anti-Welsh campaign, the allegations served to heighten national consciousness in the game. In 1931, the year in which the sense of persecution peaked, the depression also reached its worst point, and the situation in soccer reflected a wider feeling in Wales that an English-based government was ignoring its suffering. Amongst soccer clubs and administrators, this may have developed national consciousness, but neither in the game nor in society and politics was the perceived solution seen in nationalistic terms. Outside soccer, the feeling of marginalization raised class consciousness and developed socialist sympathies, while within the game the resulting attitude was a sense of frustration. The financial and emotional importance of playing in the English soccer system was simply too great to allow the sense of persecution to develop into any separatist sense of anti-Englishness.

CONCLUSION

Sport can give life to national identities that otherwise often remain unarticulated and subconscious in everyday life. In creating the 'imagined communities' that Benedict Anderson famously described nations as, it is more real and accessible than any vague notion of a common history or inheritance.[100] For nations without a state, ethnic basis or even linguistic unity, sport takes on an added significance. For many people in the so-called Celtic fringes of Britain, it is one of the few pieces of tangible evidence that their nation exists. The team concerned does not actually have to play under the title of a nation or consist of players from that country. Sides like Cardiff City, composed of men from the four corners of the UK, became representatives of Wales when playing against English opposition in prestigious matches. Just as in war, sport provided an identifiable 'other' that united people

[99] *FE*, 5 September 1936.
[100] Benedict Anderson, *Imagined Communities* (London, 1991).

behind a sense of who they were not. Yet, despite the patriotic rhetoric surrounding important club matches, it was not reflective of an overriding wider unity between south and north. Regional identity in the north of England was contained within the locality; it was neither a separate nor a distinctive identity. Thus Yorkshire saw its identity as synonymous with northernness.[101] Similarly, in south Wales, national identity was based on, and intertwined with, a sense of regional pride. The south was a fragmented unit with no cultural signs or language of its own. It thus appropriated those of Wales. Nowhere is this clearer than in the claim of rugby union in south Wales to be the national sport.

Industrial south Wales was undoubtedly proud of its Welshness, but without really identifying with the rural north. When the press spoke of the 'big three' Welsh clubs, they did not think of including Wrexham in the number.[102] Like Britain as a whole,[103] Wales enjoyed both unity and diversity. In line with the nature of the communities this Welsh identity represented, it incorporated anyone who could cement it, as long as they retained a connection with the region. In the case of professional soccer players, their strongest bond was with the club they played for every week. An Englishman playing for Cardiff City was more of a local representative than a man from Merthyr playing for Arsenal. Therefore, men in the national side who had left the region, or came from the north, did not always easily fit into a national identity rooted in regionalism. They were not completely excluded from the equation, as the pride in Bryn Jones or Billy Meredith showed, but it was those who lived in the south who were most prominent in it. Good soccer was always going to be appreciated and the region still felt a pride in a wider Wales, but for it to be a regional, and thus patriotic celebration, it had to be clearly associated with the south. The regional nature of this national identity reinforced its concern with recognition from England, rather than competing with the north or seeking separation from the British context. If English players and competitions offered a route to glory on a wider platform, they

[101] Richard Holt, 'Heroes of the North: sport and the shaping of regional identity', in Hill and Williams (eds.), *Sport and Identity*, p. 140.

[102] For example, *FE*, 29 August 1936.

[103] Keith Robbins, *Nineteenth-century Britain: Integration and Diversity* (Oxford, 1988), p. 183.

were adopted. To the people of south Wales, loyalties and identities were complex, intertwined and even contradictory. A multi-national team could be turned into Welsh heroes, whilst a side of Welshmen bearing the name of Wales could be given a less euphoric reception. Soccer not only reflected this diversity, it helped to shape it. The songs and dress of supporters and the patriotic talk of the press represent a symbolic flagging of nation-hood by the media, fans and players. As Hill points out, they 'are the routine signs through which the sense of nation is daily communicated. They are probably more important for under-standing nationhood than the more obvious manifestations of national propaganda.'[104]

Above the level of Welsh identity was the question of Wales's Britishness. Farmer and Stead argue that 'true Britishness was more fully evident in the players of the English league system . . . than in anything since Lord Kitchener's armies in the First World War'.[105] As commemorations of the war illustrated, for a majority a pride in Wales sat comfortably alongside a sense of Britishness. Indeed, the whole shared experience of the Great War had probably intensified that sense of belonging to Britain.[106] The commitment of clubs and supporters to English competitions illustrated how Wales was not particularly interested in asserting its independence. The local press's prominent quotation of extracts from English newspapers that praised south Wales teams after a notable win illustrated Welsh pride in any recognition of its equal place in Britain. Similarly, Wales played only two internationals against non-British sides in the period and declined invitations from Germany and Italy, amongst others, in the late 1930s. To risk losing against Fascist regimes was to risk damaging British prestige.[107] Popular Welsh patriotism not only sat comfortably within a British state and culture, it was emotionally and politically committed to the United Kingdom.

[104] Hill, 'Cocks, cats, caps', p. 3.
[105] David Farmer and Peter Stead, *Ivor Allchurch MBE: The Authorised Biography of the Legendary Golden Boy* (Swansea, 1998), p. 8.
[106] Gaffney, *Aftermath*, ch. 8; Chris Williams, ' "Welsh soldiers in a British army": the experience of the First World War' (unpublished paper, 2000).
[107] Wales's two overseas internationals were against France in 1933 and 1939. *SWE*, 19 April 1939. The FAW secretary denied that the refusal was because of the international situation. Instead, he unconvincingly said that, because of the position of some clubs, he felt unable to ask them to release players. See Beck, *Scoring for Britain*, for an examination of the increasing political role of international soccer.

CONCLUSION:
'IRREDEEMABLY PROLETARIAN AND ENGLISH'[1]

A man in my town was a strong enemy of Welshness . . . He had some
spare cash and dreamed of being a Tory demagogue after the style of
Joseph Chamberlain. He wanted to take the town's mind off the fears
raised by the slump that started in Wall Street, America, and ran in a
straight line to Dinas, Rhondda Fawr.

He decided to start a soccer team. 'Rugby players tend to talk Welsh,' he
said. 'I don't want them. That oval ball is the symbol of deviousness. A
round, candid ball and no pawing of bodies, that's the honest English way.'

The soccer did not flourish. The pitch was riven by subsidence and the
dirt surface collapsed beneath the striker's feet when he was poised to score
his only goal of the season.

Gwyn Thomas, 'Confusion as a culture in itself'[2]

Between 1900 and 1939, south Wales was transformed from a
Liberal bastion to a class-conscious Labour heartland. That
process also saw the establishment of soccer as an integral component of the region's popular culture. The basis of the sport's
development was the very working-class in-migration that undermined Liberal Wales. This contributed to the view of soccer as
'irredeemably proletarian and English'. In this light, the growth
of association football and class consciousness in south Wales
initially seem interrelated. Yet soccer also became a vehicle for
Welsh national identity in the region between the wars, while
control of the game lay in the hands of the middle classes. This
conclusion examines the interpretation of association football in
south Wales as an un-Welsh and working-class sport.

In 1914, the *Welsh Outlook*, a new publication expounding a
Liberal, Nonconformist ethos, declared:

The Association Code in Wales is new and alien and comes in the back of
its popularity elsewhere: it is the game of the alien of the valleys whose

---

[1] Williams, *When was Wales?*, p. 221.
[2] *High on Hope* (Cowbridge, 1985), pp. 23–4.

immigration and denationalising tendency is one of the major problems of our country. It is best reported in alien newspapers . . .[3]

Soccer's growth was recognized as a portent of wider changes. The article argued that the game itself was 'fine' and 'manly' with benefits for the community and individual. It even defended professionalism to an extent. What concerned its author was that soccer would cause a realignment in the focus of popular culture in Wales:

> The centres of interest will consequently be in Newcastle, Manchester, London, and the eyes of its followers will be outward and not inward. The intimate value of internal rivalry will be absent and the social context of the game will be cosmopolitan.

In contrast, he saw Welsh rugby as 'a discovery of democracy which acts as participant and patron . . . A game democratic and amateur is a rare thing – a unique thing to be cherished.' Such a game reflected well on the nation that supported it. The writer felt that the rise of a sport with no Welsh characteristics, and whose popularity threatened rugby, should be resisted. As Dai Smith points out, it was similar fears for Wales's democracy that characterized the condemnation of riotous behaviour and strikes.[4] The bonds of community and nation, which were thought to be manifested in rugby, were sacred and to be held on to in a changing world.

In drawing a direct analogy between the rise of soccer and the threats to Liberal Wales, the *Welsh Outlook* article is an exception. Little of the disdain and hostility that the dribbling code had to face can be attributed directly to any feeling that the game was a signal of profound socio-cultural change. On the eve of the Great War, Liberal Wales appeared safe and stable. Its values, traditions and symbols still bound together the communities and classes of the south and the cracks that had begun to emerge seemed to be closing. The scale of industrial disputes had receded, syndicalism remained only the creed of a small, if vocal, minority of miners, while the Labour Party continued to find

---

[3] *Welsh Outlook*, 1 (February 1914).
[4] David Smith, 'Wales through the looking-glass', in David Smith (ed.), *A People and a Proletariat: Essays in the History of Wales, 1780–1980* (London, 1980), p. 228.

parliamentary success elusive.[5] Even the key Labour figure of
Keir Hardie MP continued to poll fewer votes than the Liberals
in his two-seat constituency of Merthyr Boroughs. Few could
have anticipated how radically the political and economic map
of south Wales would change in the next decade.

Soccer was not marginalized because of professionalism or any
equating of it with the proletarianizing of the workers.[6] Its
development was based on the financial support of middle-class
patrons who spoke of community values, and while there was a
distaste for overt professionalism in the higher echelons of Welsh
rugby, rugby's own liberal interpretations of expenses meant that
there was hardly a strong antipathy towards paying players. The
commitment to amateurism owed more to a desire to remain
within the British rugby union community than a belief that
professionalism highlighted class differences. As the patrons of
the association code in England and Wales knew, one could
openly pay a player and promote his game as a social harmon-
izer. Instead, the bulk of the onslaughts that soccer faced before
1914 represented the fears of the rugby fraternity that their sport
was being pushed into the background. While professionalism
may not have been equated with proletarianism, neither was it
equated with the kind of cross-class democracy that Welsh rugby
took pride in. Professional games were played by workers, not by
the social mix that made Welsh rugby, and by implication Wales,
unique. A decline in rugby would mean that Wales lost something more than just a game. For this reason, Liberal Wales was
keen to uphold the sport. Yet there was little reason to suppose
that a decline in the game's popularity was part of an impending
cataclysm for Liberal Wales. The democratic harmony that
rugby was thought to promote was not based on sport alone.
Soccer's threat to the popularity of rugby may have been
obvious, but the threat of a proletarian culture to the Wales that
rugby represented was not, and to equate the two took a leap of
the mind that only the most prophetic took.

By 1930, the Welsh economy seemed in ruins. In the coal
industry, prices had collapsed and markets disappeared, while
unemployment was becoming a near-epidemic. Alongside the

---

[5] Morgan, *Rebirth of a Nation*, pp. 153–5.
[6] Contrary to the argument in Evans, 'Football on the edge', p. 27

economic upheavals was an equally significant political realignment. In the 1929 general election, the Labour Party won twenty-five of Wales's thirty-six seats, including every constituency in Cardiff and the coalfield, and the Liberals were driven back to the rural periphery. It was clear for all to see that the nation's 'Edwardian high noon' had come to an end in a decade of tumultuous change. The maturation of soccer in the 1920s was yet more evidence that south Wales was experiencing a profound change that went beyond economics. It is from the early 1920s that the majority of nationalistic attacks on the dribbling code date. The internationalist language that socialism spoke, and which had been given a new heroic impetus by the 1917 Russian revolution, was an increasing threat to the Liberals' patriotic vision of Wales. Every general election and strike brought more evidence that the threat was real. The growth of soccer with its 'foreign' heroes at the expense of the honestly Welsh sport of rugby could not be divorced from the wider political picture. Compounding this idea that the association code was at odds with Liberal, imperial Wales was the memory of the soccer authorities' decision in 1914 to play on while others fell on the fields of France.

Soccer's alien image meant that it began to draw attacks, not only from the rugby fraternity, but also from Welsh nationalist and cultural figures too. The ideology of inter-war Welsh nationalism was anti-industrial and in favour of a rural, Welsh-speaking society. Spectator sports, with their urban roots, were out of sorts with such a vision. Iorwerth Peate, a prominent folk writer, historian and cultural nationalist, saw the reading of the *Football Echo* as one of the symbols of a community adopting English customs at the expense of traditional Welsh ones.[7] Meanwhile, Caradoc Evans, a prominent writer and exposer of the hypocrisy of traditional Wales, saw the Welsh ideal as acting with humility and decorum in victory. To him, the 'fuss' that followed the 1927 cup final was organized by Cardiff Scots, while most Welshmen were not 'leavened with any great pride or sinful vanity', knowing that, had the team been all-Welsh, it would have scored as many goals as it had players.[8] The jubilation and indecorum of

---

[7] *SWE*, 13 January 1927.
[8] *Sunday Express*, 1 May 1927.

the victory did not fit with his vision of the nation. Despite its popular impact, the Welsh-language press and periodicals gave scant coverage to the 1927 cup final. The pastimes of their Wales were the traditional cultural, religious and linguistic practices rather than the vulgarities of the football field.

To the masses, such high-minded disdain was irrelevant. They neither drew distinctions between amateurs and professionals nor argued over the subtleties of what was Welsh. For the majority of miners, dockers and their peers, the Liberal agenda had always been somewhat out of touch, while the nationalists were simply an irrelevance. Even before the First World War, disestablishment, temperance and the other staple Liberal values were of increasingly marginal interest to south Wales's working class. In retrospect, the popularity of soccer after 1910 can be seen as further evidence that the Liberal definition of Edwardian Wales was far from all-encompassing. By 1914, at club level at least, rugby could no longer claim to be the national game in south Wales, while in the north that assertion had always been false. Yet, with the achievements of the Welsh rugby fifteen over-shadowing the changes in domestic sport, the place of soccer in a popular national identity was yet to be defined. That national identity was built on the achievements and successes that had sprung from the economic confidence of Edwardian Wales. Soccer in south Wales had yet to provide comparable triumphs. The game still awaited its 1905.

The rise of left-wing politics was not, for all but a minority of extremists, incompatible with national pride. Chris Williams has argued that in the Rhondda national identity was marginal although not irrelevant compared with the 'intermeshing of class and community solidarities'.[9] In the everyday experience of the Valleys it may have been marginal, but, as the great cup-runs of the 1920s and the continuing popularity of the rugby inter-nationals demonstrated, it was still something to be celebrated should the right circumstances arise. Indeed, in the depressed economic conditions of south Wales, the psychological need for any celebration must have been all the greater. On the back of economic problems, the bitter legacy of the war and Lloyd George's failure to build his 'land fit for heroes', the people of the

<hr>

[9] Williams, *Democratic Rhondda*, p. 212.

industrial south had redefined what Wales meant in their eyes. Welshness, like any identity, is fluid and the people of Wales have consistently reinvented themselves throughout history.[10] The achievements in the 1920s of Cardiff City and others provided the success that soccer needed to be incorporated into a definition of what was Welsh. Soccer in south Wales could now take its place alongside rugby as a Welsh sport in a remade Wales.

The proliferation of English-based players meant that the association code's international matches could not rival its rugby counterparts in their expressions of patriotism but, as long as success was forthcoming at club level, south Wales could unite and rejoice in soccer's achievements. The cup and league competitions offered attractive and exciting opportunities to achieve what Wales had always sought: recognition in a British context. The successes of the likes of Cardiff City were too short-lived for soccer to be permanently connected with Wales in the eyes of outsiders or even later Welsh generations. However, during the inter-war years, working-class south Wales celebrated its Welshness wherever it could, and the 'people's game' offered a vehicle alongside the rugby international for the people to do so. Compared with war, religion and other agencies of modernity, sport may be minor in creating national identities but it is still significant.[11] With the decline of the chapel, the Welsh language, its associated culture and the Welsh rugby team, soccer did much to keep a popular and active sense of national pride alive in inter-war south Wales. Amidst the social and economic upheavals of the inter-war years, the evidence which soccer provided that national pride could still unite fragmented communities was a relief to many. Thus, the press was keen to emphasize and flag the patriotic side of soccer occasions and the supporters who attended them. Yet the patriotic celebrations were not evidence that the message of the left was not reaching home. Socialism may have spoken an international language but many of those who preached and believed it were still proud of their nation. As in times of war, it was a case of my country right or left. Indeed, the power and popularity of socialism were incorporating the left into the evolving definitions of Wales.

[10]   This is the central theme in Williams, *When was Wales?*
[11]   Hill, 'Cocks, cats, caps', p. 18.

This pride in Wales and Welshness signified neither a strong sense of unity with north Wales nor a lack of British patriotism. North Wales was a distant and rural world to people in the south and patriotic language in the south was often primarily articulating a regional pride. McKibbin argues that the 'English industrial working class was neither politically nor culturally homogeneous, but love of football united them almost more than anything else'.[12] Despite historians' arguments of an 'alternative culture' in the coalfield, and the expressions of a Welsh identity that were seen in soccer, association football was something that united Welsh workers with a wider British working-class culture.[13] Nor was there really any such thing as Welsh soccer: instead, there was soccer in Wales. Patriotism on the terraces did not change what was on the pitch or in the boardroom. Indeed, the game in Wales took an active pride in being part of a Britain that had invented the sport, taken it to the world and still enjoyed the respect of foreign teams. This international popularity that soccer enjoyed also gave the game a status that rugby could not match. When England played Italy in 1934, the Welsh press could be found hoping for an English win in the interest of British prestige, and to put Italy in its place for using the title of world champions when the home nations had not entered that year's World Cup.[14] Through soccer, Wales enjoyed a place at the heart of what was becoming a global culture.

To the outside world, south Wales was an intensely class-based society, a hotbed of communists and revolutionaries threatening to call to revolt the aimless masses standing in the long dole queues. Class was unquestionably an important concept in the region and played a defining role in the politics of south Wales. To the poor and the ill-treated, it was at the root of the injustices they suffered and socialism drew on this in promising an answer to their problems. Yet the impact of the rise of socialism and class consciousness on sport was less obvious. Professional soccer clubs portrayed themselves as community bodies, representatives of a town and its people. However, broadly speaking, they were run by the middle classes and supported by the workers.

[12] McKibbin, *Classes and Cultures*, p. 340.
[13] Hywel Francis and David Smith, *The Fed: A History of the South Wales Miners in the Twentieth Century* (London, 1980).
[14] *SWE*, 13 November 1934.

Conflicts arose between the two groups but they did not degenerate into the class-ridden battles that were often prevalent elsewhere. Nor did the British Labour movement incorporate sport into its political outlook. It drew its support from its economic and social promises and the personal appeal of its leaders, rather than from preaching an all-encompassing ideo-logical message. Despite soccer's integral place in working-class culture, there is no evidence that the workers who followed it looked upon the game as their exclusive preserve or a site of resistance. The game's professional status meant that it was reliant on the financial support of middle-class patrons. If they ran clubs fairly and ensured a reasonable level of success on the pitch, then their presence was accepted. This does not mean that supporters passively embraced the narratives espoused by club directors and the press of an integral relationship between soccer and community. A club perceived to be run badly could not expect unconditional support. Yet, even then, socialist calls to replace the incompetents at the top, or even the system itself, were not repeated in soccer. Even in the radical hotbed that was the Rhondda, the collapse of senior soccer clubs met with resigned acceptance rather than calls to end the capitalist nature of professional sport. Finding oneself hungry and out of work may have been a reason to turn to radical solutions – one's team's failures were not. Similarly, in the junior game, the failures of the like of the BWSF further illustrate how south Wales's support of socialism was not, for most, the adoption of an all-encompassing ideology. Radicalism was the political solu-tion turned to by a disillusioned people rather than the popular ethos of a revolutionary working class. The experience of soccer suggests that class was not a dominant concept in south Wales. It was not the only window through which workers looked at life, and neither should it be used as a basis from which to study all aspects of the region's history.

It is often argued that there was an inherent degree of con-servatism amongst the British working class, with identities and values beyond class continuing to retain strong meanings.[15] Yet the interests of community were paramount to the Labour

---

[15] For example, see Ross McKibbin, *The Ideologies of Class: Social Relations, 1880–1950* (Oxford, 1990), ch. 1.

movement and closely equated with class. In turn, its domination of the region associated the left with Welsh identity.[16] Soccer provides evidence that class consciousness was indeed part of a much wider, more complex, and even contradictory system of values. Most of south Wales's working class felt other loyalties such as family, neighbourhood, community and nation; the values so cherished by the Liberals in Edwardian Wales did not die out with the growth of socialism. A man or woman could vote Labour, or even Communist, and still give money to a local soccer team that was run by the middle class and operated within a capitalist system. Such loyalties to local clubs show that popular perceptions of the community, even in the industrial Valleys, incorporated the middle classes, a group often marginalized or even forgotten in the inter-war history of south Wales. The game also neatly illustrates the different communities to which people could relate. A miner could support his village team, the Welsh League club representing his valley, the Football League side in the nearby coastal town and his country on international day. This would not detract from his class consciousness or his associated political beliefs. Class, community and radical politics were not incompatible and, especially in the coalfield, were closely equated for many.

Community identities were as malleable and complex as those of class. The actual extent of the loyalty which a club received depended on its performances and its supporters' economic circumstances. The attachment to a Football League club of a soccer fan from the Valleys was strongest when the team was doing well and he could afford the 1s. entry and the train fare to the ground. The attraction of good soccer in a neighbouring town might develop an affinity with a place that he never really felt before. In times of hardship, the free entertainment the village side offered on the local welfare ground held considerable appeal. Today's view of the game's 'good old days', when everyone supported their local club, has a degree of romanticism running through it. For the inter-war soccer supporter, 'local' often meant an easy train journey (or a long walk) rather than the nearest club.

---

[16] See R. Merfyn Jones, 'Beyond identity? the reconstruction of the Welsh', *Journal of British Studies*, 31, 4 (1992), 339–43.

The nostalgic picture of soccer's history has much to do with the commercial domination of the modern game. Yet finance also underpinned all aspects of soccer between 1900 and 1939. The relationship between supporters and directors was shaped by beliefs about how much money was available and how it should be spent. The wider economic climate shaped soccer's Edwardian rise and then its inter-war decline. The apathetic attitude of the region's senior clubs towards the Welsh Cup and League would have been different had there been trainloads of supporters willing to part with their shillings to watch matches in these competitions. Even junior soccer, which existed outside the commercial sector, was vulnerable to wider economic upheavals. Soccer was part of a capitalist system in which finance shaped all aspects of leisure, not least the time, space and money available to play and watch. Commercialization had brought sport in from the margins of public life, and once it was there it governed its existence.

Recent literature has lamented the failure of pre-war supporters to push for representation and the reluctance of clubs and authorities to work with them.[17] When their team was meeting expectations, to demand consultation or financial openness did not occur to most fans. In times of trouble, directors did co-operate with supporters, even if, as the case of Cardiff City shows, there was a degree of hesitation at larger clubs. Each side had expectations of the other; they complained when these were not met, but also tried to work together to help their clubs. This may not have given supporters a genuine democratic and influential voice, but it is difficult to see just what running a club in, say, the manner of a trade union would have achieved. As long as the wider game operated in a capitalist system, then no amount of democratic control would have increased clubs' fortunes. To succeed, a beleaguered soccer club needed a large injection of capital, and no working-class supporter could provide that.

Despite the fears of the rugby fraternity and the commercial nature of the sport, soccer was a democratic game to the extent that it conformed to the patriarchal conception of democracy

---

[17] See the work of Rogan Taylor, in particular his *Football and its Fans* and 'Walking alone together: football supporters and their relationship with the game', in Williams and Wagg (eds.), *British Football and Social Change: Getting into Europe*.

prevalent at the time. Just as work, politics and play were primarily male arenas, so soccer was dominated by men, projected masculine values and encouraged the two sexes to spend less time with each other. As Welsh international Trevor Ford wrote, 'Football is not a women's game, it's not a pastime for milksops or cissies, it's a man's game . . . a tough, rough, catch-'em-young and hit 'em hard game.'[18] The game was never watched or played by anything but a proportion of the population, but no pastime ever will be, and soccer's impact went far beyond those actively involved. Association football crossed class boundaries and contributed to a popular pride in community and nation. Like rugby, soccer in south Wales was a democratic sport, a people's game, and by the early 1920s the two stood alongside each other as integral parts of the region's popular culture.

Historians and contemporaries have measured inter-war south Wales by means of the working class and their activities. The region's sport was no different and, despite its cross-class involvement, it had a working-class identity derived from the faces and ethics of the popular banks and players. As Patrick Joyce argues, culture is the foundation of consciousness. Watching professional soccer was an integral part of a working-class culture that helped to define that class.[19] Yet soccer (and rugby) also illustrated how popular or mass culture could not be neatly equated with class. Sport articulated and helped to shape the different community, economic and geographic identities that divided the working class. What those identities actually were was contextual and could range from a street to a nation. Furthermore, not every working man could afford to watch soccer or even wanted to. Yet the working class in south Wales was proud of its Welshness, no matter how marginal it was in everyday life. Thus, the enduring popularity of rugby union and the national celebrations that accompanied soccer's successes were evidence of the diversity of the British working class. Just as pride in rugby league in the north of England and in association football in central Scotland showed, the rising class consciousness of inter-war Britain did not bring a uniform working-class culture. Other

---

[18] Ford, *I Lead the Attack*, p. 50.
[19] Patrick Joyce, *Democratic Subjects: Self and the Social in Nineteenth-century England* (Cambridge, 1994), p. 12; Hobsbawm, *Worlds of Labour*, chs. 10, 11.

identities, although often submerged in the world of politics, retained too much meaning to be completely superseded. The articulation of identities was essentially situational; a class, conscious and proud of itself, did not abandon the different allegiances that gave it a diverse and complex meaning. The brotherhood of workers may have been a popular political call in south Wales, but many of those same workers still enjoyed their team being top of the league, especially if it was at the expense of the English.

APPENDIX A

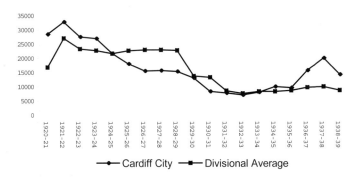

Average Football League Attendances in South Wales, 1920–1939

1920–1 promoted to Division One
1928–9 relegated to Division Two
1930–1 relegated to Division Three (South)

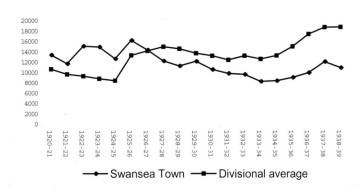

1924–5 promoted to Division Two

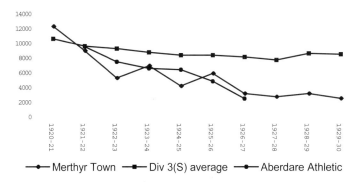

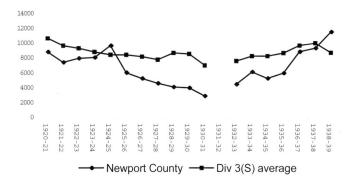

Summer 1931 failed to secure re-election to Division Three (South)
Summer 1932 re-elected to Division Three (South)

These figures were compiled from information in Brian Tabner, *Through the Turnstiles* (Harefield, 1992). For the post-1925 figures Tabner used the ledgers of the Football League, while for the earlier information he relied on reports in the *Athletic News* and the contemporary local and national press.

APPENDIX B

Comparison of directorates at selected English (pre-1914) and south Wales clubs by occupational group (percentages)[1]

	South Wales pre-1915	post-1918	English non-league	Football League
A: Aristocracy and gentry	–	–	11.1	3.6
B: Upper professional	22.4	14.6	7.8	11.3
C: Lower professional	5.3	4.9	5.6	7.8
D: Proprietors and employers associated with drink trade	17.1	12.2	6.7	12.4
E: Other proprietors and employers	27.6	35.4	28.9	38.4
F: Managers and higher administration	6.6	7.3	13.3	9.1
G: Clerical	6.6	2.4	2.2	7.5
H: Foremen, supervisors and inspectors	6.6	4.9	13.3	1.5
I: Skilled manual	9.2	17.1	2.2	7.8
J: Semi-skilled manual	–	–	–	0.7
K: Unskilled manual	–	–	–	–

[1] South Walian clubs represented are: Abertillery, Cardiff City, Ebbw Vale, Llanelly, Mid Rhondda, Newport County, Risca District, Tredegar and Swansea Town. One-year sample used for each club. Lists of directors in company files and registers at the PRO and Companies House, Cardiff. Figures for England calculated from Vamplew, *Pay Up*, p. 171. English non-league is defined as selected clubs outside the Football League. Vamplew's methodology of occupational classification has been followed.

BIBLIOGRAPHY

1. NEWSPAPERS AND PERIODICALS (PLACE OF PUBLICATION)

Aberdare Leader
Athletic News
Bluebirds Journal (Cardiff)
Cardiff Post
Cardiff and Suburban News
Cardiff Times
Cynon Valley Leader
Daily Record and Mail (Glasgow)
Daily Worker
The Economist
Empire News and Sunday Chronicle (Cardiff)
Football Argus (Newport)
Football Post (Newport)
Merthyr Express
Montgomeryshire and Radnor Times
Rhondda Gazette
Rhondda Leader
Sporting News and Football Leader (Swansea)

Sporting Post (Swansea)
South Wales Argus (Newport)
South Wales Daily News (Cardiff)
South Wales Daily Post (Swansea)
South Wales Echo (Cardiff)
South Wales Evening Post (Swansea)
South Wales Football Argus (Newport)
South Wales Football Echo (Cardiff)
South Wales Football Express (Cardiff)
South Wales Graphic (Cardiff)
South Wales News (Cardiff)
Spectator
Sports Budget
Sunday Express
The Times
Welsh Outlook
Western Mail (Cardiff)
World of Sport (Swansea)

2. ARCHIVAL SOURCES

Aberdare Athletic AFC Ltd (Aberdare Public Library)
    Minutes of board meetings, 1920–1
    Illustrated handbook, 1921
    Annual report and statement of accounts, 1926
Aberdare Athletic Supporters' Club, handbooks (Aberdare Public Library)
Abergavenny and District United AFC, balance sheet, 1920–1 (NLW)
Abertillery AFC Ltd, company records (PRO, BT31/22480/137375)
Barry and District Association Football League, official handbooks (NLW)
Caerau Association Football and Athletic Club Ltd, company records (PRO, BT31/252422/162477)
Caerphilly Town AFC Ltd, company records (PRO, BT31/26061/168919)
Cardiff and District Football League, official handbooks (King George V Drive, Cardiff)

Cardiff City AFC Ltd, company records (Companies House, Cardiff, company no. 109065)

Cardiff City Police, annual reports (Cardiff Central Library)

Cardiff Schools Football League, annual sports day programmes (Cardiff Central Library)

City of Cardiff, reports of council and committees (Cardiff Central Library)

Ebbw Vale Association Football and Athletic Club Ltd, company records (PRO, BT31/22028/133682)

Evans, Len, Diary entitled 'Short notes of my tour through Canada with the Welsh International Team – May 24th to July 12th [1929]' (Parker Road, Cardiff)

Football Association of Wales (Westgate Street, Cardiff)
  Annual reports
  Memorandum of association
  Minutes of council and committee meetings
  Rules of the association
  Statement in lieu of prospectus

International Board, minutes of annual meetings (Westgate Street, Cardiff)

Llanelly AFC Ltd, company records (PRO, BT31/20801/123192)

Llawlyfr Cynghrair Pel-droed yr Urdd (NLW)

Merthyr Town AFC Ltd, company records (PRO, BT31/20094/116486)

Merthyr Town AFC, official handbook, 1912–13 (Merthyr Tydfil Library)

Merthyr Tydfil Association Football League, minutes, 1930–9 (Merthyr Tydfil Library)

Mid Rhondda AFC Ltd, company records (PRO, BT31/20937/124400)

New Tredegar and District AFC Ltd, company records (PRO, BT31/26712/176010)

Newport County AFC Ltd, Prospectus, 1936 (Newport Public Library)

Newport and Monmouthshire County AFC Ltd, company records (PRO, BT31/20798/123163)

Ocean Area Recreation Union, rules of the union (Aberdare Public Library)

Pontypridd Association Football League, minutes (King George V Drive, Cardiff)

Risca District AFC Ltd, company records (PRO, BT31/20119/116760)

South Wales and Monmouthshire Football Association (NLW)
  Annual reports
  Minutes
  Rules of the association

Swansea Town AFC Ltd, company records (Companies House, Cardiff, company no. 123414)

Tredegar AFC Ltd, company records (PRO, BT31/13277/110013)

Welsh Schools Football Association (NLW)
  Official handbooks
  Statements of Accounts, 1934–6

3. INTERVIEWS AND CORRESPONDENCE

Arnol, Richard (letters to author, 1998)
Barrett, Bill (interview with author, 1998)
Brooks, Jack (interview with author, 1999)
Charlesworth, Margaret (letter to Derrick Jenkins, 1981)
Curtis, Ernie (unbroadcast interview with HTV, 1986)
Harris, H. K. (letters to Derrick Jenkins, 1981)
Harris, Ivor (interview with author, 1998)
Howell, Dorothy (interview with author, 1998)
Jones, Charles (interview with author, 1998)

King, W. R. (interview with author, 1998)

Newport County AFC (letters to John Warner, 11 June, August 1937; Newport Public Library)

Thomas, Tom (unbroadcast interview with HTV, 1986)

Tucker, Iris (interview with author, 1998)

Williams, Ralph A. (letter to Derrick Jenkins, 1987)

Wilson, Jim (unbroadcast interview with HTV, 1986)

4. PRIMARY WORKS: BOOKS, ARTICLES AND CLUB/ASSOCIATION PUBLICATIONS

Aberdare Athletic miscellaneous match programmes.

Abse, Dannie, *Selected Poems* (London, 1970).

Abse, Dannie, 'Only sixty-four years', in Simon Kuper (ed.), *Perfect Pitch: 1) Home Ground* (London, 1997), pp. 115–31.

Anon., *On Behalf of the South Wales Collier Boy* (Treorchy, 1929).

Anon., *Let's Talk about Cardiff City*, Football Handbook Series, no. 14 (London, 1946).

Barnes, Walley, *Captain of Wales* (London, 1953).

Barrett, Bill, 'I was born on Rat Island', in Stewart Williams (ed.), *The Cardiff Book*, vol. 3 (Barry, 1977), pp. 9–20.

Barry Town miscellaneous match programmes.

Bowen, D. H., 'Welsh football', in T. Stephens (ed.), *Wales: Today and Tomorrow* (Cardiff, 1907), pp. 294–6.

Burgess, Ron, *Football: My Life* (London, 1952).

Capel-Kirby, W. and Carter, Frederick W., *The Mighty Kick: Romance, History and Humour of Football* (London, 1934).

Cardiff City miscellaneous match programmes.

Cardiff City FA Cup final souvenirs 1925 and 1927.

'Citizen' (Dewi Lewis), *A Short History of Cardiff City AFC* (Cardiff, 1952 edn).

Davies, Rhys, *My Wales* (London, 1934).

Davies, Walter Haydn, *The Right Place, The Right Time: Memories of Boyhood Days in a Welsh Mining Community* (Swansea, 1975 edn).

Dictionary of Welsh Biography (London, 1959).

Edwards, H. W. J., *The Good Patch* (London, 1938).

Edwards, Wil Jon, *From the Valley I Came* (London, 1956).

Fabian, A. H. and Green, Geoffrey (eds.), *Association Football* (London, 1960).

Ford, Trevor, *I Lead the Attack* (London, 1957).

Gibson, Alfred and Pickford, William, *Association Football and the Men who Made it* (London, 1906).

Godwin, Paul, 'Soccer at the pithead', in *FA Book for Boys* (n.d.), pp. 29–32.

Griffiths, Mervyn, *Man in the Middle* (London, 1958).

International championship miscellaneous match programmes.

Jenkins, E. J., *The Splott I Remember* (Cowbridge, 1983).

Jenkins, Islwyn (ed.), *The Collected Poems of Idris Davies* (Llandysul, 1980 edn).

Jennings, Hilda, *Brynmawr: A Study of a Distressed Area* (London, 1934).

Johns' Newport Directory (Newport, various editions).

Jones, Lewis, *Cwmardy* (London, 1978 edn).

—— *We Live* (London, 1978 edn).

Kelly's Directory of Monmouthshire and South Wales (London, various editions).

Kelsey, Jack, *Over The Bar* (London, 1958).

Kennard, E. F. K., *The Remarkable Career of a Well Known Athlete* (Cardiff, ?1914).

Lerry, G. G., *Association Football in Wales, 1870–1924* (Oswestry, 1924).

—— *The Football Association of Wales: 75th Anniversary, 1876–1951* (Wrexham, 1952).

— (writing as XYZ), *The Story of the Welsh Cup* (Oswestry, 1933).

Little, Kenneth L., *Negroes in Britain: A Study of Racial Relations in English Society* (London, 1947).

Llewellyn, Richard, *How Green was my Valley* (Harmondsworth, 1991 edn).

Lush, A. J., *The Young Adult in South Wales* (Cardiff, 1941).

Massey, Philip, 'Portrait of a mining town', *Fact*, 8 (November 1937).

Meara, Gwynne, *Juvenile Unemployment in South Wales* (Cardiff, 1936).

Merthyr Town miscellaneous match programmes.

Ministry of Health, *Report of the South Wales Regional Survey Committee* (London, 1921).

Morgan, J. H., '. . . Reviews fifty years of sport in Cardiff', in Stewart Williams (ed.), *The Cardiff Book*, vol. 1 (Barry, 1973), pp. 19–36.

Murphy, Jimmy, *Matt . . . United . . . and Me* (London, 1968).

Newport County miscellaneous match programmes.

Orwell, George, *The Road to Wigan Pier* (Harmondsworth, 1962 edn).

Paul, Roy, *A Red Dragon Of Wales* (London, 1956).

PEP, 'The football industry', *Planning*, XVII, 324 (26 February 1951) and 325 (5 March 1951), 157–208.

Pickford, R. W., 'How soccer is controlled', *The Listener*, 29 September 1937, 656–7.

— 'The psychology of the history and organization of association football', *British Journal of Psychology*, 31 (1940), 80–143.

Pilgrim Trust, *Men without Work* (Cambridge, 1938).

Pressdee, Harry, 'Sporting days', in Anne Eyles (ed.), *In the Shadows of the Steelworks II* (Cardiff, 1995), pp. 109–15.

Priestley, J. B., *The Good Companions* (London, [1929] 1976 edn).

— *English Journey* (London, [1934] 1968 edn).

Seed, Jimmy, *The Jimmy Seed Story: Forty-three Years in First-class Football as Player and Manager* (London, 1957).

South Wales and Monmouthshire Council of Social Service, *A Social Approach to Unemployment in South Wales* (Cardiff, 1935).

Sully, E., 'Physical training and character' in T. Stephens (ed.), *Wales: Today and Tomorrow* (Cardiff, 1907), pp. 289–93.

Sutcliffe, C. E., Brierley, J. A. and Howarth, F., *The Story of the Football League* (Preston, 1938).

Swansea Town miscellaneous match programmes.

Thomas, George, *My Wales* (London, 1986).

Twamley, Bill, *Cardiff and Me Sixty Years Ago: Growing Up during the Twenties and Thirties* (Newport, 1984).

Veitch, Colin, 'Soccer for sixpence', *The Labour Magazine*, 1, 7 (November 1922), 318–19.

Western Mail Directory of Cardiff (Cardiff, various editions).

5. SECONDARY WORKS: BOOKS AND ARTICLES

Allison, Lincoln (ed.), *Taking Sport Seriously* (Aachen, 1998).

Ambrosen, Tony, 'Newport Go Out', *The Footballer*, 1, 1 (1988).

— *Ironsides: A Lifetime in the League: A Who's Who of Newport County* (Harefield, 1991).

— *Amber in the Blood: A History of Newport County* (Harefield, 1993).

Anderson, Benedict, *Imagined Communities: Reflections on the Origin and Spread of Nationalism* (London, 1991 edn).

Andrews, David, 'Sport and the masculine hegemony of the modern nation: Welsh rugby, culture and society, 1890–1914', in John Nauright and Timothy J. L. Chandler (eds.), *Making Men: Rugby and Masculine Identity* (London, 1996), pp. 50–69.

Andrews, David L. and Howell, Jeremy W., 'Transforming into a tradition: rugby and the making of imperial Wales, 1890–1914', in A. G. Lingham and J. W. Loy (eds.), *Sport in Social Development* (Leeds, 1993), pp. 77–96.

Arnold, A. J., *A Game that would Pay: A Business History of Professional Football in Bradford* (London, 1988).
— '"Not playing the game"? Leeds City in the Great War', *International Journal of the History of Sport*, 7, 1 (1990), 111–19.
Baber, Colin and Thomas, Dennis, 'The Glamorgan economy, 1914–45', in Arthur H. John and Glanmor Williams (eds.), *Glamorgan County History*, vol. V: *Industrial Glamorgan* (Cardiff, 1980), pp. 519–80.
Bailey, Peter, *Popular Culture and Performance in the Victorian City* (Cambridge, 1998).
Bale, John, 'Geographical diffusion and the adoption of professionalism in England and Wales', *Geography*, 63 (1978), 188–97.
— *The Development of Soccer as a Participant and Spectator Sport: Geographical Aspects* (London, 1979).
— *Sport and Place: A Geography of Sport in England, Scotland and Wales* (London, 1982).
— *Sport, Space and the City* (London, 1993).
Beck, Peter J., 'England v Germany, 1938', *History Today*, 32 (1982), 29–34.
— *Scoring for Britain: International Football and International Politics, 1900–1939* (London, 1999).
Beddoe, Deirdre, *Back to Home and Duty: Women between the Wars, 1918–1939* (London, 1989).
Benson, John, *The Working Class in Britain, 1850–1939* (London, 1989).
Berry, David, *Wales and Cinema: The First Hundred Years* (Cardiff, 1994).
Billig, Michael, *Banal Nationalism* (London, 1995).
Billot, John, *History of Welsh International Rugby* (Ferndale, 1971).
Birley, Derek, *Land of Sport and Glory: Sport and British Society, 1887–1910* (Manchester, 1995).
— *Playing the Game: Sport and British Society, 1910–50* (Manchester, 1995).
Boyle, Raymond and Haynes, Richard, *Power Play: Sport, the Media and Popular Culture* (Harlow, 2000).
Bradley, Joseph M., 'Football in Scotland: a history of political and ethnic identity', *International Journal of the History of Sport*, 12, 1 (1995), 81–98.
Brailsford, Dennis, *British Sport: A Social History* (Cambridge, 1997).
Bull, David, 'More balls than most', *New Statesman and Society*, 1 March 1996, pp. 24–5.
Burgum, John, *Swansea City FC (Illustrated History)* (Manchester, 1988).
Cantelon, H. and Hollands, R. (eds.), *Leisure, Sport and Working-Class Cultures: Theory and History* (Toronto, 1988).
Cashmore, Ellis, *Making Sense of Sports* (London, 2000 edn).
Clapson, Mark, *A Bit of a Flutter: Popular Gambling and English Society, c. 1823–1961* (Manchester, 1992).
Clarke, John and Critcher, Chas, *The Devil Makes Work: Leisure in Capitalist Britain* (London, 1985).
Clarke, John, Critcher, Chas, and Johnson, Richard (eds.), *Working Class Culture: Studies in History and Theory* (London, 1979).
Clarke, Peter, *Hope and Glory: Britain, 1900–1990* (Harmondsworth, 1996).
Coles, R. W., 'Football as a sociological religion', in Michael Hill (ed.), *A Sociological Yearbook of Religion in Britain*, no. 8 (London, 1975), pp. 61–77.
Colley, Linda, *Britons: Forging the Nation, 1707–1837* (London, 1994 edn).
Collins, Tony, *Rugby's Great Split: Class, Culture and the Origins of Rugby Football League* (London, 1998).
Collins, Tony and Vamplew, Wray, 'The pub, the drinks trade and the early years of modern football', *Sports Historian*, 20, 1 (2000), 1–17.
Corrigan, Peter, *100 Years of Welsh Soccer* (Cardiff, 1976).
Cosslett, John (ed.), *The Century Collection: An Anthology of Best Writing in the Western Mail through the Twentieth Century* (Derby, 1999).

Cox, Richard W., *Sport in Britain: A Bibliography of Historical Publications* (Manchester, 1991).
— *History of Sport: A Guide to the Literature and Sources of Information* (Frodsham, 1994).
— *The Internet as a Resource for the Sports Historian* (Frodsham, 1995).
Cox, Richard, Jarvie, Grant and Vamplew, Wray (eds.), *Encyclopedia of British Sport* (Oxford, 2000).
Critcher, Chas, 'Football and cultural values', *Working Papers in Cultural Studies*, 1 (1971), 103–19.
Croll, Andy, 'From bar stool to choir stall: music and morality in late-Vicotorian Merthyr', *Llafur*, 6, 1 (1992), 17–27.
— 'Street disorder, surveillance and shame: regulating behaviour in the public spaces of the late Victorian British town', *Social History*, 24, 3 (1999), 250–68.
— *Civilizing the Urban: Popular Culture and Public Space in Merthyr c.1870–1914* (Cardiff, 2000).
Crooks, John, *Cardiff City Chronology, 1920–86* (Cardiff, 1986).
— *The Bluebirds: A Who's Who of Cardiff City Football League Players* (Pontypool, 1987).
— *Cardiff City Football Club: The Official History of the Bluebirds* (Harefield, 1992).
Crossick, Geoffrey (ed.), *The Lower Middle Class in Britain* (London, 1977).
Crump, Jeremy, 'Recreation in Coventry between the Wars', in Bill Lancaster and Tony Mason (eds.), *Life and Labour in a 20th Century City: The Experience of Coventry* (Warwick, 1986), pp. 261–87.
Cunningham, Hugh, 'Leisure and culture', in F. M. L. Thompson (ed.), *The Cambridge Social History of Britain, 1750–1950*, vol. 2: *People and their Environment* (Cambridge, 1990), pp. 279–339.
Daunton, Martin J., *Coal Metropolis: Cardiff, 1870–1914* (Leicester, 1977).
Davies, Gareth, M., *Soccer: The International Line-ups and Statistics Series: Wales, 1876–1960* (Cleethorpes, 1995).
Davies, Gareth M. and Garland, Ian, *Who's Who of Welsh International Soccer Players* (Wrexham, 1991).
Davies, Gwennant, *The Story of the Urdd* (Aberystwyth, 1973).
Davies, Iolo, *A Certaine Schoole: A History of Cowbridge Grammar School* (Cowbridge, 1967).
Davies, James A. (ed.), *The Heart of Wales: An Anthology* (Bridgend, 1994).
Davies, John, *A History of Wales* (London, 1993).
— *Broadcasting and the BBC in Wales* (Cardiff, 1994).
Davies, Russell, *Secret Sins: Sex, Violence and Society in Carmarthenshire, 1870–1920* (Cardiff, 1996).
DeGroot, Gerard J., *Blighty: British Society in the Era of the Great War* (London, 1996).
Delaney, Trevor, *The Grounds of Rugby League* (Keighley, 1991).
— *The International Grounds of Rugby League* (Keighley, 1995).
Dobbs, Brian, *Edwardians at Play: Sport, 1890–1914* (London, 1973).
Dunning, Eric, *The Sociology of Sport* (London, 1971).
— *Sport Matters: Sociological Studies of Sport, Violence, and Civilization* (London, 1999).
Dunning, Eric, Murphy, Patrick and Williams, John, *The Roots of Football Hooliganism: An Historical and Sociological Study* (London, 1988).
— *Football on Trial: Spectator Violence and Development in the Football World* (London, 1990).
Dunning, Eric, and Sheard, Kenneth, *Barbarians, Gentleman and Players: A Sociological Study of the Development of Rugby Football* (Oxford, 1979).
Eckley, Simon, *The Old Photograph Series: Pontypridd* (Stroud, 1994).
Eckley, Simon and Jenkins, Emrys, *Rhondda: A Second Series* (Stroud, 1995).
Edgell, Stephen and Jary, David, 'Football: a sociological eulogy', in Michael A. Smith, Stanley Parker and Cyril A. Smith (eds.), *Leisure and Society in Britain* (London, 1987), pp. 214–29.
Edwards, E. E., *Echoes of Rhymney* (Newport, 1974).
Evans, Neil, 'Urbanisation, elite attitudes and philanthropy: Cardiff, 1850–1914', *International Review of Social History*, 27 (1982), 290–323.

— 'The Welsh Victorian city: the middle class and civic and national consciousness in Cardiff, 1850–1914', *Welsh History Review*, 12, 3 (1985), 350–87.

— 'Writing the social history of modern Wales: approaches, achievements and problems', *Social History*, 17, 3 (1992), 479–92.

— (ed.), *National Identity in the British Isles*, Coleg Harlech Occasional Papers in Welsh Studies, no. 3 (Harlech, 1989).

Farmer, David, *Swansea City 1912–82* (London, 1982).

— *The Life and Times of Swansea RFC: The All Whites* (Swansea, 1995).

— *The Official 'Biography' of the Swans, Town and City* (Swansea, 2000).

Farmer, David and Stead, Peter, *Ivor Allchurch MBE: The Authorised Biography of the Legendary Golden Boy* (Swansea, 1998).

Fishwick, Nicholas, *From Clegg to Clegg House: The Official Centenary History of the Sheffield and Hallamshire County Football Association, 1886–1986* (Sheffield, 1986).

— *English Football and Society, 1910–50* (Manchester, 1989).

Francis, Hywel and Smith, David, *The Fed: A History of the South Wales Miners in the Twentieth Century* (London, 1980).

Francis, Lionel, *Seventy Five Years of Southern League Football* (London, 1969).

Frankenberg, Ronald, *Village on the Border: A Social Study of Religion, Politics and Football in a North Wales Community* (London, 1957).

Fuller, J. G., *Troop Morale and Popular Culture in the British and Dominion Armies, 1914–1918* (Oxford, 1990).

Gaffney, Angela, *Aftermath: Remembering the Great War in Wales* (Cardiff, 1998).

Garland, Ian, *The History of the Welsh Cup, 1877–1993* (Wrexham, 1993).

Garland, Ian and Gray-Thomas, Wyn, *The Canaries Sing Again: A History of Caernarfon Town FC* (Caernarfon, 1986).

Gearing, Brian, 'More than a game: the experience of being a professional footballer in Britain', *Oral History*, 25, 1 (1997), 63–70.

Gramich, Katie, 'Cymru or Wales? Explorations in a divided sensibility', in Susan Bussnett (ed.), *Studying British Cultures: An Introduction* (London, 1997), pp. 97–112.

Gray-Jones, Arthur, *A History of Ebbw Vale* (Risca, 1970).

Green, Geoffrey, *The History of the Football Association* (London, 1953).

— *Soccer: The World Game – A Popular History* (London, 1953).

— *The Official History of the FA Cup* (London, 1960 edn).

Giulianotti, Richard, *Football: A Sociology of the Global Game* (Cambridge, 1999).

Harding, John, *Football Wizard: The Story of Billy Meredith* (Derby, 1985).

— *For the Good of the Game: The Official History of the Professional Footballers' Association* (London, 1991).

Hargreaves, John, *Sport, Power and Culture: A Social and Historical Analysis of Popular Sports in Britain* (London, 1987 edn).

Harrison, Paul, *Southern League Football: The First Fifty Years* (Gravesend, 1989).

Hayes, Nick and Hill, Jeff (eds.), *'Millions Like Us'? British Culture in the Second World War* (Liverpool, 1999).

Herbert, Trevor and Jones, Gareth Elwyn (eds.), *Wales between the Wars* (Cardiff, 1988).

Hignell, Andrew, *The History of Glamorgan County Cricket Club* (London, 1988).

— *The Skipper: A Biography of Wilfred Wooller* (Royston, 1988).

— *A Favourit' Game: Cricket in South Wales before 1914* (Cardiff, 1992).

Hill, Jeff, 'Reading the stars: towards a post-modernist approach to sports history', *Sports Historian*, 14 (1994), 45–55.

— 'British sports history: a post-modern future?', *Journal of Sport History*, 23, 1 (1996), 1–19.

— 'The legend of Denis Compton', *Sports Historian*, 18 (1998), 19–33.

— 'Cocks, cats, caps and cups: a semiotic approach to sport and national identity', *Culture, Sport, Society*, 2, 2 (1999), 1–21.

Hill, Jeff and Varrasi, Francesco, 'Creating Wembley: the construction of a national monument', *Sports Historian*, 17, 2 (1997), 28–43.

Hill, Jeff and Williams, Jack (eds.), *Sport and Identity in the North of England* (Keele, 1996).

Hobsbawm, Eric, *Worlds of Labour: Further Studies in the History of Labour* (London, 1984).

Hobsbawm, Eric, and Ranger, Terence (eds.), *The Invention of Tradition* (Cambridge, 1983).

Hoggart, Richard, *The Uses of Literacy* (Harmondsworth, 1957).

Holt, Richard, 'Working class football and the city: the problem of continuity', *British Journal of Sports History*, 3, 1 (1986), 5–17.

— *Sport and the British: A Modern History* (Oxford, 1992 edn).

— 'Sport and history: the state of the subject in Britain', *Twentieth Century British History*, 7, 2 (1996), 231–52.

— 'Golf and the English suburb: class and gender in a London club, *c*.1890–*c*.1960', *Sports Historian*, 18, 1 (1998), 76–89.

— (ed.), *Sport and the Working Class in Modern Britain* (Manchester, 1990).

Holt, Richard, Mangan, J. A. and Lanfranchi, Pierre (eds.), *European Heroes: Myth, Identity, Sport* (London, 1996).

Holt, Richard and Mason, Tony, *Sport in Britain, 1945–2000* (Oxford, 2000).

Hopcraft, Arthur, *The Football Man: People and Passions in Soccer* (London, 1968).

Horne, John, Tomlinson, Alan and Whannel, Gary, *Understanding Sport: An Introduction to the Sociological and Cultural Analysis of Sport* (London, 1999).

Huggins, Mike, *Flat Racing and British Society, 1790–1914: A Social and Economic History* (London, 2000).

— 'Second-class citizens? English middle-class culture and sport, 1850–1910: a reconsideration', *International Journal of the History of Sport*, 17, 1 (2000), 1–35.

Humphries, Steve, *Hooligans or Rebels? An Oral History of Working-Class Childhood and Youth, 1889–1939* (Oxford, 1981).

Hutchinson, John, *The Football Industry: The Early Years of the Professional Game* (Glasgow, 1982).

Inglis, Simon, *Soccer in the Dock: A History of British Football Scandals, 1900 to 1965* (London, 1985).

— *The Football Grounds of Great Britain* (London, 1987 edn).

— *League Football and the Men who Made it: The Official Centenary History of the Football League* (London, 1988).

Jackson, Peter, *The Cardiff City Story* (Cardiff, 1974).

James, Royston (gol.), *Can Llwyddiant! Cyfrol i Ddathlu Canmwlyddiant Undeb Rygbi Cymru* (Abertawe, 1981).

Jarvie, Grant (ed.), *Sport in the Making of Celtic Cultures* (Leicester, 1999).

Jarvie, Grant and Maguire, Joseph, *Sport and Leisure in Social Thought* (London, 1994).

Jarvie, Grant and Reid, I. A., 'Sport, nationalism and culture in Scotland', *Sports Historian*, 19, 1 (1999), 97–124.

Jarvie, Grant and Walker, Graham (eds.), *Scottish Sport and the Making of the Nation: Ninety Minute Patriots?* (Leicester, 1994).

Jenkins, Derrick, 'Football in Cardiff, 1888–1939' (unpublished, 1984).

Jenkins, Derrick and Stennett, Ceri, *Wembley 1927* (Cardiff, 1985).

Jenkins, Geraint H., *Cewri'r Bel-droed yng Nghymru* (Llandysul, 1977).

Jenkins, Geraint H. and Smith, J. Beverley (eds.), *Politics and Society in Wales, 1840–1922: Essays in Honour of Ieuan Gwynedd Jones* (Cardiff, 1988).

Jenkins, Gwyn, *The History of the Aberystwyth and District League, 1934–1984* (Aberystwyth, 1984).

Jenkins, John M., Pierce, Duncan and Auty, Timothy, *Who's Who of Welsh International Rugby Players* (Wrexham, 1991).

John, Angela V., *Our Mothers' Land: Chapters in Welsh Women's History* (Cardiff, 1991).

Johnes, Martin, 'Fred Keenor: a Welsh soccer hero', *Sports Historian*, 18, 1 (1998), 105–19.

— 'Irredeemably English? Association football and Wales', *Planet: The Welsh Internationalist*, 133 (1999), 72–9.
— 'Hooligans and barrackers: soccer and crowd disorder in south Wales, *c.*1906–39', *Soccer and Society*, 1, 2 (2000), 19–35.
— 'Eighty minute patriots? National identity and sport in modern Wales', *International Journal of the History of Sport*, 17, 4 (2000), 93–110.
— ' "Heads in the Sand": Football, Politics and Crowd Disasters', unpublished paper given at British Society of Sports History annual conference, University of Liverpool, 2000.
— ' "Poor man's cricket": Baseball, class and community in south Wales, c.1880–1950', *International Journal of the History of Sport*, 17, 4 (2000), 149–62.
— 'Mushrooms, scandal and bankruptcy: the short life of Mid Rhondda Football Club', *The Local Historian*, 32, 1 (2002), 41–53.
Johnson, Paul (ed.), *20th Century Britain: Economic, Social and Cultural Change* (London, 1994).
Jones, Aled, *Press, Politics and Society: A History of Journalism in Wales* (Cardiff, 1993).
Jones, David J. V., *Crime and Policing in the Twentieth Century: The South Wales Experience* (Cardiff, 1996).
Jones, Gareth Elwyn and Smith, Dai (eds.), *The People of Wales* (Llandysul, 1999).
Jones, Glyndwr G., *Cronicl Caerffili*, no. 8 (Bromley, n.d.).
Jones, H. J., *Nelson Handball Court: A History of the Court and its Players, 1860–1940* (published by the author, n.d.).
Jones, Howard C., *Old Caerphilly and District in Photographs* (Barry, 1979).
Jones, Peter, *Wrexham: A Complete Record* (Derby, 1992).
Jones, R. Merfyn, 'Beyond identity? The reconstruction of the Welsh', *Journal of British Studies*, 31, 4 (1992), 330–57.
Jones, Stephen G., 'The economic aspects of association football in England 1918–39', *British Journal of Sports History*, 1, 3 (1984), 286–99.
— 'Sport, politics and the labour movement: the British Workers' Sport Federation, 1923–35', *British Journal of Sports History*, 2, 2 (1985), 154–78.
— *Workers at Play: A Social and Economic History of Leisure, 1918–39* (London, 1986).
— 'Work, leisure and unemployment in Western Europe between the wars', *British Journal of Sports History*, 3, 1 (1986), 55–81.
— *Sport, Politics and the Working Class* (Manchester, 1988).
Jones, William D., *Wales in America: Scranton and the Welsh, 1860–1920* (Cardiff, 1993).
Jose, Colin, 'Across Canada with Wales in 1929', *The Footballer*, 2, 4 (1990).
Joyce, Patrick, *Visions of the People: Industrial England and the Question of Class, 1848–1914* (Cambridge, 1991).
— *Democratic Subjects: Self and the Social in Nineteenth-century England* (Cambridge, 1994).
Judt, Tony, 'A clown in regal purple: social history and the historians', *History Workshop*, 7 (1979), 66–93.
Kelly, Stephen F., *Back Page Football: A Century of Newspaper Coverage* (London, 1988).
Kinealy, Christine, *A Disunited Kingdom? England, Ireland, Scotland and Wales, 1800–1949* (Cambridge, 1999).
King, W., *Towards the Light: The Story of Cardiff High School for Boys, 1898–1970* (Llanharan, 1992).
Kirk, Neville, ' "Traditional" working-class culture and "the rise of Labour": some preliminary questions and observations', *Social History*, 16, 2 (1991), 203–16.
— *Change, Continuity and Class: Labour in British Society, 1850–1920* (Manchester, 1998).
— (ed.), *Northern Identities: Historical Interpretations of 'The North' and 'Northernness'* (Aldershot, 2000).
Korr, Charles, 'West Ham United Football Club and the beginning of professional football in east London, 1895–1914', *Journal of Contemporary History*, 13, 2 (1978), 211–32.

— *West Ham United: The Making of a Football Club* (London, 1986).

Krüger, Arnd and Riordan, James (eds.), *The Story of Worker Sport* (Leeds, 1996).

Lanfranchi, Pierre and Taylor, Matthew, 'Professional football in World War Two Britain', in Pat Kirkham and David Thoms (eds.), *War Culture: Social Change and Changing Experience in World War Two Britain* (London, 1995), pp. 87–197.

Laybourn, Keith (ed.), *Social Conditions, Status and Community, 1860–c.1920* (Stroud, 1997).

Lewis, E. D., *The Rhondda Valleys* (Cardiff, 1963 edn).

Lewis, R. W., 'Football hooliganism in England before 1914: a critique of the Dunning thesis', *International Journal of the History of Sport*, 13, 3 (1996), 310–39.

Lieven, Michael, *Senghennydd: The Universal Pit Village, 1890–1930* (Llandysul, 1994).

Lile, Brian, 'Nice one Cyril!' *The Footballer*, 2, 7 (1990).

Lile, Brian and Farmer, David, 'The early development of association football in south Wales, 1890–1906', *Transactions of the Honourable Society of Cymmrodorion* (1984), 193–215.

Lloyd, Grahame, *C'mon City: A Hundred Years of the Bluebirds* (Bridgend, 1999).

Lloyd, Howard (gol.), *Crysau Cochion: Cymry ar y Maes Chwarae* (Llandybïe, 1958).

— *Chware Teg* (Llandybïe, 1967).

Lowerson, John, *Sport and the English Middle Classes, 1870–1914* (Manchester, 1993).

Lush, Peter and Farrar, Dave (eds.), *Tries in the Valleys: A History of Rugby League in Wales* (London, 1998).

McInery, Jeff, *The Linnets: An Illustrated History of Barry Town AFC* (Cardiff, 1993).

McKibbin, Ross, 'Working class gambling in Britain, 1880–1939', *Past and Present*, 82 (1979), 147–78.

— 'Work and hobbies in Britain, 1880–1950', in Jay Winter (ed.), *The Working Class in Modern British History* (Cambridge, 1983), pp. 127–46.

— *The Ideologies of Class: Social Relations in Britain* (Oxford, 1990).

— *Classes and Cultures: England, 1918–1951* (Oxford, 1998).

McLean, Iain and Johnes, Martin, *Aberfan: Government and Disasters* (Cardiff, 2000).

McMillan, James, *The Way We Were, 1900–14* (London, 1978).

Mangan, J. A., *Athleticism in the Victorian and Edwardian Public School: The Emergence and Consolidation of the Educational Ideology* (Cambridge, 1981).

— (ed.), *Pleasure, Profit, Proselytism: British Culture and Sport at Home and Abroad, 1700–1914* (London, 1988).

— (ed.), *Tribal Identities: Nationalism, Europe, Sport* (London, 1996).

— (ed.), *Sport in Europe: Politics, Class, Gender* (London, 1999).

Marples, Morris, *A History of Football* (London, 1954).

Marwick, Arthur, *The Deluge: British Society and the First World War* (London, 1991 edn).

Mason, Tony, *Association Football and English Society 1863–1915* (Brighton, 1980).

— 'Sporting News, 1860–1914', in Michael Harris and Alan Lee (eds.), *The Press in English Society from the Seventeenth to Nineteenth Centuries* (London, 1986), pp. 168–86.

— 'Football and the historians', *International Journal of the History of Sport*, 5, 1, (1988), 136–41.

— *Sport in Britain* (London, 1988).

— 'All the winners and the half times . . .', *Sports Historian*, 13 (1993), 3–13.

— (ed.), *Sport in Britain: A Social History* (Cambridge, 1989).

Matthews, B. E., *The Swansea City Story* (Swansea, 1976).

— *The Swans: A History of Swansea City FC, 1912–82* (Swansea, 1987).

Matthews, John E., *From Pit to Pitch: A Pictorial History of Football in Rhos* (Rhosllannerchrugog, 1991).

Meacham, Standish, *A Life Apart: The English Working Class, 1890–1914* (London, 1977).

Meller, Helen, E., *Leisure and the Changing City, 1870–1914* (London, 1976).

Melling, Althea, ' "Plucky lasses", pea soup, and politics: the role of ladies' football during the 1921 miners' lock-out in Wigan and Leigh', *International Journal of the History of Sport*, 16, 1 (1999), 38–64.

Melling, Philip H., *Man of Amman: The Life of Dai Davies* (Llandysul, 1994).

Mellor, Gavin, 'The social and geographical make-up of football crowds in the north-west of England, 1946–1962: "super-clubs", local loyalty and regional identities', *Sports Historian*, 19, 2 (1999), 25–42.

— 'The genesis of Manchester United as a national and international "super-club", 1958–68', *Soccer and Society*, 1, 2 (2000), 151–66.

Mennell, James, 'The service football program of World War One: its impact on the popularity of the game', *Journal of Sport History*, 16, 3 (1989), 248–60.

Metcalfe, Alan, 'Organized sport in the mining communities of south Northumberland, 1880–1889', *Victorian Studies*, 25, 4 (1982), 469–95.

— 'Football in the mining communities of east Northumberland 1882–1914', *International Journal of the History of Sport*, 5, 3 (1988), 269–91.

— 'The control of space and the development of sport: a case study of twenty two sports in the mining communities of east Northumberland, 1880–1914', *Sports Historian*, 15 (1995), 23–33.

Moorhouse, Geoffrey, *A People's Game: The Official History of Rugby League, 1895–1995* (London, 1995).

Moorhouse, H. F., 'Professional football and working class culture: English theories and Scottish evidence', *Sociological Review*, 32, 2 (1984), 285–313.

— 'Scotland against England: football and popular culture', *International Journal of the History of Sport*, 4, 2 (1987), 189–202.

— 'One state, several countries: soccer and nationality in a "United Kingdom"', *International Journal of the History of Sport*, 12, 2 (1995), 55–74.

Morgan, Kenneth O., *Rebirth of a Nation: Wales 1880–1980* (Oxford, 1982 edn).

— *Modern Wales: Politics, Places and People* (Cardiff, 1995).

Morris, Desmond, *The Soccer Tribe* (London, 1981).

Murphy, Patrick, Dunning, Eric and Maguire, Joseph, 'Football spectator violence and disorder before the First World War: a reply to R. W. Lewis', *International Journal of the History of Sport*, 15, 1 (1998), 141–62.

Nash, Kath, *Town on the Usk: A Pictorial History of Newport* (Cwmbran, 1983).

Newsham, Gail J., *In a League of their Own! The Dick, Kerr's Ladies Football Team* (London, 1994).

Nielson, Niels Kayser, 'Welfare-nationalism? Comparative aspects of the relation between sport and nationalism in Scandinavia in the inter-war years', *Sports Historian*, 17, 2 (1997), 63–79.

O'Leary, Paul, *Immigration and Integration: The Irish in Wales, 1798–1922* (Cardiff, 2000).

Oliver, Liz, ' "No hard-brimmed hats and hat pins please!" Bolton women cotton workers and the game of rounders, 1911–39', *Oral History*, 25, 1 (1997), 40–5.

Opie, Iona and Peter, *Children's Games in Street and Playground* (Oxford, 1969).

Osborne, John M., ' "To keep the life of the nation on the old lines": the *Athletic News* and the First World War', *Journal of Sport History*, 14, 2 (1987), 137–50.

Owen, John A. and Jacob, Carolyn, *The Unconquerable Spirit: Merthyr Tydfil and District in the 1930s* (Merthyr Tydfil, 1993).

Parratt, Catriona, M., 'Athletic "womanhood": exposing sources for female sport in Victorian and Edwardian England', *Journal of Sport History*, 16, 2, (1989), 140–57.

Parry, Peter, Lile, Brian and Griffiths, Donald, *The Old Black and Green: Aberystwyth Town, 1884–1984* (Aberystwyth, 1987).

Parry-Jones, David (ed.), *Taff's Acre: A History and Celebration of Cardiff Arms Park* (London, 1984).

Phillips, Jim, 'Football and British–Soviet relations: the Moscow Dynamo and Moscow Spartak tours of 1945 and 1954', *The Historian*, 51 (1996), 20–3.

Polley, Martin, *Moving the Goalposts: A History of Sport and Society since 1945* (London, 1998).

Pritchard, Katie Olwen, *The Story of Gilfach Goch* (Newport, 1973).

Protheroe, G., 'Aberdare Athletic', *Programme Monthly*, 147 (June 1993), 28–30.

Pyke, Philip, 'The Jones Dynasty', *The Footballer*, 7, 4 (1990).

Richards, Huw, Stead, Peter and Williams, Gareth (eds.), *Heart and Soul: The Character of Welsh Rugby* (Cardiff, 1998).

— *More Heart and Soul: The Character of Welsh Rugby* (Cardiff, 1999).

Ridgwell, Stephen, 'South Wales and the cinema in the 1930s', *Welsh History Review*, 17, 4 (1995), 590–615.

Robbins, Keith, *Nineteenth-Century Britain: Integration and Diversity* (Oxford, 1988).

Rogers, W. M., *Camp ar Gamp* (Pontypridd, 1969).

Rollin, Jack, *Soccer at War, 1939–45* (London, 1985).

Routh, Guy, *Occupation and Pay in Great Britain, 1906–79* (London, 1980 edn).

Rowlands, A., 'Roy Paul: Red Dragon of Wales', *The Footballer*, 2, 7 (1990).

Rubenstein, David, 'Sport and the sociologist, 1890–1914', *British Journal of Sports History*, 1, 1 (1984), 14–23.

Russell, Dave, ' "Sporadic and curious": the emergence of rugby and soccer zones in Yorkshire and Lancashire c.1860–1914', *International Journal of the History of Sport*, 5, 2 (1988), 185–205.

— 'Amateurs, professionals and the construction of social identity', *Sports Historian*, 16 (1996), 64–80.

— 'Sport and identity: the case of Yorkshire County Cricket Club, 1890–1939', *Twentieth Century British History*, 7, 2 (1996), 206–30.

— *Football and the English: A Social History of Association Football, 1863–1995* (Preston, 1997).

— 'Associating with football: social identity in England, 1863–1998', in Gary Armstrong and Richard Giulianotti (eds.), *Football Cultures and Identities* (London, 1999), pp. 15–28.

— 'Football and society in the north-west, 1919–1939', *North West Labour History*, 24 (1999/2000), 3–14.

Say, Tony, 'Herbert Chapman: football revolutionary?', *Sports Historian*, 16 (May 1996), 81–98.

Seddon, Peter J., *A Football Compendium* (Boston Spa, 1995).

Seward, Andy, 'Cornish rugby and cultural identity: a socio-historical perspective', *Sports Historian*, 18, 2 (1998), 78–94.

Shepherd, Richard, *The History of Newport County FC, 1912/13–1972/73* (Newport, 1973).

— *Newport County '79/80: A Season of Triumph* (Newport, 1980).

— *Seventy Years of Newport County: A Pictorial History, 1912–82* (Newport, 1982).

— *Cardiff City Football Club, 1899–1947: From Riverside to Richards* (Chalford, 1996).

— *Newport County Football Club, 1912–1960* (Chalford, 1997).

— *Swansea Town Football Club, 1912–1964* (Chalford, 1998).

Signy, Dennis, *A Pictorial History of Soccer* (London, 1969 edn).

Slade, Arthur, 'Cardiff Corinthians A.F.C.', *The Cardiff Spectator*, 2, 13 (1961).

Smith, Dai, 'Tonypandy 1910: definitions of community', *Past and Present*, 87 (1980), 158–84.

— 'People's theatre: a century of Welsh rugby', *History Today*, 31 (1981), 31–6.

— *Wales! Wales?* (London, 1984).

— 'The Valleys: landscape and mindscape', in Prys Morgan (ed.), *Glamorgan County History*, vol. VI: *Glamorgan Society, 1780–1980* (Cardiff, 1988), pp. 129–49.

— *Aneurin Bevan and the World of South Wales* (Cardiff, 1993).

— *Wales: A Question for History* (Bridgend, 1999).

— (ed.), *A People and a Proletariat: Essays in the History of Wales, 1780–1980* (London, 1980).

Smith, David, and Williams, Gareth, *Fields of Praise: The Official History of the Welsh Rugby Union, 1881–1981* (Cardiff, 1980).

Smith, Malcolm, *Democracy in a Depression: Britain in the 1920s and 1930s* (Cardiff, 1998).

Smith, Sean, *The Union Game: A Rugby History* (London, 1999).

Soar, Phil and Tyler, Martin, *Encyclopaedia of British Football* (London, 1987 edn).

Stead, Peter, and Richards, Huw (eds.), *For Club and Country: Welsh Football Greats* (Cardiff, 2000).

Stedman Jones, Gareth, 'Class expression versus social control? A critique of recent trends in the social history of "leisure" ', *History Workshop*, 4 (1977), 163–70.

Stennett, Ceri, *The Soccer Dragons* (Cardiff, 1987).

Stevenson, John and Cook, Chris, *The Slump: Society and Politics during the Depression* (London, 1977).

Stradling, Rob, *Cardiff and the Spanish Civil War* (Cardiff, 1996).

Studd, Stephen, *Herbert Chapman – Football Emperor: A Study in the Origins of Modern Soccer* (London, 1981).

Tabner, Brian, *Through the Turnstiles* (Harefield, 1992).

Tanner, Duncan, Williams, Chris and Hopkin, Deian (eds.), *The Labour Party in Wales, 1900–2000* (Cardiff, 2000).

Taylor, Matthew, 'Football archives and the historian', *Business Archives: Sources and History*, 78 (1999), 1–12.

— 'Labour relations and managerial control in English professional football, 1890–1939', *Sports History Review*, 31 (2000), 80–99.

Taylor, Matthew and Coyle, John, 'The election of clubs to the Football League 1888–1939', *Sports Historian*, 19, 2 (1999), 1–24.

Taylor, Rogan, *Football and its Fans: Supporters and their Relations with the Game, 1885–1985* (Leicester, 1992).

Taylor, Rogan and Ward, Andrew, *Kicking and Screaming: An Oral History of Football in England* (London, 1995).

— 'Kicking and screaming: broadcasting football oral histories', *Oral History*, 25, 1 (1997), 57–62.

Thomas, Gwyn, *High on Hope* (Cowbridge, 1985).

Thomas, Iris Roderick, *Remember When: Memories of Yesteryear* (Abertillery, 1993).

Thomas, J. B. G., *The Men in Scarlet: The Story of Welsh Rugby Football* (London, 1972).

Thompson, Paul, *The Edwardians: The Remaking of British Society* (London, 1992 edn).

Tischler, Steven, *Footballers and Businessmen: The Origins of Professional Soccer in England* (New York, 1981).

Tomlinson, Alan (ed.), *Explorations in Football Culture* (Brighton, 1983).

Tranter, Neil, *Sport, Economy and Society in Britain, 1750–1914* (Cambridge, 1998).

Turner, Dennis and White, Alex, *The Breedon Book of Football Managers* (Derby, 1993).

Twydell, Dave, 'Ghosts of the League . . . no. 1: Aberdare Athletic', *The Footballer*, 2, 1 (1988).

— *More Defunct FC: Club Histories and Statistics* (Harefield, 1990).

— *Rejected FC*, vol. 1: *Histories of the Ex-Football League Clubs* (Harefield, 1992 edn).

— *Rejected FC*, vol. 2: *Histories of the Ex-Football League Clubs* (Harefield, 1995 edn).

Underwood, Terry, *Yesterday's Newport* (Newport, 1980).

Vamplew, Wray, 'Ungentlemanly conduct: the control of soccer-crowd behaviour in England, 1888–1914', in T. C. Smout (ed.), *The Search for Wealth and Stability: Essays in Economic and Social History Presented to M. W. Flinn* (London, 1979), pp. 139–54.

— *Pay Up and Play the Game: Professional Sport in Britain, 1875–1914* (Cambridge, 1988).

Vasili, Phil, 'Walter Daniel Tull, 1888–1918: soldier, footballer, black', *Race and Class*, 38, 2 (1996), 51–69.

— *The First Black Footballer: Arthur Wharton 1865–1930 – An Absence of Memory* (London, 1998).

— *Colouring over the White Line: The History of Black Footballers in Britain* (Edinburgh, 2000).

Veitch, Colin, ' "Play up! play up! and win the war!" Football, the nation and the First World War, 1914–15', *Journal of Contemporary History*, 20, 3 (1985), 363–78.

Vernon, James, *Politics and the People: A Study in English Popular Culture, c.1815–1867* (Cambridge, 1993).

Waddington, Ivan, and Roderick, Martin, 'American exceptionalism: soccer and American football', *Sports Historian*, 16 (1996), 42–63.

Wagg, Stephen, *The Football World: A Contemporary Social History* (Brighton, 1984).
— (ed.), *Giving the Game Away: Football, Politics and Culture on Five Continents* (Leicester, 1995).
Walton, John K., *The English Seaside Resort: A Social History, 1750–1914* (Leicester, 1983).
— *The British Seaside: Holidays and Resorts in the Twentieth Century* (Manchester, 2000).
Walton, John K. and Walvin, James (eds.), *Leisure in Britain, 1780–1939* (Manchester, 1983).
Walvin, James, *The People's Game: A Social History of English Football* (London, 1975).
— *Leisure and Society, 1830–1950* (London, 1978).
— *A Child's World: A Social History of English Childhood, 1800–1914* (Harmondsworth, 1982).
— 'Sport, social history and the historian', *British Journal of Sports History*, 1, 1 (1984), 5–13.
— *The People's Game: The History of Football Revisited* (London, 1994).
Waters, Chris, *British Socialists and the Politics of Popular Culture, 1884–1914* (Manchester, 1990).
Watkins, David, 'Merthyr Town A.F.C., 1908–34', in Huw Williams (ed.), *Merthyr Tydfil: Drawn from Life* (Merthyr, 1981), pp. 70–89.
Webb, Harri, *Rampage and Revel* (Llandysul, 1977).
West, Gordon, *A Century on the Beat: A History of 100 Years of Police Rugby Football in the South Wales Constabulary Area* (Cardiff, 1992).
Whannel, Gary, *Fields in Vision: Television Sport and Cultural Transformation* (London, 1992).
Wheeler, Robert F., 'Organized sport and organized labour: the workers' sports movement', *Journal of Contemporary History*, 13, 2 (1978), 191–210.
White, Carol and Williams, Sian Rhiannon (eds.), *Struggle or Starve: Women's Lives in the South Wales Valleys between the Two World Wars* (Dinas Powys, 1998).
Williams, Chris, *Democratic Rhondda: Politics and Society, 1885–1951* (Cardiff, 1996).
— *Capitalism, Community and Conflict: The South Wales Coalfield, 1898–1947* (Cardiff, 1998).
— ' "Going underground"? The future of coalfield history revisited', *Morgannwg*, 42 (1998), 41–58.
Williams, Gareth, ' "How's the Tenors in Dowlais?" Hegemony, harmony and popular culture in England and Wales, 1600–1900', *Llafur*, 5, 1 (1988), 70–80.
— *1905 and All That: Essays on Rugby Football, Sport and Welsh Society* (Llandysul, 1991).
— 'The road to Wigan Pier revisited: the migration of Welsh rugby talent since 1918', in John Bale and Joseph Maguire (eds.), *The Global Sports Arena: Athletic Migration in an Interdependent World* (London, 1994), pp. 25–38.
— 'Postponing death: sport and literature in Wales', *New Welsh Review*, 35 (1997), 37–46.
— *Valleys of Song: Music and Society in Wales, 1840–1914* (Cardiff, 1998).
Williams, Glanmor (ed.), *Swansea: An Illustrated History* (Swansea, 1990).
Williams, Graham, *The Code War: English Football under the Historical Spotlight* (Harefield, 1994).
Williams, Gwyn A., *When Was Wales? A History of the Welsh* (Harmondsworth, 1991 edn).
Williams, Jack, ' "A wild orgy of speed": responses to speedway in Britain before the Second World War', *Sports Historian*, 19, 1 (1999), 1–15.
— *Cricket and England: A Cultural and Social History of the Inter-war Years* (London, 1999).
Williams, John, *Digest of Welsh Historical Statistics* (Griffithstown, 1985).
Williams, John and Wagg, Stephen (eds.), *British Football and Social Change: Getting into Europe* (Leicester, 1991).
Williams, L. J., 'Capitalists and coalowners', in Prys Morgan (ed.), *Glamorgan County History*, vol. VI: *Glamorgan Society, 1780–1980* (Cardiff, 1988), pp. 109–28.
Williams, M. and Daniel, H. (eds.), *Swansea Schools FA 75th Anniversary* (Swansea, 1989).
Winter, J. M., *The Great War and the British People* (London, 1986).
Yeo, Eileen and Stephen (eds.), *Popular Culture and Class Conflict, 1590–1914: Explorations in the History of Labour and Leisure* (Brighton, 1981).
Yeo, Stephen, *Religion and Voluntary Organisations in Crisis* (London, 1976).
Young, Percy M., *A History of British Football* (London, 1959).

6. Unpublished theses

Barclay, Martin, 'Aberdare, 1880–1920: class and community' (MA, University of Wales, 1985).

Croll, Andrew J., 'Civilizing the urban' popular culture, public space and urban meaning, Merthyr c.1870–1914' (Ph.D., University of Wales, 1997).

Day, R., 'The motivation of some football club directors: an aspect of the social history of association football, 1890–1914' (MA, University of Warwick, 1976).

Evans, Alun, 'Football on the edge: the relationship between Welsh football policy-making and the British international championship' (MA, De Montfort University, 1996).

Fishwick, Nicholas, 'Association football and English social life, 1910–1950' (D.Phil., University of Oxford, 1984).

French, Carl, 'The history of the Welsh Schools Rugby Union, 1903–39' (M.Ed., University of Wales, 1991).

Johnes, Martin, 'That other game: a social history of soccer in south Wales, 1906–39' (Ph.D., University of Wales, 1998).

Lile, Emma, 'Women and sport in Aberystwyth, 1870–1914' (MA, University of Wales, 1995).

Pincombe, Ian, '"Out of Rexville": G. F. Lovell and the south Wales confectionery industry, c.1830–1940' (Ph.D., University of Wales, 2000).

Redhead, Stephen, 'A study of some aspects of the legal status and employment conditions of association football players in England and Wales from the late 19th century to the present day' (Ph.D., University of Warwick, 1984).

Stroud, Raymond J., 'The landscape of popular recreation in Newport, Monmouthshire, 1888–1914' (MA, University of Wales, 1993).

Taylor, Matthew, ' "Proud Preston": a history of the Football League, 1900–39' (Ph.D., De Montfort University, 1997).

Thomas, E. J., 'The history of physical education in Wales to 1970' (M.Ed., University of Manchester, 1979).

7. Broadcasts

In Living Memory, BBC Radio Wales, 1993.
All our Lives: A People's History of Wales, BBC Wales, 1994–6.
Alive and Kicking, BBC 2, 1995.
That Saturday Magic, BBC 2 Wales, 1997.

INDEX